Basic Accounting
to Understand Financial Statements

An MBA Core Course Companion

Ross Jennings, Ph.D.
University of Texas at Austin

Dedication and Acknowledgements

This book is dedicated to the memory of my mentor and friend, Philip W. Bell (1924 – 2007). Phil was a noted scholar in accounting, the co-author with Edgar O. Edwards of the classic accounting book, *The Theory and Measurement of Business Income*, and an inductee into the Accounting Hall of Fame. We first met when I was an undergraduate foreign exchange student at the University of Nairobi in Kenya and Phil was the faculty director of my exchange program. Back in the United States, Phil advised me to enter an MBA program to achieve my dream of returning to Africa. After my graduation, he diverted that dream by recruiting me to a faculty position at Rice University. At Rice, I found both my career and my wife.

This book has benefited both directly and indirectly from many others, including Bruce Baron, Skylar DeTure, Matthew Scott, and especially Karen Jennings and Sara Toynbee. I have also benefited from many conversations with colleagues at the University of Texas, especially Steve Limberg and Eric Hirst, who have taught this material with me for many years. Finally, I have benefited from my interactions with the hundreds of master's students in business and accounting that I have taught at the University of Texas.

Contents

PART I – Accounting Concepts

PART II – Accounting in Practice

PART III – Bookkeeping

PART IV – Using Accounting Information

Basic Accounting to Understand Financial Statements

An MBA Core Course Companion

Introduction

Who Should Read This Book

Financial accounting is commonly taken in the first semester of MBA programs, and in many of these courses the overall objective is to understand financial statements. The pace is usually fast, and students in the course have a wide variety of backgrounds. Having taught such a course to many hundreds of MBA students over the years, I have seen the value of students completing some "pre-work" in accounting before beginning their MBA program. This pre-work levels the playing field for students with little or no background in accounting, and helps them to get more out of the class and enjoy the class more. This book was written with that goal in mind.

This book can also be useful as a review for both undergraduate and graduate students prior to taking more advanced courses in intermediate accounting or financial statement analysis. Indeed, this book can be useful for <u>anyone</u> wanting to learn more about accounting.

What's in This Book

Part I – Accounting Concepts – The six chapters in the first part of the book cover the main concepts of accrual accounting and the elements of the two main financial statements, the balance sheet and the income statement. Each chapter provides intuitive explanations for the accounting concepts and connects those concepts to the resulting financial statements.

Part II – Accounting in Practice – This part of the book applies the concepts from the first part to understanding an actual company's financial statements. Starbucks is the example company and each chapter provides a line-by-line explanation for one of their five financial statements.

Part III – Bookkeeping – This part mainly explains the system of bookkeeping by which business entities of all sizes keep track of the economic activity recorded in their accounting systems. The first chapter explains debits and credits and T-Accounts, the second chapter provides a comprehensive example of the entire accounting cycle, and the third chapter goes into more depth on a few additional accounting topics.

Part IV – Using Accounting Information – This part provides a brief overview of academic research on (a) whether accounting information is useful for investors and (b) whether managers use accounting information to mislead investors. As we will see throughout this book, because accrual accounting measures "wealth," not cash, accountants must make many subjective judgments and apply many estimates. These estimates may not be accurate either because they are difficult to make or because managers are influenced by their economic incentives to bias the estimates. Thus, these estimates may either be so inaccurate that the resulting information is not useful, or so biased that the resulting information is misleading.

How to Read This Book
Everyone should read the first part of the book first, whether this is their first exposure to accounting or whether this material is a review. What to read next depends on the reader's primary interest. If that interest is understanding actual financial statements, they should read the second part of the book next and skip the third part of the book. If that interest is understanding the bookkeeping system by which accounting records are kept, they should read the third part of the book next, especially the first two chapters, before returning to the second part of the book. Though this bookkeeping material is not necessary to understand financial statements, I am a firm believer that understanding bookkeeping helps to deepen understanding of accounting and facilitates communication with others.

The third chapter in the third part of the book briefly explains the accounting for a few topics that are often covered in introductory accounting classes. As such, this chapter can serve as an alternative explanation for students during their financial accounting class or as a review for students about to take more advanced classes.

The fourth part of the book is for readers who are interested in the effect on financial statements of economically-motivated managers making the many estimates that are required in accrual accounting. These well-informed financial managers have superior information about their company that they can communicate through accounting. On the other hand, these managers may have economic incentives to mislead investors into thinking the company is performing better than it actually is. The two chapters in this part of the book summarize academic research that examines whether the resulting accounting information is useful and whether it can sometimes be used to mislead investors.

Part I – Accounting Concepts

Chapter 1 – A Simple Start

The foundational concepts underlying accounting are not difficult to understand. At the beginning of any accounting period, typically a quarter or year, a person or a company has an amount of "wealth." During the period, if the person or company performs well, the wealth increases by "income." That's about it.

The picture below shows a bag of money at the beginning of a year (beginning wealth), that increases by a flow of small bags during the year (income for the year), resulting in a larger bag at the end of the year (ending wealth). Keep this picture in mind because as things get more complicated this is still what is happening over and over again.

But of course there will be some complications along the way. That's why classes are offered in accounting and why people read books about accounting. The complications arise from several sources.

First, is the challenge of <u>what to include</u> in the definition of wealth, i.e., what is in the bags in the picture above. As we will see, some important sources of wealth (think about your college degree or the skills of the employees where you work) are just too difficult to measure and so we are not able to include them.

Second, is the challenge of <u>when to count</u> increases in wealth as income. As a person or company moves from a vague idea of how to increase wealth to having in hand an increase in cash, uncertainty is slowly resolved about whether wealth has successfully been increased. The challenge is deciding how much uncertainty must be resolved before we are comfortable "counting" the increase in wealth.

These two challenges become more difficult as business transactions become more complex. However, in spite of these complications and difficulties, the underlying concepts remain the same. Most importantly, the central idea of wealth (the two big bags above) growing each year by that period's income (the flow of small bags above) does not change.

To get us started, I want to introduce only two concepts in this first chapter: the difference between stocks and flows and the difference between cash and wealth.

Stocks and Flows
Stocks and flows are concepts from economics, but we see these concepts often and intuitively understand them in our daily life. In accounting a "stock" represents financial "position," an amount at a point in time. A "flow" represents financial "performance," the change in a stock that occurs over time. Here are two simple examples that have nothing to do with accounting.

Assume that a mother measures her daughter's height on her birthday each year. On the girl's seventh birthday she is 48 inches tall and on her eighth birthday she is 50 inches tall. The girl's height is her "stock," her "position," at that point in time. The change in her height from her seventh birthday to her eighth birthday is her "flow," her "performance," the amount by which she grew during the year. Her mother will never confuse the stock with the flow or vice versa. If someone asks how tall her daughter was on her last birthday, she will never say "about two inches." If someone asks how much her daughter grew last year, she will never say "50 inches." We want to learn to apply that same easy intuition to accounting.

For another example, assume a baseball team is keeping track of attendance for the season at their stadium and the total prior to the most recent game was 486,000. 40,000 people attended the most recent game so the new total for the season is 526,000. The beginning "stock," or "position," just prior to the most recent game, was 486,000, and the ending stock, just after the most recent game, is 526,000. The "flow," the change in the stock or the "performance," was 40,000. If asked how many people attended the most recent game, the general manager will not say 526,000 because he intuitively knows they are asking for a flow, not a stock.

Now let's move closer to accounting by applying the same stock and flow concepts to your money. Your "stock" of money is how much you have at a point in time, for example at the beginning of the year, and measures your "position." The "flow" is the amount by which your stock changed during the year, and measures your "performance." When we apply these concepts to money, we often refer to the stock as "wealth" and to the flow as "income," which is the amount by which your wealth changes during a period.

Here's a simple example. Assume you want to keep track of your checking and savings accounts, and you call the sum of those two accounts your wealth. Over time, as you earn a salary and pay your living expenses, your account balances go up and down. Those balances are like the little girl's height, except of course, her height only goes up.

Naturally you are interested in how well you did during the year, how your wealth changed that year. This change in your wealth, your income, is a measure of your performance. You can measure the change in your wealth during the year, your income, in two ways.

The first way is to compute the difference between the sum of the balances in your two accounts at the end of the year minus the sum of the balances in your two accounts at the beginning of the year. That difference is your income for the year. But measuring your income this way does not provide the ability to see <u>why</u> your income was what it was. For example, if your income was low because you spent too much money eating out in restaurants, you would not be able to see that.

The second way to measure the change in your wealth is to directly measure the deposits (cash inflows from your salary) and the withdrawals (cash outflows to pay your living expenses). If your deposits are greater than your withdrawals, then the sum of the balances in your two accounts will have increased and your wealth will have increased by the difference. On the other hand, if your deposits are less than your withdrawals, then the sum of the balances in your two accounts will have decreased and your wealth will have decreased by the difference.

Using this method, if you also assign your deposits and withdrawals to categories, you will have information about why your income was high or low that year. For example, your deposits might be related to salary and birthday gifts you received, and your withdrawals might have separate categories for groceries and eating out. This is a simple accounting system that provides you with information that may help you to make a decision, such as spending less money eating in restaurants.

To see this more clearly, let's use some numbers. Make the following assumptions:

- At the beginning of the year you have $1,000 in your checking account and $10,000 in your savings account, so that your wealth is $11,000

- During the year you earn a salary of $60,000 that was deposited in your checking account

- During the year you had withdrawals from your checking account for living expenses of $55,000

- At the end of the year you have $6,000 in your checking account and the original $10,000 in your savings account

- You then transfer $4,000 from your checking account to your savings account, leaving $2,000 in your checking account and increasing your savings account balance to $14,000

Computing your income the first way, you ended the year with $16,000 in your two accounts and you began the year with $11,000 in your two accounts, so your wealth increased by $5,000 ($16,000 - $11,000).

We can formalize this by means of the following equation

Ending Wealth – Beginning Wealth = Income

Which, in our example is

$16,000 - $11,000 = $5,000

This is just like computing the difference between the little girl's height on her two birthdays to determine her growth, and just like computing the difference between the season's baseball attendance before and after a game to determine that game's attendance.

Finally, we can put all of this in the form of a "statement" that reports your wealth at the beginning and end of the year as follows:

	End of Period	Beginning of Period
Checking	$ 2,000	$1,000
Savings	14,000	10,000
Wealth	$16,000	$11,000

The side-by-side columns clearly show that your change in wealth during the period, your income, was $5,000 (16,000 – 11,000).

Computing your income the second way, you made deposits of your salary of $60,000 minus withdrawals for living expenses of $55,000, so your net income, your performance for the year, was an increase of $5,000 ($60,000 - $55,000).

We can formalize this by means of the following equation

Deposits – Withdrawals = Income

Which, in our example is

$60,000 - $55,000 = $5,000

We can put this in the form of a "statement" that reports your deposits and withdrawals during the year as follows:

Deposits	$60,000
Withdrawals	-55,000
Income	$ 5,000

Notice that both methods arrive at the same measure of income, the change in your wealth of $5,000 ($16,000 - $11,000) is equal to the difference between your deposits and withdrawals of $5,000 ($60,000 - $55,000).

The first statement above is called a "balance sheet" or "statement of position" because it reports the balances (stocks) at a point in time. The second statement above is called an "income statement" or "profit and loss statement" because it reports the income (flows) during the period. These two statements "articulate," which means that the difference in wealth on the balance sheet is always equal to the income on the income statement.

I used the terms "position" and "performance" several times above, where stocks measure position and flows measure performance. Now, to be perfectly clear as to how these terms relate to accounting

- Balance sheets report an individual's or company's <u>position</u>, the amount of wealth at a point in time

- Income statements report an individual's or company's <u>performance</u>, the amount by which wealth has changed during a period of time

As was stated above, you can assign the deposits and withdrawals in the second statement to categories that provide more information about where your money came from and where it went.

To see this, suppose that your only deposits were from your salary and that you assign your withdrawals to three categories, rent, eating out, and other. In this case, your expanded income statement would look like this:

Salary	$60,000
Rent	-24,000
Eating Out	-4,000
Other	-27,000
Income	$ 5,000

If you had a budget to spend only $3,600 on eating out, you would now be able to see that you spent more than that and you could decide whether you wanted to increase your budget or try to spend less.

In this way, the information provided by an accounting system as simple as this one can help you make better decisions about how you spend your money. Providing information to make better decisions is a main objective of accounting and one that we will emphasize throughout this book.

Cash versus Wealth
In the previous example we considered your wealth as the sum of the cash in your checking and savings accounts. But that's not right, is it? You probably have more things you own that you consider part of your wealth.

To see how this might affect what we have said so far, let's extend the previous example by assuming that during the year you had a car that you want to include as part of your wealth. To be more specific, assume that

- You originally paid $20,000 for the car
- As of the beginning of the current year your car is two years old and has declined in value by $6,000 so that the current value of the car is $14,000
- As of the beginning of the year you have a car loan with an outstanding balance of $8,500

Including the car but not the loan in the calculation of your wealth at the beginning of the current year should increase your wealth by $14,000, right? Well, yes, but if we also consider the outstanding loan that you took out to pay for the car then you don't own the whole car, only the part that is not owed to the bank for your loan—the bank owns the rest of the car.

The car is an example of the more general fundamental equation of accounting that we introduce below. In the case of the car, your ownership in the car is the difference between the total value of the car you own and the amount that you owe on the car, and can be represented in the following equation:

Value of Car – Owed for Car = Wealth in Car

Which, at the beginning of the year in our example is

$14,000 - $8,500 = $5,500

Thus, including the car and the loan increases your wealth by $5,500, so that your wealth at the beginning of the year is $16,500, which is $10,000 in your savings account, $1,000 in your checking account, and $5,500 for your car.

Now let's see how including the car and the loan as part of your wealth effects the change in your wealth (your income) during the year.

To answer this question, we have to make additional assumptions about what happened during the year:

- You estimate that during the year your car fell in value by $3,000 as you drove it around
- During the year you made payments on the car loan of $375 per month ($375 x 12 = $4,500 for the year), of which $400 is interest and the other $4,100 reduces your outstanding balance to $4,400 ($8,500 - $4,100)

- Thus, your wealth in the car at the end of the year is $11,000 - $4,400 = $6,600

- Total deposits and withdrawals from your checking account are the same as in the previous example, $60,000 of deposits and $55,000 of withdrawals.

As we did above, we can compute the effect of the car and the car loan on your income in two ways. Let's start by taking the difference between the "stock" of wealth at the end of the year and the "stock" of wealth at the beginning of the year. Here are comparative balance sheets including the car and the car loan as part of your wealth.

	End of Period	Beginning of Period
Checking	$ 2,000	$1,000
Savings	14,000	10,000
Car	11,000	14,000
Assets	$27,000	$25,000
Car Loan	-4,400	-8,500
Wealth	$22,600	$16,500

By comparing the wealth at the end of the period with the wealth at the beginning of the period, you can see that wealth increased during the year by $6,100 ($22,600 - $16,500).

Now let's compute the change in your wealth during the period, using the "flows." First, we have the inflow of your salary of $60,000 that was deposited in your checking account.

Next, we have the $55,000 of withdrawals you made from your checking account for living expenses. We previously said that you spent $24,000 on rent, $4,000 on eating out and $27,000 on "other." Here we have to be careful. Were the withdrawals for "other" all for living expenses? Most of it was, but $4,100 of it reduced your car loan, which in turn increased your ownership in your car and your wealth. Thus, the amount of withdrawals from your checking account for "other" that reduced your wealth was $22,900 ($27,000 - $4,100). Note that the $400 of interest on the car loan is implicitly included in "other" and reduces income and wealth.

But we also have to consider that the value of the car fell by $3,000 as you used it during the year. This reduced your ownership in the car and your wealth.

So, at the end of the year the net value of your car has actually increased from $5,500 (the value of the car of $14,000 minus the outstanding loan balance of $8,500) to $6,600 (the value of the car of $11,000 minus the outstanding loan balance of $4,400).

This illustrates an important point, your wealth in the car decreases when the value of the car falls from driving it around, but increases as you pay off the loan so that the bank owns less of the car and you own more.

Putting all of this together, we have the following income statement:

Deposits (Salary)	$60,000
Rent	-24,000
Eating Out	-4,000
Other Cash Expenses	-22,900
Decrease in Car	-3,000
Income	$ 6,100

This income statement and the discussion in the previous paragraphs are very important, make sure you understand it.

Your wealth, including the car and the loan, can be summarized by a simple equation. First, as we discussed above, when we included your car as part of your wealth, your wealth increased by the value of the car net of the amount you owed the bank. In the same way, viewed more broadly your wealth is the sum of the things you own (assets) less the amounts you owe (liabilities), which equals your net ownership of the things you own.

This relationship between what you own, what you owe, and your wealth is captured in the fundamental equation of accounting

$$\text{Assets} \quad - \quad \text{Liabilities} \quad = \quad \text{Wealth}$$

At the beginning of the year you had total assets of $25,000 ($1,000 in checking, $10,000 in savings, and $14,000 in the car) and total liabilities of $8,500 (just the car loan), for wealth of $16,500. Using the fundamental accounting equation, your position at the beginning of the year is

$$\textbf{\$25,000} \qquad \textbf{\$8,500} \qquad \textbf{\$16,500}$$
$$\text{Assets} \quad - \quad \text{Liabilities} \quad = \quad \text{Wealth}$$

At the end of the year you had total assets of $27,000 ($2,000 in checking, $14,000 in savings, and $11,000 in the car) and total liabilities of $4,400 (the car loan), for wealth of $22,600. Using the fundamental accounting equation, your position at the end of the year is

$$\begin{array}{ccc} \textbf{\$27,000} & \textbf{\$4,400} & \textbf{\$22,600} \\ \text{Assets} \quad - & \text{Liabilities} \quad = & \text{Wealth} \end{array}$$

The net effect of all of this was that your wealth increased by $6,100, from $16,500 to $22,600. This is captured in the following equation, which represents the changes between the beginning and end of the year.

$$\begin{array}{ccc} \uparrow\textbf{\$2,000} & & \uparrow\textbf{\$6,100} \\ \text{Assets} \quad - & \text{Liabilities} \quad = & \text{Wealth} \\ & \downarrow\textbf{\$4,100} & \end{array}$$

Much of the rest of this book is about using this equation to keep track of the transactions of an individual (like you) or a company. We will use arrows to show changes in the equation as we account for various transactions and events. In all cases it is important to maintain the equality or "keep the equation in balance." This concept is important enough to repeat.

As we enter transactions and events into the accounting system, the fundamental accounting equation must <u>always</u> remain in balance.

From the two examples above, one that excludes the car and loan in your wealth and one that includes the car and loan in your wealth, we have two alternative measures of your performance during the year. The example that views your wealth as only what is in your checking and savings accounts measures your income for the year as $5,000. The example that expands the definition of your wealth to include your car and the loan measures your income as $6,100.

Which is the better measure of your performance?

Many view the second measure as the better one because it is more comprehensive; it includes not only your cash, but also non-cash assets that increase your wealth, net of loans that decrease your wealth.

How do the two measures differ? The second measure includes everything included by the first, but <u>also</u> recognizes that

(a) $4,100 of your cash outflows lowered your loan balance and were not therefore a decrease in your wealth, and

(b) Your use (consumption) of $3,000 worth of the car by driving it around during the year lowered your wealth

The combination of adding back $4,100 and subtracting $3,000 increased income from the first method to the second method by $1,100.

The first method is <u>cash accounting</u>, which defines wealth as only cash, and the second method is <u>accrual accounting</u>, which expands the definition of wealth to include things we own (assets) and owe (liabilities) beyond just cash.

This second method, the one referred to as accrual accounting, is the type of accounting that is required for many companies and the type of accounting we will discuss in the remainder of this book.

In our example of accrual accounting above, we only expanded your definition of wealth to include your car and car loan. But why stop there? You probably own lots of things like a computer, a cell phone, furniture, clothing, sports equipment, etc. Why not assign a value to all of these things you own to get a more accurate (complete) measure of your wealth?

You can do that, but if you do, you will also need to keep track of their decline in value as you use them up. Keeping track of all of the things you own and their decline in value as you use them would be time consuming (costly). You need to decide whether it is worth it to spend so much time keeping track of these things.

The test for whether or not it is worth your time is whether you will be able to make better decisions if you spend the time necessary to keep track of ALL of your assets and liabilities.

Here is how this worked out for me. Several years ago I began using the popular personal finance software, Quicken, to keep track of my family's finances. Each month I spent time assigning the various outflows to separate categories so I would know how much we were spending on food, utilities, mortgage, entertainment, travel, etc. After several years I realized that we had not made one decision based on this information. I was wasting my time.

This is an important concept in accounting. Accounting records are costly to maintain and one of the main benefits of incurring that cost is to have better information to make decisions. In the case of companies, this is better information for creditors to make better lending decisions, and better information for current and potential stockholders to make better investing decisions.

Returning to you, suppose you conclude that the information provided by accounting for some, but maybe not all, of your assets and liabilities would justify the effort involved. When you attempt to expand your definition of wealth beyond your cash assets, you will face several challenges.

The first challenge is what to include and not include in your definition of wealth. You might exclude some items, like your college degree, even though they are important, because they are too difficult to measure. You might exclude other items, like your socks, because they are too trivial to worry about.

The second challenge is in assigning a monetary value to the assets and liabilities that you decided to include in your definition of wealth. You might value your assets based on (a) what you paid for the item, (b) what you paid reduced by the amount you have used, or (c) what the item is worth to you, regardless of what you paid.

When you were just counting cash in your checking and savings accounts you didn't face these questions. But as you shift from cash accounting to accrual accounting and expand your definition of wealth from cash to include "things" you own and amounts you owe, you will face these challenges.

On the other hand, accrual accounting is more comprehensive in the sense that it provides information not just about cash, but a more expansive view of the economic resources (assets) and obligations (liabilities) of an individual or a company. That's why in spite of the costs of preparing accrual-basis financial statements, and the potential inaccuracy of the estimates used in those statements, accounting rule makers believe that accrual-basis financial statements provide better information than cash accounting. What's more, substantial academic research in accounting supports this conclusion.

As a result, even though most individuals will not incur the costs of a full accrual accounting system, the accounting rule makers have decided that accrual accounting is worth the effort for many companies. In fact, accrual accounting financial statements are required of all publicly-traded companies in the U.S. and indeed around the world, and that's what the rest of this book is about.

In the next two chapters we will look more deeply at how an individual or a company applies the expanded definition of wealth used by accrual accounting to report their financial position on their balance sheet and their financial performance on their income statement.

Chapter 2 – The Balance Sheet

Your Financial Position

A main point from the last chapter was the difference between cash accounting and accrual accounting. Cash accounting, as the name implies, keeps track of increases and decreases in cash, a narrow definition of wealth. Accrual accounting, in contrast, expands the definition of wealth to include other things that are owned (assets) and amounts that are owed (liabilities).

This chapter focuses in more detail on reporting "financial position," the amounts that are owned and owed at a point in time. These are the "stocks" we talked about in the last chapter. Companies report their financial position on their balance sheet, sometimes called their statement of financial position.

But we're not going to start with a company. Let's start with an individual, someone like you. What are you worth? What is your wealth or your financial position?

We could limit your wealth to your checking and savings accounts as we started with in the last chapter, but that seemed too restrictive. In the example in the last chapter we expanded wealth to include a car and the loan to pay for the car. In this chapter we expand the definition of wealth further to include more things that are owned (assets) and amounts that are owed (liabilities).

To begin, what are your assets? They are anything of value to you that you own or control. For example, your assets may include a car, a house, sports equipment, jewelry, furniture, clothes, cash, investments, etc. These are all assets.

To figure out what you're worth, you need to assign a dollar value to each of these assets. For some assets this will be very easy. For example, the dollar value of your savings or checking account is just the balance. Assigning a value to other assets is more difficult. For example, the value of the furniture in your house or apartment is not obvious, but you can probably come up with an estimate that is reasonable.

But there are other assets that are so difficult to measure that you will probably leave them out altogether. For example, although you may be able to reasonably estimate the value of the furniture in your house or apartment, it will be much more difficult to assign a dollar value to your work experience, your friends, or your personality. These are important assets, but they are just too difficult to measure objectively. To make this point, consider the following story.

You and your significant other are planning to be married. Your future father-in-law is old fashioned and he has asked you to prepare a statement of financial position that lists all of your assets with dollar values assigned. He also asked you to list these assets from easiest to measure to hardest to measure. Here is an abbreviated version of the list you might give him (excluding the dollar amounts):

> Cash
> Bank Account
> Mutual Fund
> Car
> House
> Education
> Work Experience
> Friends
> Personality

When your future father-in-law examined the list, he drew a line between "House" and "Education." He told you that he would not accept the items below the line because he was worried you might use the subjectivity in those measures to inflate their values. He told you he had no way to verify whether the values you assigned were realistic or inflated, so he wasn't going to "count" them.

Now, suppose I told you that you could keep either the items above your future father-in-law's line or below that line, but not both, which would you choose? Most people would choose to keep the items below the line. Those items are the essence of who you are, and with those items you are likely to be able to replace the items above the line.

The items above the line are financial and tangible assets, i.e., they are either money or near money or something you can touch. The items below the line are referred to as intangible assets. There is nothing there that you can touch. Ironically, these intangible assets are both our most valuable personal assets and also the most difficult to measure in monetary terms. As we will soon see, it is the same for a business entity.

Pause here, and write down <u>your</u> most important financial and tangible assets, assign values to them, and add them up.

Likely you left off very small items such as a pair of shoes, or a half-consumed gallon of milk, or a flashlight. Omitting these items from your list of assets saved effort (cost), but will not make much difference because their cumulative dollar amount is likely to be small.

For those assets you did list, did you have a hard time trying to estimate the values for some of them? Assigning or measuring values is a critical part of accounting.

The next step in calculating your wealth (or net worth or financial position) is to add up all of the amounts you owe—your liabilities. A liability is an amount that you are <u>currently obligated</u> to pay at some time in the future, like the outstanding balance on a car loan, a home mortgage, or your credit card.

Pause again and list your most important liabilities and add them up. Liabilities are usually easier to measure than assets because they are usually for contracted amounts such as your credit card balance or your student loan balance.

But be sure to only include current obligations, i.e., obligations you have <u>as of today</u>. You can think of current obligations as the amounts you would owe if the world came to an end right now and we went to the great settling up where everyone paid each other what is owed. Next month's rent or electric bill are not current obligations because you have not yet consumed those services and therefore you do not currently owe for them. On the other hand, your entire mortgage or MasterCard balances are current obligations, even if you don't intend to pay them off for a while.

Now that you have a list of your assets and liabilities, their values, and the totals for each, you can compute your wealth (or net worth) using the fundamental accounting equation we saw in the previous chapter:

$$\text{Assets} - \text{Liabilities} = \text{Wealth}$$

Remember, the three items in the equation are all "stocks," amounts at a point in time that measure the financial position of an individual or company.

Balance Sheet Transactions

Obviously, the amounts for assets and liabilities reported on the balance sheet can change over time. To begin to see how this happens, we consider three common transactions that change the amounts in assets and liabilities <u>without changing wealth</u>. We refer to these as balance sheet transactions because they only affect the balance sheet. In the next chapter we will expand the balance sheet equation to capture the "flows," changes in assets and liabilities that change wealth (income) and that measure the financial performance of an individual or company.

The three balance sheet transactions that do not change wealth are

- Purchase an asset for cash. This is just an exchange of one asset for another and so does not change wealth.

- Purchase an asset on credit or borrow cash. This results in an equal increase in an asset and increase in a liability, but does not change in wealth.

- Payback a loan. This results in an equal decrease in an asset and decrease in a liability, but does not change in wealth.

Here are examples of these three types of transactions. For the first transaction, assume you spend $1,000 to buy a new computer. This does not change your wealth as long as you value the computer at the $1,000 you just paid for it. The effect on the accounting equation is:

$$↑\$1,000$$
$$\text{Assets} \quad - \quad \text{Liabilities} \quad = \quad \text{Wealth}$$
$$↓\$1,000$$

For the second transaction, assume you buy a bicycle for $500 by charging it to your credit card. This increases an asset and a liability, but does not change wealth. The effect on the accounting equation is:

$$↑\$500 \qquad\qquad ↑\$500$$
$$\text{Assets} \quad - \quad \text{Liabilities} \quad = \quad \text{Wealth}$$

For the third transaction, assume you pay $100 toward your credit card balance. This decreases an asset and a liability, but does not change wealth. The effect on the accounting equation is:

$$\text{Assets} \quad - \quad \text{Liabilities} \quad = \quad \text{Wealth}$$
$$↓\$100 \qquad\quad ↓\$100$$

Notice that for all three of these examples (a) the accounting equation remains "in balance" (the equality is maintained) and (b) there is no effect on wealth.

Accounts

The way we have written the accounting equation suppresses a lot of information by hiding the various types of assets and liabilities. To provide more information we can divide (disaggregate) assets and liabilities into categories that are similar to each other called "accounts." For example, you might group all of your assets into the following accounts:

- Cash
- Bank accounts
- Other investments
- Vehicles
- Clothing
- Personal property.

We can do the same with your liabilities:

- Credit card balances
- Car loan
- Student loan.

For your wealth (for now) we have only one account

- Wealth

Each person can decide how many accounts they want so that they can retrieve from the accounting system the information they want to help them make better decisions. For example, someone who doesn't spend much on clothes might decide that there is no reason to have an account for clothing that is separate from personal property. On the other hand, someone who spends a lot on clothes and jewelry might want to keep track of these two items separately with separate accounts for each.

This decision on the number of accounts depends on the information you wish to retrieve from the accounting system. However, the more accounts you have the more costly it is to maintain your accounting system. You should expand the number of accounts only if you are going to use the information to make better decisions.

You can add and delete accounts as your life changes and your accounts need not be the same as your friends' if they have different assets and liabilities or want to be able to retrieve different information from their accounting systems.

Now let's look at an example balance sheet that you might have prepared for your future father-in-law:

Your Name
Balance Sheet as of December 31, 20x1

Cash	$200
Investments	3,500
Vehicles	12,000
Personal Property	4,200
Total Assets	$19,900
Student Loan	4,600
Total Liabilities	$4,600
Wealth	15,300
Total Liabilities and Wealth	$19,900

Note that the balance sheet is as of a certain date. This says that as of midnight on December 31st of 20x1 these were your assets and liabilities. These are "stocks," amounts at a point in time.

Note also that the last line of this balance sheet is labeled "Total Liabilities and Wealth," which is equal to "Total Assets," reported above. Total liabilities and wealth are the sources of funding (paying for) your assets. To see this more clearly, we can rearrange the terms in the fundamental accounting equation, moving liabilities to the right-hand side of the equals sign, as follows:

$$Assets = Liabilities + Wealth$$

In this version of the equation we can clearly see that the assets are paid for either by your own funds (wealth) or by borrowing money from someone else (liabilities).

Accounting for a Business Entity

Now we want to shift from accounting for a person to accounting for a business entity. A business entity can take several different forms. A common form, and the one we will focus on in this book, is a corporation. In this form, the business entity creates "shares" in the corporation, which are equal units of ownership, and sells the shares to investors.

For example, a corporation might issue (sell) one hundred shares, one share each to one hundred different people. The individuals (for example) may each pay $10 to the company for their single share. In this case, each person owns one percent of the business entity and the business entity has the $1,000 the one hundred owners have paid to the company in exchange for each investor's one percent ownership.

When we change from an individual to a corporation, there is one important change in terminology: we replace the term "wealth" with the term "owners' equity," so that the accounting equation becomes

Assets - Liabilities = Owners' Equity

The concept underlying owners' equity for a business entity is the same as the concept of wealth for an individual, but rather than referring to you owning yourself it refers to the various owners collectively owning the company. The definition I will use is

Owners' Equity is the wealth that investors have invested in the company, as measured by the accountants.

This illustrates an important difference between accounting for a person and accounting for a company. In the case of a person, there is no difference between the entity and the owner of the wealth. No one can own a share of you. You own all of you.

In contrast, a business entity cannot own itself. Rather people, one or many, own the business. This not only applies to corporations, but also to other forms of business such as partnerships and sole proprietorships. In a partnership there are multiple owners as with a corporation, but usually they are fewer, their ownership shares are more difficult to transfer to others, and the owners' legal liability and tax status differs from shareholders in a corporation. In a sole proprietorship, there is only one owner, and again that person's legal liability and tax status differ from shareholders in a corporation.

It is important to emphasize that in all three cases, a corporation, a partnership, and a sole proprietorship, there is a distinction between the business as an economic entity and the owners as separate economic entities, and they need to be accounted for separately. Even with a sole proprietorship, if the owner invests $10,000 in the business, she is transferring $10,000 from her personal account (entity), to her business account (a separate entity).

Here are examples of the three balance sheet transactions we discussed above, but this time applied to a corporation.

For the first transaction, assume the company paid cash of $32,000 to buy a new delivery van. The effect on the accounting equation is:

↑**$32,000**

Assets – Liabilities = Owners' Equity

↓**$32,000**

For the second transaction, assume the company borrows $15,000 from a bank. The effect on the accounting equation is:

↑**$15,000**   ↑**$15,000**

Assets – Liabilities = Owners' Equity

For the third transaction, assume the company pays $1,000 toward their bank loan. The effect on the accounting equation is:

Assets – Liabilities = Owners' Equity

↓**$1,000**   ↓**$1,000**

As we saw with accounting for an individual, for all three of these examples (a) the accounting equation remains "in balance" (the equality is maintained) and (b) there is no effect on wealth.

The Accounting Rule Makers
An individual is free to create a personal accounting system or not, as they wish. If they do create a personal accounting system, they are free to establish many accounts or few accounts and to record or fail to record any assets or liabilities, again, as they wish. There are no binding rules.

For small private companies the situation is basically the same. There are no binding accounting rules for whether or how they should keep their accounting records and prepare financial statements. However, as with individuals, probably all small businesses can benefit from some form of accounting to help the owners and managers make better decisions.

There are two situations under which there are rules of accounting that companies must follow. First, if a company is publicly traded on a stock exchange and subject to the jurisdiction of the Securities Exchange

Commission, they must follow the rules of accounting. Second, if a company is audited, the auditor will require that they follow the rules of accounting in order to obtain an audit. Publicly-traded companies are required to be audited, but many private companies are also audited, either because they are preparing to go public, or because a bank that loaned them money requires an audit, or for some other reason.

Ultimately, the U.S. Congress has authority to set accounting rules in the U.S. but for more than eighty years they have delegated that authority to the Securities Exchange Commission (SEC). The SEC in turn has delegated that authority to a series of private accounting standard setting bodies. The current standard setting body is the Financial Accounting Standards Board (FASB), a private, non-profit organization that establishes most of the U.S. accounting rules.

The rules of accounting are commonly referred to as Generally Accepted Accounting Principles, or GAAP for short.

The FASB was established in 1973, and is currently headquartered in Norwalk, CN. The Board has seven full-time Board members serving five-year terms with a two-term limit. Board members generally have backgrounds in auditing, financial statement preparation, use of financial statements, or academic accounting research.

The FASB adds a topic to their agenda when the Board decides that the current standards are outdated or incomplete. The Board then goes through a lengthy and public deliberative process that includes issuing an "exposure draft" of a proposed new accounting standard and giving the public several months to comment on the proposal. The voting rules for approving a new accounting standard have changed over time from requiring a four-vote majority to requiring a five-vote super majority. The current voting rule is a four-vote majority.

Most of the rest of the world follows a different set of accounting standards that are set by the International Accounting Standards Board (IASB), which is headquartered in London. The IASB has a similar make-up and similar procedures as the FASB, except that the IASB Board is larger and its membership is international, including two U.S. members (out of 12). The FASB and the IASB work closely together to facilitate "convergence" of the two different sets of accounting rules, which are slowly becoming more similar over time.

Chapter 3 – The Income Statement

Reporting Performance versus Position

In the last chapter we focused on financial position, both for an individual and for a company, in which assets, liabilities and wealth/owners' equity are reported on a balance sheet. In this chapter we focus on performance, the change in wealth/owners' equity over time. In both cases, for individuals and companies, the measure of performance is net income. We begin with an individual and then consider a company.

Revenue and Expense

Three types of accounts, or "elements" of accounting report financial position on the balance sheet: assets, liabilities and wealth. Now we introduce the two main types of accounts that report performance on the income statement: revenue and expense.

The accounting equation we have been using to this point shows when wealth goes up and down, but it does not show why wealth is going up and down. To get more information about why wealth is going up and down we need to expand the equation.

To do this we replace increases and decreases in wealth with "revenue" and "expense."

A revenue is an increase in wealth as a result of providing a customer with a good or service.

As we will see later, this can occur either when an asset increases or when a liability decreases.

An expense is a decrease in wealth when a resource is consumed (used up) in the process of providing a customer with a good or service.

As we will see later, this can occur either when an asset decreases or when a liability increases.

Thus, we have

$$\Delta \text{Wealth} \;=\; \text{Revenue} \;-\; \text{Expense}$$

The Greek letter delta (Δ) represents "change," so that ΔWealth is the change in wealth from the beginning of the year to the end of the year.

Revenue and expense are <u>temporary</u> wealth accounts that collect the change in wealth during the period.

Let's begin by applying the concepts of revenue and expense to an individual. For an individual, wealth only changes when revenue is earned or expense is incurred. We can expand the fundamental equation of accounting to show this. When we expand the accounting equation to add revenue and expense, we have the following as of the beginning of the year:

$$\text{Assets}_{\text{Beg}} \quad - \quad \text{Liab}_{\text{Beg}} \quad = \quad \text{Wealth}_{\text{Beg}} \quad + \quad \text{Revenue} \quad - \quad \text{Expense}$$

In this equation assets, liabilities and wealth are their beginning balances and revenue and expense are zero. As we move through the year, assets and liabilities change as revenue is earned and expense is incurred. During the period wealth remains at the beginning balance so that at the end of the period the accounting equation is

$$\text{Assets}_{\text{End}} \quad - \quad \text{Liab}_{\text{End}} \quad = \quad \text{Wealth}_{\text{Beg}} \quad + \quad \text{Revenue} \quad - \quad \text{Expense}$$

Notice that assets and liabilities are now their ending balances, wealth is still its beginning balance, and all of the changes in wealth are captured by the revenue and expense accounts which are no longer zero. This is important enough to repeat.

In the equation above, wealth is still its beginning balance because all of the changes in wealth are captured by the revenue and expense accounts, which are no longer zero, and which combined are the net income (increase in wealth) for the period.

As a last step, at the end of the accounting period, the revenue and expense accounts are "closed" into the wealth account, transferring all of their value to that account so that wealth is now also the ending balance.

$$\text{Assets}_{\text{End}} \quad - \quad \text{Liab}_{\text{End}} \quad = \quad \text{Wealth}_{\text{End}} \quad + \quad \boxed{\text{Revenue} \quad - \quad \text{Expense}}$$

After closing the revenue and expense accounts to wealth, the revenue and expense accounts have been returned to zero balances to prepare to count performance (net income) in the next period.

This last statement is critical to understanding how accounting works, and is emphasized in the next section.

More on Closing Revenue and Expense to Wealth

The process of closing the revenue and expense accounts and transferring their net value (net income) to wealth is an important concept. Here are two intuitive examples to illustrate how this works. The first is an example that we have already discussed—keeping track of attendance at a baseball stadium. Although this example is more physical than financial, revisiting it may help to see the intuition for what happens when we close revenue and expense accounts into wealth.

Assume that you are managing a baseball stadium in which there is only one gate into the stadium and the gate has only one turnstile. You want to keep track of each game's attendance (performance) and also keep a running total of attendance for the season (position). There is a counter on the turnstile that counts each fan that enters. When the last fan has entered for a particular game, you can record the count for that day and add it to the running total for the season. You then reset the counter to zero so it is ready to count the attendance (performance) for the next day's game.

Revenue and expense accounts operate just the same as the counter on that turnstile. They count the gross inflows and outflows of wealth during the accounting period (performance), and at the end of the period the amounts in these accounts are transferred to the wealth account (position) and the balances are reset to zero.

The second example is more financial, but still very simple. Assume a boy sells popcorn at a baseball stadium. At the stadium he wears an apron with pockets for his change, and at home he has a cigar box in his bedroom for his profits. Each day he goes to the stadium with an empty apron, a distributor gives him popcorn, he sells the popcorn in the stands, and he pays the distributor at the end of the day. When he is back home, he puts all of the money from his apron into the cigar box.

One day when the boy leaves for the stadium he has $365 dollars in his cigar box. This is his position at the beginning of the day. At the stadium that day he sells $100 of popcorn and pays the distributor $70. When he returns home, he transfers the $30 in his apron to his cigar box. This is his performance (income) for the day. He now has $395 in the cigar box (365 + 30). This is his position at the end of the day.

When the boy takes the $30 of income for the day out of his apron and puts it into the cigar box (wealth) that is exactly the same as the accounting system closing revenue and expense to wealth (the cigar box). Now that the boy has transferred his day's earnings from his apron to his cigar box, he has reset his apron pockets to zero, and his apron is ready to "count" his increase in wealth the next day he goes to the stadium to sell popcorn.

Again, this is just how revenue and expense accounts are used. They count the gross inflows and outflows of wealth during the accounting period. At the end of the period the amounts in these accounts are transferred to the wealth account, and their balances are reset to zero.

Returning to Our Previous Example

To illustrate how all of this works, we extend the example from the previous chapter on the balance sheet. For convenience, here is your ending balance sheet for 20x1 from that example, which is also your beginning balance sheet for 20x2.

Your Name
Balance Sheet
as of December 31

	20x1
Cash	$200
Investments	3,500
Vehicles	12,000
Personal Property	4,200
Total Assets	$19,900
Student Loan	$4,600
Total Liabilities	$4,600
Wealth	$15,300
Total Liabilities and Wealth	$19,900

Assume the following economic activity during 20x2:

- You started a new job on January 1, 20x2. During the year you received $66,000 in cash for eleven months of the $72,000 of your gross salary earned this year. You will receive your December salary of $6,000 early in January of 20x3.

- You paid cash of $58,000 for taxes, eleven months of rent, travel, and other living expenses. You will pay $2,000 for your December rent in early January of 20x3.

- You paid cash of $2,250 toward the balance on your student loan, of which $120 was for interest and the remainder reduced the principle.

- You recognized that your vehicle declined in value (depreciated) by $1,500.

- You paid cash of $2,500 for a nice racing bicycle, your main hobby.

- You added the remainder of the cash you received for your salary to your investments so that you ended the year with the same $200 balance in your cash account with which you began the year.

Here is a summary of your cash inflows and outflows:

Salary		$66,000
Taxes, Rent and Living Expense	$58,000	
Student Loan	2,250	
Bicycle	2,500	
Total Spent		$62,750
Surplus to Investments		$3,250

But this just tells us that you ended the year with $3,250 more cash than you began the year and that you transferred that amount to investments. We can think of that as one measure of your performance during the year, the "excess" cash you generated, but you might be more interested in what happened to a more complete measure of your wealth.

To expand from cash as a definition of your wealth to one that includes other assets and liabilities, consider the following additional items

- You are owed $6,000 in salary at the end of the year

- You owe $2,000 in rent at the end of the year

- $2,130 of the $2,250 you paid on your student loan reduced the liability and did not reduce your wealth

- Your vehicle has declined by $1,500 during the year even though this was not a cash outflow

- You paid $2,500 for a bicycle, but that was an exchange of one asset for another that did not decrease your wealth

Let's consider each of these in turn.

First, you are owed salary at the end of the year. Suppose you were meticulous about accounting for your personal finances such that every time anything happened that affected your wealth you recorded it in your accounting records. If this were the case, each time as you left work and got in your car to go home you would update your accounting records, recording an increase in your wealth for the salary you had earned during that day. Suppose the amount you earned that day was $300, the effect on the accounting equation would be

$$\begin{array}{cccccccc} \uparrow 300 & & & & & & \uparrow 300 & \\ \Delta\text{Assets} & - & \Delta\text{Liab} & = & \text{Wealth}_{\text{Beg}} & + & \text{Revenue} & - & \text{Expense} \end{array}$$

The Greek letter delta (Δ) in front of Assets and Liabilities indicates changes in those two financial statement elements. No delta is necessary in front of Wealth because Revenue and Expense capture the changes in wealth during the period.

What is the asset you have? We can call it "salary receivable." It is the amount that your employer owes you for working that you have not yet been paid. To see that this is an asset, suppose the world came to an end and we went to the great settling up. Would you expect your employer to pay you this $300? I expect the answer is "yes."

How will this asset behave between paydays? Each day that you work it will increase by $300. Those amounts will cumulate until the next payday when you receive the money. Assume that during December you worked 20 days so that at the end of December your employer owes you $6,000 (20 x $300).

Second, you owe rent at the end of the year that you have not yet paid. This is similar to, but the opposite of, the previous transaction. Again, suppose you record everything in your accounting records that affects your wealth as it happens. In this case, each morning when you get up you record the fact that you owe your landlord rent for sleeping in your apartment the night before. If the amount you owe your landlord for each night is $67 (rounding), the effect on the accounting equation would be

$$\begin{array}{cccccccc} & & \uparrow 67 & & & & & \uparrow 67 & \\ \Delta\text{Assets} & - & \Delta\text{Liab} & = & \text{Wealth}_{\text{Beg}} & + & \text{Revenue} & - & \text{Expense} \end{array}$$

What is the liability you have? We can call it "rent payable." It is the amount you owe your landlord for having used the apartment that you have not yet paid. To see that this is a liability, at the great settling up would your landlord expect you to pay her this $67? I expect the answer is "yes."

How will this liability behave between rent payments? Each day the liability will increase by $67 (rounded). Those amounts will cumulate until the next time you pay your rent. At the end of December you will owe your landlord $2,000, which you will pay in early January.

Third, $2,130 of the $2,250 you paid for your student loan reduced the liability and did not reduce your wealth. Loan payments of this type (student loans, car loans, mortgages, etc.) are normally a mixture of interest, which compensates the lender for lending the money, and principle, which reduces the outstanding balance owed to the lender. The interest portion ($120 in this case) reduces wealth; it is the cost of borrowing. The principle portion ($2,130 in this case) does not affect wealth; it is a reduction in an asset and a reduction in a liability.

Let's look more closely at the interest portion of the loan payment. Interest for the year was $120, which amounts to about $0.33 per day. If you were recording everything that happened to you every day, the effect on the equation of incurring interest expense on your student loan each day would be

$$\overset{\uparrow \textbf{0.33}}{\Delta\text{Assets}} \quad - \quad \Delta\text{Liab} \quad = \quad \text{Wealth}_{\text{Beg}} \quad + \quad \text{Revenue} \quad - \quad \overset{\uparrow \textbf{0.33}}{\text{Expense}}$$

Why is your wealth decreasing? Because you are using someone else's money and will need to pay them for that. What is the liability that is increasing? We can call it "interest payable." This is the amount you owe to whomever has lent you the money for your student loan. It is a liability because they will expect to be paid at the great settling up.

If we assume you did not account for interest expense each day, and that you make the entire $2,000 payment for your student loan on the last day of the year? The effect on your accounting equation would be

$$\underset{\downarrow\textbf{2,250}}{\Delta\text{Assets}} \quad - \quad \underset{\downarrow\textbf{2,130}}{\Delta\text{Liab}} \quad = \quad \text{Wealth}_{\text{Beg}} \quad + \quad \text{Revenue} \quad - \quad \overset{\uparrow\textbf{120}}{\text{Expense}}$$

Cash of $2,250 is paid (the decrease in assets) and $120 of that amount is a reduction in your wealth, the cost of being able to borrow your student loan balance for the year. The remaining $2,130 is applied to your student loan, reducing the outstanding balance by that amount.

Fourth, your vehicle has declined in value by $1,500 during the year. The effect on your accounting equation is

$$\Delta\text{Assets} \quad - \quad \Delta\text{Liab} \quad = \quad \text{Wealth}_{\text{Beg}} \quad + \quad \text{Revenue} \quad - \quad \overset{\uparrow\textbf{1,500}}{\text{Expense}}$$
$$\underset{\downarrow\textbf{1,500}}{}$$

Even though this was not a cash outflow it is a decrease in the value of your assets as a result of using up or consuming one of your assets (the car won't last forever), and is therefore a decrease in your wealth.

Fifth, you paid $2,500 for a bicycle. The effect on the accounting equation is

$$\overset{\uparrow\textbf{2,500}}{\Delta\text{Assets}} \quad - \quad \Delta\text{Liab} \quad = \quad \text{Wealth}_{\text{Beg}} \quad + \quad \text{Revenue} \quad - \quad \text{Expense}$$
$$\underset{\downarrow\textbf{2,500}}{}$$

In this case the asset cash decreased and the asset bicycle increased, with no effect on wealth. It was just an exchange of one asset for another. We will include the bicycle in the asset line item for personal property.

At the end of the period you transferred $3,250 into your investment account. Again, this is an exchange of one asset (cash) for another (investment), and the effect on the accounting equation is

$$\overset{\uparrow\textbf{3,250}}{\Delta\text{Assets}} \quad - \quad \Delta\text{Liab} \quad = \quad \text{Wealth}_{\text{Beg}} \quad + \quad \text{Revenue} \quad - \quad \text{Expense}$$
$$\underset{\downarrow\textbf{3,250}}{}$$

Finally, you closed the revenue and expense accounts and transferred net income of $10,380 to wealth.

$$\Delta\text{Assets}_{\text{End}} \quad - \quad \Delta\text{Liab}_{\text{End}} \quad = \quad \overset{\uparrow\textbf{10,380}}{\text{Wealth}_{\text{Beg}}} \quad + \quad \underset{\downarrow\textbf{72,000}}{\text{Revenue}} \quad - \quad \underset{\downarrow\textbf{61,620}}{\text{Expense}}$$

This last transaction changes wealth from its beginning balance to its ending balance, and returns the revenue and expense accounts to zero so they can begin counting performance (net income) in the next period.

Reconciling Cash and Accrual Accounting

Accounting for the previous example results in the following accrual-basis income statement. Take a few moments to make sure you understand how the transactions above resulted in this income statement.

Your Name
Income Statement
for the period ending December 31, 20x2

		20x2
Revenue (Salary)		$72,000
Taxes, Rent and Living Expense	$60,000	
Interest Expense	120	
Depreciation	1,500	
Total Expense		$61,620
Net Income		$10,380

Contrast this accrual-basis income statement with the following statement of cash inflows and outflows that considers only a narrow definition of wealth that consists of cash.

Your Name
Statement of Cash Inflows and Outflows
for the period ending December 31, 20x2

Salary		$66,000
Taxes, Rent and Living Expense	$58,000	
Student Loan	2,250	
Bicycle	2,500	
Total Spent		$62,750
Surplus to Investments		$3,250

These two statements present two alternative measures of performance for the period, one based on cash inflows and outflows and the other based on accrual accounting which employs an expanded view of wealth to include other assets and liabilities beyond cash. In this section we examine each of the differences between the cash statement and the accrual statement to see how they differ from each other.

First, we see that the salary line item increased by the $6,000 from $66,000 on a cash basis to $72,000 on an accrual basis. This increase is for the salary you earned but have not yet received for working during December.

Second, Taxes, Rent and Living Expense increased by $2,000 from $58,000 on a cash basis to $60,000 on an accrual basis for the December rent you have not yet paid.

Third, the line item for the student loan is eliminated. Of that $2,250, $120 is reported as interest expense, and $2,130 reduced your outstanding loan balance, but did not change your wealth.

Fourth, the $2,500 cash outflow for the bicycle is eliminated because it was an exchange of one asset for another and did not reduce your wealth.

Finally, a line is added for depreciation, the non-cash decrease in the value of your vehicle of $1,500, which is a decrease in your wealth by $1,500.

The result of all of this is to convert your net cash inflow of $3,250 into accrual-basis net income of $10,380. To summarize, the difference of $7,130 is from

- Adding salary earned but not received of $6,000
- Subtracting rent owed but not paid of $2,000
- Adding $2,130 of cash paid to decrease your student loan
- Adding $2,500 paid for a bicycle that did not decrease your wealth
- Subtracting $1,500 for the decrease in the value of your vehicle

Combining these items, we have

$$6,000 - 2,000 + 2,130 + 2,500 - 1,500 = 7,130$$

At this point you might conclude that preparing an accrual-basis income statement is more work than preparing a statement of cash inflows and outflows. If so, you would be correct. The question is

Is the extra work of an accrual accounting system worth the effort?

On the one hand, as an individual this additional information may not help you make any decisions. It may be enough for you to know that you increased your investment account by $3,250 and are that much closer to meeting your long-term saving goal.

On the other hand, the accounting standard setters have concluded that the extra effort of implementing an accrual accounting system is worth the effort for audited business entities. This is based on the assumption that the accrual basis measure of net income is a more comprehensive measure of economic performance during the year that provides important information for creditors and investors that is useful in making their decisions. We will see in Chapter 15 that academic research supports this assumption.

In the next section we discuss accrual-basis net income for business entities. But before we do, here is the final 20x2 accrual-basis balance sheet for the example above alongside the beginning balance sheet (the ending balance sheet for 20x1).

Your Name
Balance Sheet
as of December 31

	20x2	20x1
Cash	$200	$200
Investments	6,750	3,500
Salary Receivable	6,000	0
Vehicles	10,500	12,000
Personal Property	6,700	4,200
Total Assets	$30,150	$19,900
Rent Payable	2,000	0
Student Loan	2,470	4,600
Total Liabilities	$4,470	$4,600
Wealth	$25,680	15,300
Total Liabilities and Wealth	$30,150	$19,900

Notice that the change in wealth during the period, from $15,300 to $25,680, is equal to the accrual-basis net income reported above of $10,380.

Accounting for a Business Entity

Now we shift from accounting for an individual to accounting for a business entity. As in the previous chapter, we focus on the corporate form of a business where the main differences from an individual are

- The term "wealth" that we used for an individual is changed to the term "owners' equity" for a business entity

- In contrast to an individual, a business entity cannot own itself, it is owned by one or more persons or other business entities

- Also in contrast to an individual, a business entity can have transactions between the entity and its owners because a business entity is owned by others

Recall that the definition of owners' equity is

The wealth that investors have invested in the company, as measured by the accountants.

After substituting owners' equity for wealth in our expanded accounting equation that includes revenue and expense, we have the following as of the beginning of the period when revenue and expense are zero.

$$\text{Assets}_{Beg} \ - \ \text{Liab}_{Beg} \ = \ \text{Owners' Equity}_{Beg} \ + \ \text{Revenue} \ - \ \text{Expense}$$

A business entity can have the following two general types of transactions that result in a change in owners' equity

- Transactions between the entity and <u>all non-owners</u> – these transactions affect income
- Transactions between the entity and its <u>owners</u> – these transactions do not affect income

The first set of transactions are those by which the business entity makes money for its owners. These are primarily transactions between the entity and its customers, suppliers, employees, and the government. These transactions are recorded as revenue and expense and are then closed (transferred) to owners' equity at the end of the accounting period.

The second set of transactions, those between the business and its owners, are transactions in which the owners increase or decrease their investment in the company. These transactions are analogous to making a deposit or withdrawal in a bank account. The three general types of these transactions, which are recorded directly to owners' equity, are

- The business sells shares of its stock to someone for cash (or some other asset). As a result, assets increase and owners' equity increases.
- The business declares a dividend to the owners. As a result, owners' equity decreases and liabilities increase.

- The business repurchases shares of its own stock from one or more of the owners. As a result, assets (cash) decrease and owners' equity decrease.

To distinguish between these two general types of transactions, we modify the accounting equation as follows

$$\text{Assets}_{Beg} \quad - \quad \text{Liab}_{Beg} \quad = \quad \text{POE}_{Beg} \quad + \quad \text{Revenue} \quad - \quad \text{Expense}$$

In this version of the equation, POE_{Beg} is "Permanent" Owners' Equity as of the beginning of the period. This amount will change during the period only if and when owners invest more in the company (buy stock) or withdraw some of their investment from the company (receive a dividend or sell their stock back to the company). **These transactions are recorded directly to permanent owners' equity.**

Revenue and expense accounts are "temporary" owners' equity accounts that accumulate changes in wealth from earning income during the period and then are reset to zero at the end of the period. All transactions other than those between the company and its owners are recorded to these temporary owners' equity accounts (or a few other temporary owners' equity accounts to be added in a later chapter).

At the end of the accounting period, after all of the transactions and other events are recorded, but before the revenue and expense accounts are closed and transferred to owners' equity, the equation will look like this

$$\text{Assets}_{End} \quad - \quad \text{Liab}_{End} \quad = \quad \text{POE}_{Pre\text{-}Close} \quad + \quad \text{Revenue} \quad - \quad \text{Expense}$$

In this version of the equation, assets and liabilities are their ending balances, reflecting all of the changes that have occurred, whether from transactions with owners that were made directly to Permanent Owners' Equity (POE) or transactions with others, that were recorded as revenue and expense. $\text{POE}_{Pre\text{-}Close}$ is "Permanent" Owners' Equity" before closing revenue and expense. Permanent Owners' Equity may have changed during the period as a result of transactions with owners, but it does not yet reflect the changes in owners' equity due to transactions with non-owners.

In the final step, the revenue and expense accounts are closed to owners' equity and the equation will look like this.

$$\text{Assets}_{End} \quad - \quad \text{Liab}_{End} \quad = \quad \text{POE}_{End} \quad + \text{Revenue} \quad - \quad \text{Expense}$$

In this version of the equation, Permanent Owners' Equity has changed from "Pre-Close" to the ending balance and the revenue and expense accounts have been reset to zero.

A Simple Example

Here is an intuitive example to help make these points clear. Assume you have a bank account that you consider to be a separate entity that you want to account for separately from the rest of your economic activity. **You own the bank account.**

You make deposits and withdrawals during the year, which are transactions between you and the bank account. These are your additional investments in this entity and withdrawals of your investment from this entity.

Also, during the year the bank account (as a separate entity) earns interest and incurs fees. The interest is revenue earned by the bank account entity and the fees are expenses incurred by the bank account entity. The difference between the interest earned and the fees incurred is the net income earned by the bank account entity on your behalf as the owner.

To put numbers to this example, assume that you began a recent year with a balance in your account of $1,000 and during the year:

- You made deposits of $640
- You made withdrawals of $300
- The account earned interest of $26
- The account incurred fees of $12

The bank account's <u>position</u> changed during the year from a beginning balance of $1,000 to an ending balance of $1,354 (1,000 + 640 − 300 + 26 − 12).

The bank account's <u>performance</u> during the year was revenue of $26 and expense of $12, for net income of $14.

Let's see how this would be represented in a series of equations. Here is the equation at the beginning of the period when there is $1,000 in the account, and since there are no liabilities, your wealth in this entity (as the owner) is also $1,000. Because it is the beginning of the period, revenue and expense are both zero.

$$
\begin{array}{ccccccccc}
\textbf{1,000} & & \textbf{0} & & \textbf{1,000} & & \textbf{0} & & \textbf{0} \\
\text{Assets}_{\text{Beg}} & - & \text{Liab}_{\text{Beg}} & = & \text{POE}_{\text{Beg}} & + & \text{Revenue} & - & \text{Expense}
\end{array}
$$

When you make deposits and withdrawals, these are transactions between the entity and its owner (you) in which you are increasing and decreasing your investment in this entity. Notice, this does not affect the income the bank account entity earns, revenue and expense are still zero.

$$
\begin{array}{ccccccccc}
\uparrow\textbf{640} & & & & \uparrow\textbf{640} & & & & \\
\textbf{1,000} & & \textbf{0} & & \textbf{1,000} & & \textbf{0} & & \textbf{0} \\
\text{Assets}_{\text{Beg}} & - & \text{Liab}_{\text{Beg}} & = & \text{POE}_{\text{Beg}} & + & \text{Revenue} & - & \text{Expense} \\
\downarrow\textbf{300} & & & & \downarrow\textbf{300} & & & &
\end{array}
$$

Now we add the interest and fees. The interest is revenue to the bank account and the fees are an expense to the bank account. These are transactions with non-owners, i.e., the bank. The bank has paid revenue to the bank account for the right to use the money in the account, and the bank has charged the account for services provided.

$$
\begin{array}{ccccccccc}
\uparrow\textbf{26} & & & & & & & & \\
\uparrow\textbf{640} & & & & \uparrow\textbf{640} & & & & \\
\textbf{1,000} & & \textbf{0} & & \textbf{1,000} & & \uparrow\textbf{26} & & \uparrow\textbf{12} \\
\text{Assets}_{\text{Beg}} & - & \text{Liab}_{\text{Beg}} & = & \text{POE}_{\text{Beg}} & + & \text{Revenue} & - & \text{Expense} \\
\downarrow\textbf{300} & & & & \downarrow\textbf{300} & & & & \\
\downarrow\textbf{12} & & & & & & & &
\end{array}
$$

At the end of the period we close the revenue and expense accounts to owners' equity. This transfers the amount in revenue and expense to owners' equity and resets the revenue and expense accounts to zero.

$$
\begin{array}{ccccccccc}
\uparrow\textbf{26} & & & & \uparrow\textbf{14} & & & & \\
\uparrow\textbf{640} & & & & \uparrow\textbf{640} & & & & \\
\textbf{1,000} & & \textbf{0} & & \textbf{1,000} & & \uparrow\textbf{26} & & \uparrow\textbf{12} \\
\text{Assets}_{\text{Beg}} & - & \text{Liab}_{\text{Beg}} & = & \text{POE}_{\text{Beg}} & + & \text{Revenue} & - & \text{Expense} \\
\downarrow\textbf{300} & & & & \downarrow\textbf{300} & & \downarrow\textbf{26} & & \downarrow\textbf{12} \\
\uparrow\textbf{12} & & & & & & & &
\end{array}
$$

At the end of the year, which is the beginning of the next year, we have

$$\underset{Assets_{End}}{\textbf{1,354}} \; - \; \underset{Liab_{End}}{\textbf{0}} \; = \; \underset{POE_{End}}{\textbf{1,354}} \; + \; \underset{Revenue}{\textbf{0}} \; - \; \underset{Expense}{\textbf{0}}$$

This equation merely adds up all of the items represented in the previous equation to show that the balance in the bank account is equal to both assets and owners' equity for the bank account entity.

Later, when we review the actual financial statements of Starbucks, we will see that accounting for the company's activity is very analogous to accounting for this bank account, with these differences.

- Rather than only one asset Starbucks has many, including cash, receivables from customers, inventory, plant and equipment, etc.

- Rather than one revenue Starbucks has several, from selling coffee from company-owned stores, earning license fees from licensed stores, and selling Starbucks-related packaged goods.

- Rather than one expense, Starbucks has several, including for the coffee they sell, rent for their stores, wages for their employees, advertising, etc.

- Finally, Starbucks, as with all companies, has a specific owners' equity account that revenue and expense are closed (transferred) into, which is called retained earnings.

But all that lies further ahead. When we get there, think back to this simple bank account example to help you not lose track of what is happening in the complexity of a large modern business entity like Starbucks.

Ten Common Transactions

At first, accounting can seem more complicated than it actually is. However, even though a large corporation like Starbucks enters into many thousands of transactions every year, the fact is that the vast majority of these transactions represent relatively few "types" of transactions that are repeated over and over again. Many of these transactions may look different on the surface, but they are in fact economically equivalent.

To see this more clearly, I want to stop here and review ten common transactions that we will cover throughout this book, some we have already seen and others will be discussed in more depth ahead.

Three Balance Sheet Transactions
These are transactions that the company enters into to prepare to make money. These transactions do not affect income or owners' equity.

1. Buying an asset for cash. The effect on the equation is to increase an asset for the item purchased and decrease an asset for the cash used.

$$\uparrow \atop \text{Assets}_{Beg} \quad - \quad \text{Liab}_{Beg} \quad = \quad \text{POE}_{Beg} \quad + \quad \text{Revenue} \quad - \quad \text{Expense} \atop \downarrow$$

2. Buying an asset on credit or borrowing cash. The effect on the equation is to increase an asset for the cash borrowed and increase liability for the obligation to the lender.

$$\overset{\uparrow}{\text{Assets}_{Beg}} \quad - \quad \overset{\uparrow}{\text{Liab}_{Beg}} \quad = \quad \text{POE}_{Beg} \quad + \quad \text{Revenue} \quad - \quad \text{Expense}$$

3. Paying a liability. The effect on the equation is to decrease an asset for the cash paid and to decrease a liability for the reduction in the obligation to the lender.

$$\underset{\downarrow}{\text{Assets}_{Beg}} \quad - \quad \underset{\downarrow}{\text{Liab}_{Beg}} \quad = \quad \text{POE}_{Beg} \quad + \quad \text{Revenue} \quad - \quad \text{Expense}$$

Three Transactions With Owners
These are transactions between the company and its owners. These transactions do not affect income, but they do affect owners' equity.

4. The company sells (issues) its own stock to investors for cash. The effect on the equation is to increase an asset for the cash received from the investors and to increase owners' equity for the increased ownership of the investors.

$$\overset{\uparrow}{\text{Assets}_{Beg}} \quad - \quad \text{Liab}_{Beg} \quad = \quad \overset{\uparrow}{\text{POE}_{Beg}} \quad + \quad \text{Revenue} \quad - \quad \text{Expense}$$

5. The company declares a cash dividend for its investors, which is a legal liability on the part of the company. The effect on the equation

is to increase a liability for the obligation to pay the dividend to the shareholders and to decrease owners' equity for the reduced ownership of the investors.

$$\text{Assets}_{Beg} \quad - \quad \overset{\uparrow}{\text{Liab}_{Beg}} \quad = \quad \underset{\downarrow}{\text{POE}_{Beg}} \quad + \quad \text{Revenue} \quad - \quad \text{Expense}$$

6. The company repurchases from its investors some of its own stock. The effect on the equation is to decrease cash for the amount paid to the shareholders and to decrease owners' equity for the reduced ownership of the investors.

$$\underset{\downarrow}{\text{Assets}_{Beg}} \quad - \quad \text{Liab}_{Beg} \quad = \quad \underset{\downarrow}{\text{POE}_{Beg}} \quad + \quad \text{Revenue} \quad - \quad \text{Expense}$$

Four Income Statement Transactions
These are transactions are between the company and its non-owners, and are the transactions by which the company makes money. They affect the temporary owners' equity accounts, revenue and expense, and thereby affect both income and owners' equity.

We will discuss these four transactions in much greater depth in the next two chapters.

7. The company provides goods and services that are either paid for upon delivery or later. The effect on the equation is to increase assets for the cash received now or accounts receivable for the cash to be received later and to increase revenue for the amount earned from providing the goods and services.

$$\overset{\uparrow}{\text{Assets}_{Beg}} \quad - \quad \text{Liab}_{Beg} \quad = \quad \text{POE}_{Beg} \quad + \quad \overset{\uparrow}{\text{Revenue}} \quad - \quad \text{Expense}$$

8. The company provides goods and services that were paid for in advance. The effect on the equation is to decrease liabilities for the cash received previously and to increase revenue for the amount earned from providing the goods and services.

$$\text{Assets}_{Beg} \quad - \quad \underset{\downarrow}{\text{Liab}_{Beg}} \quad = \quad \text{POE}_{Beg} \quad + \quad \overset{\uparrow}{\text{Revenue}} \quad - \quad \text{Expense}$$

9. The company consumes (uses up) a good or service that is paid for at the time or earlier. The effect on the equation is to decrease assets for the cash paid now or for the asset consumed (used up) and increase expense for the resource consumed.

$$\text{Assets}_{Beg} \quad - \quad \text{Liab}_{Beg} \quad = \quad \text{POE}_{Beg} \quad + \quad \text{Revenue} \quad - \quad \overset{\uparrow}{\text{Expense}}$$
$$\underset{\downarrow}{}$$

10. The company consumes (uses up) a good or service that will be paid for later. The effect on the equation is to increase liabilities for the obligation and increase expense for the resource consumed.

$$\text{Assets}_{Beg} \quad - \quad \overset{\uparrow}{\text{Liab}_{Beg}} \quad = \quad \text{POE}_{Beg} \quad + \quad \text{Revenue} \quad - \quad \overset{\uparrow}{\text{Expense}}$$

We will return to this list of transactions numerous times in the remainder of the book.

Chapter 4 – Revenue Recognition

Review

The previous three chapters described accounting for both an individual and a company. Beginning with this chapter we will only be accounting for a company.

The topic of this chapter is an important income statement issue, the timing of revenue recognition, i.e., <u>when</u> revenue should be recorded. The timing of expense recognition is discussed in the next chapter.

Before we proceed, it is important to have clearly in mind the following essential elements of accounting for a company from the previous chapters.

- The fundamental accounting equation is

  Assets – Liabilities = Owners' Equity.

- Assets and liabilities are measures made by accountants at a point in time (stocks) of amounts the company owns and owes.

- Owners' equity is equal to assets minus liabilities and is the amount at a point in time (stock) of the wealth investors have invested in the company as measured by accountants.

- Over time, owners' equity can change from transactions between the company and its owners—when the owners invest more or make a withdrawal from the company.

- Over time, owners' equity also changes as a result of transactions between the company and non-owners, i.e., customers, employees, suppliers, the government, etc.

- Transactions with non-owners that change owners' equity are recorded as revenue and expense, which are temporary owners' equity accounts that capture the company's net income for the accounting period.

- At the end of an accounting period revenue and expense are closed (transferred) to owners' equity, resetting their balances to zero so they can record the company's performance in the next period.

Understanding this flow of value through the company, revenue flowing in from customers, expense flowing out to employees, suppliers and others, investors adjusting their position, is essential to understanding what follows.

Why is the Timing of Revenue Recognition Important?

The question of <u>when</u> to record revenue and expense is at the heart of many of the most important issues in accrual accounting. But why is it so important?

Before we get into the details, let's step back and think about why we have accounting at all. Obviously, it is to keep track of the economic position and performance of a company, but why do we want to do that?

One answer is that it provides investors with information about how well the managers have used the money the investors have invested in the company. This is referred to as stewardship.

A second answer, and the one we focus on in this book, is that financial statement users, mainly investors and creditors, but others as well, want to use the information provided by financial statements to help them make decisions about their relationship with the company. Investors need to decide whether to keep their investment, whether to buy more or to sell what they have. Creditors need to decide whether or not to lend to the company. Suppliers need to decide whether to extend credit to the company. Customers need to know whether they can rely on the company to continue to supply them in the future. Prospective employees want to know if the company they are thinking of working for is financially healthy.

What do all of these decisions have in common? What do these decision makers <u>really</u> want to know? They want to know about the future, they want a crystal ball. But they don't have one.

What they do have are financial statements that provide information about the past that they can use to help predict the future. We see many such situations in which information about the past is used to predict the future in order to make decisions in the present. This is especially true in sports. For example, managers of fantasy baseball teams use player performance statistics from prior seasons as inputs to determine who to pick for their teams. Similarly, horse race handicappers use the results from prior races to determine how to bet in the current race.

How does this relate to the timing of recording revenue and expense and hence the timing of reporting income or profit?

Here is a simple example. Suppose you go to a bank for a loan to buy a car, and the bank asks for your annual income. In response you multiply your monthly salary by 13 instead of 12 and report that number. Using that number, which inflates your annual salary, the bank may project that you will earn more in the future than you are likely to earn. As a result, the bank may make a poor lending decision and lend you too much, running a higher than normal risk that the loan will not be repaid. And this is all because you reported more income in a recent period than you actually earned.

The situation is the same with a company. To help with their decisions, financial statement users often project the company's past annual income into the future on a <u>per year basis</u>. These financial statement users will make better decisions in doing so if the company reports <u>all</u> of the income earned in each period and <u>only</u> the income earned in each period.

This means that revenue must be recorded (recognized) in the period in which it is earned and expense must be recorded (recognized) in the period in which it is incurred. This is what we focus on in this and the next chapter.

The Timing of Revenue Recognition

Consider the timeline below, which represents the period over which a product is developed and sold to a customer

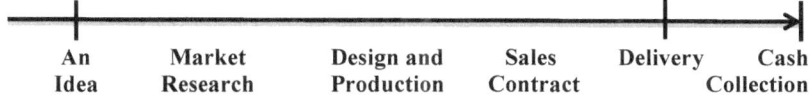

| An Idea | Market Research | Design and Production | Sales Contract | Delivery | Cash Collection |

The company starts with an idea about a product or service and conducts market research to determine potential demand. The company then designs the product and determines how and where to produce it. Once production has begun the company signs sales agreements and produces and delivers the product to the customer, often on credit. As a last step the company collects the cash.

The issue we address in this chapter is <u>when</u> along this timeline should revenue be recorded? That is, when should the company "count" an increase in owners' equity (the wealth of investors) from providing a customer with a good or service?

Remember, we are trying to provide information that is useful to financial statement users about how the company is performing. They would likely prefer to have that information as early as possible so they can use the information in their decisions. On the other hand, they do not want information that turns out not to be accurate. If the information is not accurate, they may make poor decisions, such as the bank lending you too much in the simple example above.

Further left on the timeline is earlier in the process, and recording revenue then would provide financial statement users with an early signal about the company's potential performance. However, at that early stage, it is more likely the information will turn out to be inaccurate because there is substantial <u>uncertainty</u> over how much revenue will be generated, if any.

For example, during the market research stage it is not yet clear whether there will be demand for the product. After resolving that uncertainty with market research, there is still uncertainty over whether a cost-effective product can be designed and produced. Although uncertainty is reduced after a sales contract is signed, it is still not certain that the company can satisfy the customer or that the customer won't cancel the agreement. Even after the product is delivered there remains some uncertainty over whether the customer will pay. Only after receiving payment, at the far right of the timeline, is there no uncertainty. The company has the cash.

When is the best time to record revenue so as to provide information that is both timely and sufficiently accurate? Should that decision favor timeliness or accuracy? Put differently,

when is enough of the uncertainty resolved to justify "counting" the revenue as increasing the company's wealth so that we can report it on the income statement?

You may have your own opinion about the answer to this question, and that's fine. But the answer in the accounting rules is that revenue is recognized when

... the good or service is transferred to the customer, which is when the customer has control over the good or service

This "transfer of control" can take place either (a) over time, or (b) at a point in time.

An example of transfer of control over time is when a landlord rents out an apartment or an insurance company provides insurance coverage. Each day that goes by the landlord is providing the service of use of the apartment, and each day that goes by the insurance company is standing ready to pay a claim if needed. As a result, in both cases, the company earns the revenue over time.

An example of transfer of control at a point in time is when a car dealer sells a car or when a furniture store sells a sofa. In these cases, the transfer occurs at the point in time when the car or sofa is placed under the control of the customer, usually when the car is driven off the lot or when the sofa is delivered to the customer's house. As a result, in these cases the company earns the revenue at that point in time.

We can see that the accounting rules favor accuracy over timeliness and require that nearly all of the uncertainty over revenue generation is resolved before the company is allowed to count or record the revenue. The only remaining uncertainty is whether the selling company will collect the cash, which in most cases is not very uncertain.

Why is the revenue recognition rule so conservative?

In accounting a rule is more "conservative" if it makes it more difficult for the company to record assets and income. So, why is this the case for revenue recognition?

There are two reasons for this. The first is that recognizing revenue when there is substantial uncertainty requires estimating what will happen in the future and in many cases these estimates are likely to be inaccurate. For example, if companies were permitted to record revenue on items produced but not yet sold, they may later sell fewer units or at a lower price than they originally estimated so that revenue was overstated in the earlier period. Thus, to provide decision makers with more accurate information, the rules require delaying revenue recognition until there is little uncertainty remaining about whether the revenue has actually been earned and how much has been earned.

The second reason is that allowing managers to estimate revenue earlier in the process, when substantial uncertainty remains, would give managers a great deal of discretion in determining the amount of revenue they report. The accounting rule makers recognized that the company's managers have strong incentives to report to investors and creditors that the company is performing well. These incentives, which we will discuss in more detail later, may color the manager's view of likely revenue to be earned and collected in the future, causing her to report an overly optimistic view of current revenue. The rules are designed to take most of the discretion about the amount of revenue earned in the current period out of the hands of managers, permitting them to report only revenue for goods and services for which the uncertainty is substantially resolved.

Now that we understand when revenue is recognized, let's discuss the relationship between when revenue is recognized and when cash is collected. Spoiler alert: when cash is collected is irrelevant in the timing of revenue recognition.

The Timing of Revenue Recognition versus Cash Collection

Consider another timeline. This timeline is centered on "transfer of control" and shows that the company may collect the cash from the customer before transfer of control, at the same time as transfer of control, or after transfer of control.

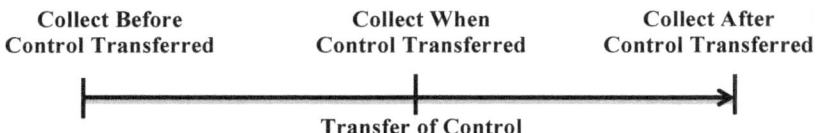

Given that revenue will be recorded when control is transferred to the customer, we want to see how the accounting is done in each of these three situations. Let's first consider these three situations in general, and then apply the concepts to a more specific example.

To illustrate these examples, we use the following "change" version of the basic accounting equation, where the change from the beginning to the end of the period is indicated by the Greek letter delta (Δ).

$$\Delta \text{Assets} \quad - \quad \Delta \text{Liab} \quad = \quad \Delta \text{Perm OE} \quad + \quad \text{Rev} \quad - \quad \text{Exp}$$

Notice that the letter delta is only applied to the "stock" accounts, assets, liabilities and owners' equity. Revenue and expense accounts are "flow" or change accounts that capture the change in owners' equity from operating the company, so no delta is necessary.

First, consider the case in which the company collects cash from the customer <u>at the same time</u> that control of the good or service is transferred. In this case the asset cash is increased and the company records revenue. The effect on the accounting equation is

$$\overset{\uparrow}{\Delta \text{Assets}} \quad - \quad \Delta \text{Liab} \quad = \quad \Delta \text{Perm OE} \quad + \quad \overset{\uparrow}{\text{Rev}} \quad - \quad \text{Exp}$$

Next, consider the case in which the company will collect the cash from the customer <u>later</u>, after the transfer of control, usually in 30 or 60 days. In this case the asset accounts receivable is increased and the company records revenue. The effect on the accounting equation is

$$\overset{\uparrow}{\Delta \text{Assets}} \quad - \quad \Delta \text{Liab} \quad = \quad \Delta \text{Perm OE} \quad + \quad \overset{\uparrow}{\text{Rev}} \quad - \quad \text{Exp}$$

Finally, consider the case in which the company collects the cash from the customer <u>in advance</u>, and control of the good or service is transferred later. In this case, when the cash is received the company records an increase in the asset cash and an increase in a liability. A liability is increased because the selling company is now obligated to provide the customer either with the good or service they have paid for or give them their money back. The effect on the accounting equation is

$$\overset{\uparrow}{\Delta \text{Assets}} \quad - \quad \overset{\uparrow}{\Delta \text{Liab}} \quad = \quad \Delta \text{Perm OE} \quad + \quad \text{Rev} \quad - \quad \text{Exp}$$

Later, when control of the good or service is transferred to the customer, the selling company records revenue and reduces its liability to the customer accordingly. The effect on the accounting equation is

$$\Delta \text{Assets} \quad - \quad \underset{\downarrow}{\Delta \text{Liab}} \quad = \quad \Delta \text{Perm OE} \quad + \quad \overset{\uparrow}{\text{Rev}} \quad - \quad \text{Exp}$$

In all three cases revenue is recorded when control is transferred, regardless of when the cash is collected. This is worth repeating.

Revenue is recorded when control is transferred, regardless of when the cash is received

And these three examples demonstrate an important part of the definition of revenue

Revenue is either an increase in an asset or a decrease in a liability.

Thus, revenue is an increase in owners' equity from providing goods and services to customers that either

- Will be collected from the customer now or in the future (increase an asset when the revenue is recognized).

- Was collected from the customer in the past (decrease a liability when the revenue is recognized).

Now let's consider more specific examples of revenue recognition using Starbucks as a convenient example.

Revenue Recognition for Starbucks

Let's start with the case in which cash is received at the same time that control is transferred and revenue is recognized. This happens every time you walk into a Starbucks and pay $5.00 cash for your beverage. In this case, the effect on the accounting equation from Starbuck's point of view is

$$\uparrow\$5.00 \qquad\qquad\qquad\qquad\qquad \uparrow\$5.00$$
$$\text{Cash} \qquad\qquad\qquad\qquad\qquad\quad \text{Revenue}$$
$$\Delta\text{Assets} \quad - \quad \Delta\text{Liab} \quad = \quad \Delta\text{Perm OE} \quad + \quad \text{Rev} \quad - \quad \text{Exp}$$

This is the end of the accounting; nothing further needs to be done. Of course, there is an expense related to providing the beverage to you, but we will ignore that for now and discuss it in detail in the next chapter.

Now, let's consider the case in which Starbucks transfers control of the product and later collects the cash. Assume that Starbucks delivered $1,000 of Frappuccino to Safeway, and 30 days later receives the cash payment. The effect on Starbucks' accounting equation for the transfer of control (delivery of the Frappuccino) is

$$\uparrow\$1,000 \qquad\qquad\qquad\qquad\qquad \uparrow\$1,000$$
$$\text{Acct Rec} \qquad\qquad\qquad\qquad\qquad \text{Revenue}$$
$$\Delta\text{Assets} \quad - \quad \Delta\text{Liab} \quad = \quad \Delta\text{Perm OE} \quad + \quad \text{Rev} \quad - \quad \text{Exp}$$

Acct Rec is an abbreviation for accounts receivable, an asset recognizing that Starbucks' customers (Safeway in this example) owe them money. Later, when the customer pays, the effect on the accounting equation is

$$\uparrow\$1,000$$
$$\text{Cash}$$
$$\Delta\text{Assets} \quad - \quad \Delta\text{Liab} \quad = \quad \Delta\text{Perm OE} \quad + \quad \text{Rev} \quad - \quad \text{Exp}$$
$$\downarrow\$1,000$$
$$\text{Acct Rec}$$

Notice that the effect on revenue is when control of the product is transferred to the customer. There is no revenue recorded when the cash is collected, this is only an exchange of one asset (accounts receivable) for another asset (cash).

Finally, let's consider the case in which Starbucks first receives cash from the customer and later transfers control of the product to the customer. This happens when you log into your Starbucks value card account on line and add $20.00 to your card, charging it to your credit card. Assume that Starbucks has an arrangement with its bank that such credit card receipts go directly into their bank account, so this is cash to Starbucks. Finally, assume that you go into a Starbucks store two weeks later and buy a $5.00 beverage using your Starbucks value card.

The effect on the accounting equation from Starbucks' point of view for the first transaction, when you added $20.00 to your value card, is

$$
\begin{array}{ccccc}
& \uparrow \$20.00 & & & \\
\uparrow \$20.00 & \text{Deferred} & & & \\
\text{Cash} & \text{Rev} & & & \\
\Delta\text{Assets} \quad - & \Delta\text{Liab} \quad = & \Delta\text{Perm OE} \quad + & \text{Rev} \quad - & \text{Exp}
\end{array}
$$

This requires some explanation. First, the increase in cash should be clear, we assumed that when you added $20.00 to your account that it was cash to Starbucks. They have your money. The question is whether at this point they have transferred control of a product to you. The answer is no. This means that Starbucks cannot yet record revenue even though they have your money.

The offsetting entry to the increase in cash is an increase in a liability. Does this make sense? Does Starbucks owe you something? Yes, they have your money and you expect that they will provide you with $20.00 of product when you ask for it. If they don't provide you with product, they should return your money. Either way, they owe you $20.00. We commonly call this liability "deferred revenue" or "unearned revenue" because the revenue is not yet earned and is being deferred until the company has transferred control of a product to the customer.

Two weeks later you go into a Starbucks store and buy a $5.00 beverage, paying with your Starbucks value card. The effect on Starbucks' accounting equation is

$$\Delta\text{Assets} \quad - \quad \underset{\substack{\downarrow\$5.00 \\ \textbf{Deferred} \\ \textbf{Rev}}}{\Delta\text{Liab}} \quad = \quad \Delta\text{Perm OE} \quad + \quad \overset{\substack{\uparrow\$5.00 \\ \textbf{Revenue}}}{\text{Rev}} \quad - \quad \text{Exp}$$

By providing you with this beverage Starbucks has reduced its obligation to you by $5.00 and recognized that much in revenue.

Notice that in all three cases, revenue is recorded when control of the good is transferred to the customer, not necessarily when the cash is received. We also see that revenue results from either an increase in an asset (cash or accounts receivable) or a decrease in a liability (deferred revenue, also referred to as unearned revenue).

We see all three of these situations in practice. Cash paid at the time control of the good or service is transferred is common in grocery stores, restaurants and other retail locations. Cash paid after control of the good or service is transferred is very common between companies and when retail customers are using a company credit card, such as buying shoes at Macy's using a Macy's credit card. Cash paid before control of the good or service is transferred is very common for certain transactions like buying insurance, airline tickets, and tickets to sporting events and concerts.

Two Common Income Statement Transactions
There is literally an infinite number of ways that companies can earn revenue by providing an endless variety of goods and services to their customers in countless ways. However, in terms of accounting there is only one of two transactions taking place when the company earns revenue. These are transactions seven and eight from our list of ten common transactions at the end of chapter three, repeated here for convenience.

7. The company provides goods and services that are either paid for upon delivery or later. The effect on the equation is to increase revenue for the amount earned from providing the goods and services, and to increase assets for the cash received now or accounts receivable for the cash to be received later.

$$\overset{\uparrow}{\text{Assets}_{\text{Beg}}} \quad - \quad \text{Liab}_{\text{Beg}} \quad = \quad \text{POE}_{\text{Beg}} \quad + \quad \overset{\uparrow}{\text{Revenue}} \quad - \quad \text{Expense}$$

8. The company provides goods and services that were paid for in advance. The effect on the equation is to increase revenue for the amount earned from providing the goods and services, and to decrease liabilities for the cash received previously.

$$\text{Assets}_{Beg} \underset{\downarrow}{\quad} - \quad \underset{\downarrow}{\text{Liab}_{Beg}} \quad = \quad \text{POE}_{Beg} \quad + \quad \overset{\uparrow}{\text{Revenue}} \quad - \quad \text{Expense}$$

The next chapter covers these same issues for expense recognition: when to recognize expense and how expense recognition relates to when the cash for the expense is paid.

Chapter 5 – Expense Recognition

The Timing of Expense Recognition

The last chapter focused on when to recognize (record) revenue. This chapter focuses on when to recognize (record) expense.

Recall that an important use of financial statements is to provide information about the past that can be used to help predict the future. In doing so, financial statement users often project a company's past annual income into the future on a <u>per year basis</u>. As a result, it is important that the company reports <u>all</u> of the income earned in each period and <u>only</u> the income earned in each period.

We can make this point regarding expense by changing the example used for revenue from the previous chapter. In that example, you went to a bank for a car loan and reported to the bank 13 months of salary as your annual salary rather than 12. We concluded this might mislead the bank into giving you a larger loan with higher than normal risk that you will not be able to make the payments.

Now, let's assume that you accurately reported to the bank your 12 months of salary, but for your living expenses you reported 11 months of rent rather than 12 as your annual rent payments. Once again, you are giving the bank a false impression of the "extra" money you have available to repay a car loan, so they might project that you will incur less expense in the future than you are likely to incur. As a result, the bank may make a poor lending decision and give you a loan that has higher than normal risk that you will not be able to make the payments.

This illustrates that just as it is important to record revenue in the period in which it is earned, it is also important to record expense in the period in which it is incurred. Recording both revenue and expense as accurately as possible in the "right" accounting period will result in the most accurate measure of income. And, as we saw in the last chapter, an accurate measure of income is important for anyone trying to project income into the future on a per period basis.

The general rule for when to record revenue is when control of the product or service has been transferred to the customer. For expense the general rule is simpler—an expense is incurred in order to generate revenue, so an expense should be recognized

. . . in the same period in which the revenue generated by that expense is recorded.

We can think of three general ways in which this might occur.

- Matched Expense – expenses that are closely associated with the revenue earned from a particular sale

- Period Expense – expenses that are not associated with a particular sale, but are associated with the revenue earned in a particular period

- Allocated Expense – expenses related to assets that are consumed or used up over multiple periods, so that the cost of the asset must be allocated as expense to the periods that benefit from the use of that asset

As we explain in the next section, regardless of which of these three is the basis for recognizing a particular expense, as with revenue, when cash is paid is irrelevant for the timing of expense recognition.

The Timing of Expense Recognition versus Cash Payment
We saw in the last chapter that revenue is not recognized when the cash is received, but when some asset is increased or a liability is decreased. In the same way, an expense is not recognized when the cash is paid, but when something is consumed in order to earn revenue and an asset is decreased or a liability is increased.

Consider the timeline below that is similar to the second timeline from the previous chapter. This timeline indicates that the company may pay for a good or service

- When the good or service is used up

- After the good or service is used up

- Before the good or service is used up

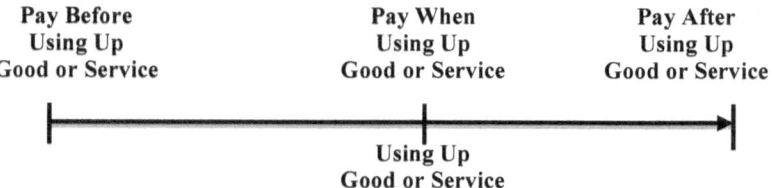

In the following example, we use a bookstore to illustrate both the three ways in which expense can be recognized and how they relate to when cash is paid.

From our discussion of revenue recognition in the previous chapter, when the clerk in the bookstore hands the customer a purchased book, control is transferred to the customer and the bookstore can record the revenue.

But what about the expenses?

The most obvious expense is the cost of the book that the clerk just gave to the customer. This is an example of the first type of expense, a matched expense, one that is closely associated with the revenue generated. The effect on the accounting equation is to decrease assets (inventory) and increase expense (cost of goods sold) as follows.

$$\Delta\text{Assets} \quad - \quad \Delta\text{Liab} \quad = \quad \Delta\text{Perm OE} \quad + \quad \text{Rev} \quad - \quad \overset{\uparrow}{\text{Exp}}$$
$$\underset{\downarrow}{}$$

In the case of inventory, the bookstore may have already paid for the book, or the bookstore may still owe the cost of the book to their supplier. It doesn't matter. The expense is recognized when the revenue is recognized, at the time control of the book is transferred to the customer, regardless of when the bookstore pays for the book.

Next, in order to operate, the bookstore must pay wages to the clerk who handed the book to the customer. This is an example of a period expense because the clerk's wages are necessary to generate that period's revenue, regardless of the amount of revenue generated and none of the clerk's current period wages will benefit future periods. The same is true for other expenditures that benefit only the current period such as rent, insurance, utilities, janitorial services to clean the building, and so on. Because current period expenditures for these services only benefit the current period regardless of how much revenue is earned in the current period, they should all be expensed in the current period.

When to expense these period expenses does not depend on when they are paid. For example, even though the clerk's wages may not be paid until the next period, they should be expensed in the current period. In this case, when the (wage) expense is recorded in the current period, the bookstore also records a liability (wages payable) for the wages owed to the clerk.

$$\Delta\text{Assets} \quad - \quad \overset{\uparrow}{\Delta\text{Liab}} \quad = \quad \Delta\text{Perm OE} \quad + \quad \text{Rev} \quad - \quad \overset{\uparrow}{\text{Exp}}$$

Later, when the clerk is paid, the bookstore reduces cash and eliminates the liability.

$$\Delta \text{Assets} \quad - \quad \Delta \text{Liab} \quad = \quad \Delta \text{Perm OE} \quad + \quad \text{Rev} \quad - \quad \text{Exp}$$
$$\downarrow \qquad\qquad \downarrow$$

On the other hand, for other period expenses the bookstore may make payment in advance of consuming the good or service. For example, insurance is normally paid for in advance resulting in a decrease in cash and an increase in an asset, pre-paid insurance, that is waiting to be consumed. At the time of purchasing insurance the bookstore records

$$\uparrow$$
$$\Delta \text{Assets} \quad - \quad \Delta \text{Liab} \quad = \quad \Delta \text{Perm OE} \quad + \quad \text{Rev} \quad - \quad \text{Exp}$$
$$\downarrow$$

Later, in the period in which some of the insurance services are consumed, the bookstore reduces the asset pre-paid insurance and records an expense.

$$\qquad\qquad\qquad\qquad\qquad\qquad\qquad\qquad\qquad \uparrow$$
$$\Delta \text{Assets} \quad - \quad \Delta \text{Liab} \quad = \quad \Delta \text{Perm OE} \quad + \quad \text{Rev} \quad - \quad \text{Exp}$$
$$\downarrow$$

Finally, examples of allocated expenses include a computerized cash register system, bookshelves, and display cases. When the bookstore invested in these items each was expected to help generate revenue in multiple future periods, so they were initially recorded as assets. Assuming the bookstore paid cash for these items, they recorded

$$\uparrow$$
$$\Delta \text{Assets} \quad - \quad \Delta \text{Liab} \quad = \quad \Delta \text{Perm OE} \quad + \quad \text{Rev} \quad - \quad \text{Exp}$$
$$\downarrow$$

As these assets were consumed over time to help the bookstore earn revenue, a portion of their initial value is allocated to expense in each period that benefits. This allocation process is called "depreciation." When depreciation expense is recorded the company decreases the previously-recognized asset for the part of the asset that has been consumed and records an expense.

$$\qquad\qquad\qquad\qquad\qquad\qquad\qquad\qquad\qquad \uparrow$$
$$\Delta \text{Assets} \quad - \quad \Delta \text{Liab} \quad = \quad \Delta \text{Perm OE} \quad + \quad \text{Rev} \quad - \quad \text{Exp}$$
$$\downarrow$$

As we discussed in previous chapters, the change in owners' equity from operating the company is captured in the accounting equation by the temporary owners' equity accounts, revenue and expense. This change is also captured on the left-hand side the balance sheet by changes in assets and liabilities. In the last chapter we learned that revenue must be either an increase in an asset or a decrease in a liability. Now, we see that

An expense must be either a decrease in an asset or an increase in a liability

Thus, an expense is something that has been consumed or used up in order to provide goods and services to customers that either

- Was paid for now or in the past (decrease an asset when expense is recognized).

- Will be paid for in the future (increase a liability when expense is recognized).

Examples of assets that are used up and become an expense include anything that is paid for in advance and later consumed, such as inventory, insurance, advertisements, etc. Examples of expenses that will be paid in the future and give rise to a liability now include anything that is consumed first and paid for later such as electricity or rent that are often paid for after we use them.

Now let's consider specific examples of expense recognition using Starbucks as a convenient example. We will ignore revenue for now, which was dealt with in the last chapter, and focus on expense.

Expense Recognition for Starbucks
When Starbucks sells coffee beans, they incur the three types of expense we described above. To begin, assume that Starbucks buys a pound of unroasted coffee for $3.00 and will pay for the coffee 30 days later. The effect of the purchase on Starbucks' accounting equation is

$$
\begin{array}{ccccccc}
 & & \uparrow\$3.00 & & & & \\
\uparrow\$3.00 & & \text{Acct} & & & & \\
\text{Inventory} & & \text{Payable} & & & & \\
\Delta\text{Assets} & - & \Delta\text{Liab} & = & \Delta\text{Perm OE} & + \text{ Rev } & - \text{ Exp}
\end{array}
$$

When they pay for that pound of coffee 30 days later the effect on Starbucks' accounting equation is

$$\Delta\text{Assets} \quad - \quad \Delta\text{Liab} \quad = \quad \Delta\text{Perm OE} \quad + \quad \text{Rev} \quad - \quad \text{Exp}$$

$$\downarrow\!\$3.00 \qquad\qquad \downarrow\!\$3.00$$
$$\text{Cash} \qquad\qquad\quad \text{Acct}$$
$$\text{Payable}$$

Acct Payable is an abbreviation for accounts payable, a liability that Starbucks owes to its supplier, in this case the company or grower who sold them the coffee beans.

Finally, when Starbucks sells the pound of coffee they record

$$\uparrow\!\$3.00$$
$$\text{COGS}$$
$$\Delta\text{Assets} \quad - \quad \Delta\text{Liab} \quad = \quad \Delta\text{Perm OE} \quad + \quad \text{Rev} \quad - \quad \text{Exp}$$
$$\downarrow\!\$3.00$$
$$\text{Inventory}$$

This is when the expense is recorded (we abbreviate cost of goods sold as COGS). This is an example of a <u>matched expense</u>. Notice there was no expense when Starbucks paid for the coffee beans, only when Starbucks used up or consumed the benefit of the coffee beans. That benefit was used up when they sold the beans, so that is when the expense was recorded.

Of course when Starbucks sold the pound of coffee beans a sales clerk waited on the customer. Assume the sales clerk will be paid her wages for that day later in the month, a few days after the end of the current pay period, and that her wages for that day were $12 per hour or $72 dollars for a six-hour shift. Her wages are an example of a <u>period expense</u>. They are an expense of that day, the day she was working, because whatever revenue Starbucks generated that day, and only revenue generated that day, benefited from that sales clerk working that day.

As of the end of the day Starbucks owes her for that day's wages and Starbucks has consumed the benefit of her labor and should record an expense. The effect on Starbucks' accounting equation is

		↑$72.00 Wages Payable						↑$72.00 Wage Expense
ΔAssets	−	ΔLiab	=	ΔPerm OE	+	Rev	−	Exp

When Starbucks pays this employee for that day's wages the effect on the Starbucks' accounting equation is

ΔAssets	−	ΔLiab	=	ΔPerm OE	+	Rev	−	Exp
↓$72.00 Cash		↓$72.00 Wages Payable						

Notice that the cost of the employee's labor is an expense of the period when she worked, which is the period that benefitted from her labor, not the period in which she was paid, which occurred after the expense was incurred. This is the main point of this example.

Don't worry that she was paid much more than the revenue from selling a pound of coffee. She likely sold a lot more than just that one pound of coffee that day. Also, don't worry about the revenue. Starbucks would have accounted for that as we discussed in the last chapter, recording the revenue when they handed the coffee to the customer. In this chapter we are focused on the expense.

This example of wage expense is a little extreme in that we have thought of one day as the accounting period to which the clerk's wages will be assigned. It is more likely that the relevant accounting period is longer, a month, or a quarter, or a year, but the idea is the same. In the case of wages, the expense recorded in any accounting period (for example that quarter) is the cost of the work done that period (quarter) regardless of whether it is paid in that period (quarter) or in the next period (quarter).

Finally, assume that Starbucks buys a large industrial coffee roaster for $100,000. They expect that the roaster will last for twenty years and have no value at the end of twenty years. Assuming they paid cash for the roaster, the effect on Starbucks' accounting equation when the roaster was purchased is

$$\uparrow\!\$100{,}000 \atop \text{Coffee Roaster}$$

$$\Delta\text{Assets} \quad - \quad \Delta\text{Liab} \quad = \quad \Delta\text{Perm OE} \quad + \quad \text{Rev} \quad - \quad \text{Exp}$$

$$\downarrow\!\$100{,}000 \atop \text{Cash}$$

Each year Starbucks consumes one-twentieth of the life of the coffee roaster, and as a result they allocate one-twentieth of the original cost as an expense to that period ($5,000 in this case). The effect on Starbucks' accounting equation is

$$\uparrow\!\$5{,}000 \atop \text{Depr Expense}$$

$$\Delta\text{Assets} \quad - \quad \Delta\text{Liab} \quad = \quad \Delta\text{Perm OE} \quad + \quad \text{Rev} \quad - \quad \text{Exp}$$

$$\downarrow\!\$5{,}000 \atop \text{Coffee Roaster}$$

We see all three of these types of expenses in practice. Cost of goods sold (or cost of services provided) is the most common matched expense. These are the costs most closely associated with the revenue generated. It could be food served in a restaurant, fuel consumed on an airplane, or services provided by a lawyer or accountant.

Period expenses can be many things, including wages, utilities, janitorial services, or anything else needed to operate the business, regardless of how much revenue was generated during the period or when the cash for that good or service is paid.

Allocated expenses can be for any asset that benefits multiple periods, such as buildings or machinery used in production, trucks or other vehicles for delivery, or the coffee roasters that Starbucks uses to roast the coffee you buy in your local store.

In all of these cases the expense is recorded in the period that benefits from consuming all or part of a good or service, regardless of when the cash was paid.

Two Common Income Statement Transactions
As we stated with revenue, so with expense, there is an infinite number of ways that companies can consume resources as they provide goods and services to their customers. However, in terms of accounting there is only one of two transactions taking place when the company incurs an

expense.   These are transactions nine and ten from our list of ten common transactions at the end of chapter three, repeated here for convenience.

9. The company consumes (uses up) a good or service that is paid for at the time or earlier. The effect on the equation is to decrease assets for the cash paid now or for the asset consumed (used up) and increase expense for the resource consumed.

$$\text{Assets}_{Beg} \quad - \quad \text{Liab}_{Beg} \quad = \quad \text{POE}_{Beg} \quad + \quad \text{Revenue} \quad - \quad \underset{\uparrow}{\text{Expense}}$$
$$\underset{\downarrow}{\phantom{\text{Assets}_{Beg}}}$$

10. The company consumes (uses up) a good or service that will be paid for later. The effect on the equation is to increase liabilities for the obligation for the resource consumed and increase expense for the resource consumed.

$$\text{Assets}_{Beg} \quad - \quad \underset{\uparrow}{\text{Liab}_{Beg}} \quad = \quad \text{POE}_{Beg} \quad + \quad \text{Revenue} \quad - \quad \underset{\uparrow}{\text{Expense}}$$

Chapter 6 – Gains and Losses

Review

So far we have introduced the balance sheet and income statement and discussed in some detail when revenue and expense are recorded and how they affect both of these statements. To review

- Revenue is recorded when control of the good or service is transferred to the customer, and is offset by an increase in cash or accounts receivable or a decrease in the liability deferred revenue.
- Expense is recorded in the period in which a resource is consumed by the company to generate revenue that period, and is offset by a decrease in an asset like inventory or pre-paid expense, or an increase in a liability like wages payable or some other payable.

Revenue and expense are "gross" (as opposed to "net") inflows and outflows from operating the business to earn a profit. Revenue is the gross amount received from a customer for purchase of a good or service. Expense is the gross amount used up to satisfy the customer. At the end of the period, revenue and expense accounts are closed (reset to zero) and the net value (profit or loss for the period) is transferred to owners' equity.

Revenue and expense transactions are the main (or "core") transactions that the company enters into to make a profit. However, companies also enter into other transactions that are not "core," but that do affect net income. These transactions are accounted for differently than revenue and expense and are the focus of this chapter.

Introduction to Gains and Losses

Companies frequently enter into transactions that are not designed to make money, but that are necessary to, for example, realign the company's assets or to recognize that an asset has fallen in value, or to record a liability. We refer to these as "non-core" transactions. The effects on net income and owners' equity of non-core transactions are not accounted for as revenue and expense, but rather as "gains" and "losses."

Gains and losses differ from revenue and expense in that they are not gross concepts, but "net" concepts. In these transactions it is often the case that the company gets something and gives up something, and the difference between the two is the "net" gain or loss the company records.

Gains and Losses versus Revenue and Expense

Here is an example to demonstrate the difference between revenue and expense on the one hand and a gain or loss on the other hand. Suppose a company has a bookcase that has a value in their accounting records of $250 and they sell it for $300 cash. If the company is a furniture store, they record two separate transactions, one for the gross amount of the revenue flowing into the company and one for the gross amount of the expense flowing out of the company.

The effect on the accounting equation for the revenue is

$$\begin{array}{ccccccccc}
\uparrow\$300 & & & & & & \uparrow\$300 & & \\
\textbf{Cash} & & & & & & \textbf{Rev} & & \\
\Delta\text{Assets} & - & \Delta\text{Liab} & = & \Delta\text{Perm OE} & + & \text{Rev} & - & \text{Exp}
\end{array}$$

The effect on the accounting equation for the expense is

$$\begin{array}{ccccccccc}
& & & & & & & \uparrow\$250 & \\
& & & & & & & \text{COGS} & \\
\Delta\text{Assets} & - & \Delta\text{Liab} & = & \Delta\text{Perm OE} & + & \text{Rev} & - & \text{Exp} \\
\downarrow\$250 & & & & & & & & \\
\textbf{Inventory} & & & & & & & &
\end{array}$$

It is easy to see that the effect of this transaction on net income is the difference between the revenue and the expense, or $50 ($300 - $250).

Now, assume a bookstore entered into the same transaction. A bookstore is not in the business of selling its bookcases to make a profit, so for a bookstore this is a non-core transaction. The bookstore may be selling the bookcase because they have too many or because they want to replace it with a newer one. In any event, the bookstore does not record revenue and expense, but rather records a gain or a loss.

To see how this affects the accounting equation, we need to expand the equation to include gains and losses as follows

$$\Delta A \quad - \quad \Delta L \quad = \quad \Delta POE \quad + \quad \text{Rev} \quad - \quad \text{Exp} \quad + \quad \text{Gain} \quad - \quad \text{Loss}$$

Gains and losses are temporary owners' equity accounts and like revenue and expense are closed to permanent owners' equity at the end of the period. Whereas revenues and expenses are gross accounts used for the core activities of the business, gains and losses are net accounts used for non-core activities.

For the sale of the bookcase, the bookstore records cash for $300 and decreases the asset bookcase for $250. To balance these two changes, they record a realized (net) gain of $50 that is reported on the income statement. The effect on the accounting equation is

$\uparrow$$300
Cash $\uparrow$$50
Gain

$$\Delta A \quad - \quad \Delta L \quad = \quad \Delta POE \quad + \quad Rev \quad - \quad Exp \quad + \quad Gain \quad - \quad Loss$$

$\downarrow$$250
Bookcase

If the bookcase had been sold for only $200, the bookstore would have experienced a realized loss of $50 ($200 - $250), and the effect on the accounting equation is

$\uparrow$$200
Cash $\uparrow$$50
Loss

$$\Delta A \quad - \quad \Delta L \quad = \quad \Delta POE \quad + \quad Rev \quad - \quad Exp \quad + \quad Gain \quad - \quad Loss$$

$\downarrow$$250
Bookcase

Realized versus Unrealized Gains and Losses

Gains and losses can either be "realized" or "unrealized." A realized gain or loss is one where the company experiencing the gain or loss has received cash (or something else of value, or nothing of value) in a completed transaction. The sale of the bookcase by the bookstore in the previous section is an example of a realized gain or loss.

An unrealized gain or loss is one where the person or company experiencing the gain or loss has an asset or liability that has changed in value, but they still own the asset or owe the liability. The transaction that determines the gain or loss has not been completed.

Here is an example. Assume a company has a small office building that is owned outright (i.e., no mortgage) and that the value of the office building on the company's balance sheet at the end of last year was $650,000. During the current year the company sold the building for $680,000 net of all commissions and other expenses. On its income statement the company records a <u>realized gain</u> of $30,000 (the net difference between the $680,000 received and the $650,000 given up).

The effect on the accounting equation of selling the building is (where the letter K indicates thousands)

↑$680K
Cash
ΔA $-$ ΔL $=$ ΔPOE $+$ Rev $-$ Exp $+$ Gain $-$ Loss
↓$650K
Building

↑$30K
Gain

This is a realized transaction because the company has the cash. They have given up the building and must record the gain to keep the accounting equation in balance. Because there is no uncertainty about the amount of this transaction, there is no controversy over whether to record this gain.

If the building had been sold for $600,000, the company would record a realized loss of $50,000. The effect on the accounting equation would be

↑$600K
Cash
ΔA $-$ ΔL $=$ ΔPOE $+$ Rev $-$ Exp $+$ Gain $-$ Loss
↓$650K
Building

↑$50K
Loss

Now, assume the company still owns the building at the end of the current year when the company estimates the building to have a value of $680,000. Thus, the company estimates that it has an <u>unrealized gain</u> of $30,000 for the year (the difference between the previous value of $650,000 and the new estimate of $680,000). If the company counts this change in value as an increase in wealth, it will record the gain and the effect on the accounting equation is

↑$30K
Building
ΔA $-$ ΔL $=$ ΔPOE $+$ Rev $-$ Exp $+$ Gain $-$ Loss

↑$30K
Gain

In contrast to accounting for realized gains, there is substantial uncertainty about unrealized gains. The gain is based on an uncertain estimate, and the gain could change as market values change in the near future. As a result, whether unrealized gains such as this should be recorded or ignored has been a controversial issue in accounting for many decades.

On the one hand, the company's wealth has increased, at least to the best of their accountant's ability to estimate the value of the building. As a result, recording this increase gives a more accurate picture of the company's income that period and wealth at the end of the period.

On the other hand, the unrealized gain is based on an uncertain estimate that may give an inaccurate picture of the company's income and wealth. This is especially a concern if the manager reporting the gain has incentives to inflate asset values and report unrealized gains to make the company's performance (and themselves) look better. For these reasons, the accounting rules generally (with few exceptions) prohibit recording unrealized gains.

The situation is different for unrealized losses. If the company estimated the value of the office building at the end of the year to be $600,000, they would record an unrealized loss of $50,000 (the difference between the previous value of $650,000 and the new estimate of $600,000), and the effect on the accounting equation would be

$$\uparrow \text{\$50K} \\ \text{Loss}$$

$$\Delta A \quad - \quad \Delta L \quad = \quad \Delta POE \quad + \quad Rev \quad - \quad Exp \quad + \quad Gain \quad - \quad Loss$$

$$\downarrow \text{\$50K} \\ \textbf{Building}$$

There is less controversy over whether to record unrealized losses. There are two reasons for this. First, it is important to disclose bad news early so that investors and creditors have a chance to react to it. Second, it is likely that the managers of the reporting company have incentives to hide bad news to make the company's performance (and themselves) look better. For these reasons, the accounting rules in many cases require companies to record unrealized losses when assets such as inventory or plant and equipment decline in value.

Types of Gains and Losses

The previous discussion focused on the concepts of realized and unrealized gains and losses. In practice, following the rules of accounting, those concepts are applied in the five situations in which gains and losses are recorded.

- A realized gain or loss is recorded when a company sells an asset for more or less than the value of the asset in the accounting records

- A realized gain or loss is recorded when a company eliminates a liability by paying more or less than the value of the liability in the accounting records
- An unrealized gain or loss is recorded when certain financial investments rise or fall in value while the company still owns them
- An unrealized loss is recorded when an asset other than a financial investment suddenly declines in value
- An unrealized loss is recorded for certain contingent liabilities

The first type of gain or loss, when a company sells an asset for more or less than its value in the accounting records, is relatively common. Companies regularly sell used assets they no longer need or that they intend to replace. The sale of the bookcase by the bookstore and the sale of the office building and in the previous sections are examples.

If the amount of cash received is greater than the recorded value of the asset being sold, a gain is recorded and the effect on the accounting equation is

$$\begin{array}{c}\uparrow\text{Cash}\\ \Delta A\\ \downarrow\text{Asset}\end{array} - \Delta L = \Delta POE + Rev - Exp + \begin{array}{c}\uparrow\text{Gain}\\ Gain\end{array} - Loss$$

If the amount of cash received is less than the recorded value of the asset being sold, a loss is recorded and the effect on the accounting equation is

$$\begin{array}{c}\uparrow\text{Cash}\\ \Delta A\\ \downarrow\text{Asset}\end{array} - \Delta L = \Delta POE + Rev - Exp + Gain - \begin{array}{c}\uparrow\text{Loss}\\ Loss\end{array}$$

The second type of gain or loss is when a company eliminates a liability by paying more or less than its value in the accounting records. Often the value required to pay off a liability may vary with interest rates, resulting in a gain if interest rates rise and a loss if interest rates fall.

If the company pays less to eliminate a liability than its recorded value, a gain is recorded and the effect on the accounting equation is

$$\begin{array}{c}\Delta A\\ \downarrow\text{Cash}\end{array} - \begin{array}{c}\Delta L\\ \downarrow\text{Liab}\end{array} = \Delta POE + Rev - Exp + \begin{array}{c}\uparrow\text{Gain}\\ Gain\end{array} - Loss$$

If the company pays more to eliminate a liability than its recorded value, a loss is recorded and the effect on the accounting equation is

$$\Delta A \quad - \quad \Delta L \quad = \quad \Delta POE \quad + \quad Rev \quad - \quad Exp \quad + \quad Gain \quad - \quad \overset{\uparrow Loss}{Loss}$$
$$\downarrow Cash \qquad \downarrow Liab$$

The third type of gain or loss, for changes in value of certain financial assets, is the only case in which a company can record an unrealized gain on the income statement. We will discuss this situation in much greater detail in a later chapter when we discuss Starbucks' statement of comprehensive income.

The final two types are also unrealized, but they involve only losses. They are unrealized because they do not involve completed transactions.

The first of these two types is when an asset the company is still using has suddenly declined in value for some reason other than using it. The decline in value could be, for example, because a new technology has made this asset obsolete, or because there has been a decline in demand for the product produced by the asset. This type of loss is referred to as an "asset impairment." In this case the company reduces the value of the asset and records a loss. The effect on the accounting equation is

$$\Delta A \quad - \quad \Delta L \quad = \quad \Delta POE \quad + \quad Rev \quad - \quad Exp \quad + \quad Gain \quad - \quad \overset{\uparrow Loss}{Loss}$$
$$\downarrow Asset$$

The opposite is not true: if the asset has risen in value the company is not permitted to record an unrealized gain.

The second of these two types of unrealized losses is when the company recognizes that they have a "contingent loss" and a "contingent liability." The word "contingent" indicates that the loss and liability will only occur if something else happens, i.e., it is contingent on something. The most common example of this is a lawsuit. In the case of a lawsuit, whether the company being sued (the defendant) has a loss and a liability is contingent on the outcome of the suit after all appeals have been exhausted.

When the suit is first filed there is substantial uncertainty over whether the defendant will ever have to pay anything. At this point the accounting rules do not require recording the loss and liability. As the suit progresses, at some point it may become "reasonably possible" that the defendant will have to pay. If that happens, the accounting rules require the defendant to disclose the suit and discuss it in the notes to their financial statements. Later, if and when it appears "probable" that the defendant will lose and will have to pay, the accounting rules require the company to record a loss and a liability to the company or individual that has sued them.

When the company recognizes this loss, the effect on the accounting equation is

$$\Delta A \quad - \quad \overset{\uparrow Liab}{\Delta L} \quad = \quad \Delta POE \quad + \quad Rev \quad - \quad Exp \quad + \quad Gain \quad - \quad \overset{\uparrow Loss}{Loss}$$

The opposite is not true: if the company has a contingent gain, the company is not permitted to record it before it is realized. In the case of winning a lawsuit, the gain can only be recorded when all of the uncertainty has been resolved.

As we discussed above, whether and when to record unrealized gains and losses has been controversial for many years. Examples of possible unrealized gains and losses include changes in the value of an asset such as an investment portfolio, a building, a piece of equipment, or inventory. Examples can also include changes in value of contracted liabilities like bonds payable and bank loans.

Some feel that these changes in value are "real" and should be recorded. Others feel they are too uncertain, and that especially unrealized gains are too subject to managerial manipulation. This second view has prevailed in the accounting rules, and as a result

Current accounting rules require companies to record unrealized losses, but not unrealized gains, with a relatively narrow exception.

Let's look at examples of each of these five types of gains and losses using hypothetical events that might have occurred with Starbucks.

Gains and Losses for Starbucks

For an example of the first type of gain or loss, assume that Starbucks has a coffee roaster that originally cost $100,000, but that after a number of years of use has a value of $65,000 in the accounting records. Also assume that they just sold the coffee roaster for $60,000 so that they can replace it with a more energy efficient model. Of course, Starbucks is not in the business of selling coffee roasters, so they do not recognize revenue and cost of goods sold for this transaction. Rather they record a realized loss for the net effect of exchanging a coffee roaster worth $65,000 in their accounting records for $60,000 in cash.

The effect on the accounting equation is

↑$60K   ↑$5K
ΔA   –   ΔL   =   ΔPOE   +   Rev   –   Exp   +   Gain   -   Loss
↓$65K

On the other hand, if they had sold the coffee roaster for $67,000, they would have realized a gain of $2,000, and the effect on their accounting equation would be

↑$67K   ↑$2K
ΔA   –   ΔL   =   ΔPOE   +   Rev   –   Exp   +   Gain   -   Loss
↓$65K

For an example of the second type of gain or loss, assume that Starbucks issued bonds to the public several years ago, borrowing $50,000. Since issuing the bonds, they have only paid interest on the bonds and the value of the bonds in the accounting records is still $50,000. Interest rates have been rising, and as a result the market price of the bonds has fallen to $48,000. Starbucks decides to retire (repurchase) the bonds at the current market price of $48,000, realizing a gain of $2,000.

The effect on their accounting equation is

                                           ↑$2K
ΔA   –   ΔL   =   ΔPOE   +   Rev   –   Exp   +   Gain   -   Loss
↓$48K   ↓$50K

On the other hand, if interest rates had fallen and the market value of the bonds had risen to $53,000, Starbucks would have realized a loss of $3,000. The effect on their accounting equation would be (in thousands)

                                           ↑$3K
ΔA   –   ΔL   =   ΔPOE   +   Rev   –   Exp   +   Gain   -   Loss
↓$53K   ↓$50K

For an example of the third type of gain or loss, assume that Starbucks paid $75,000 a few years ago to invest in the common stock of another publicly-traded company, and that investment is now worth $72,000 in the market. The accounting rules (to be discussed more fully later)

require Starbucks to record this unrealized loss of $3,000 on their income statement.

The effect on their accounting equation is

$$\begin{array}{cccccccccc}
& & & & & & & & & \uparrow\text{\$3K} \\
\Delta A & - & \Delta L & = & \Delta POE & + \text{ Rev} & - & \text{Exp} & + \text{ Gain} & - \quad \text{Loss} \\
\downarrow\text{\$3K} & & & & & & & & &
\end{array}$$

On the other hand, if the investment had risen in value to $80,000, Starbucks would record a gain of $5,000, and the effect on their accounting equation would be

$$\begin{array}{cccccccccc}
\uparrow\text{\$5K} & & & & & & & & \uparrow\text{\$5K} & \\
\Delta A & - & \Delta L & = & \Delta POE & + \text{ Rev} & - & \text{Exp} & + \text{ Gain} & - \quad \text{Loss}
\end{array}$$

This is the only example of an unrealized gain that is recorded on the income statement, i.e., unrealized gains on certain financial investments. This topic will be discussed in further detail below in the chapter on Starbucks' statement of comprehensive income.

For an example of the fourth type of gain or loss, assume that a renowned medical research team has issued a report that drinking coffee is bad for your health. As a result of this report, demand for Starbucks coffee falls to the point that the coffee roaster they have with a $65,000 value in their accounting records is no longer worth that much in the market. The accounting rules require Starbucks to write down the value of the coffee roaster to its current market or fair value. Assume that Starbucks estimates the fair value to be $40,000. Thus, Starbucks has experienced a $25,000 unrealized loss ($65,000 - $40,000) as a result of this report, and the effect on their accounting equation is

$$\begin{array}{cccccccccc}
& & & & & & & & & \uparrow\text{\$25K} \\
\Delta A & - & \Delta L & = & \Delta POE & + \text{ Rev} & - & \text{Exp} & + \text{ Gain} & - \quad \text{Loss} \\
\downarrow\text{\$25K} & & & & & & & & &
\end{array}$$

For an example of the fifth type of gain or loss, assume that a customer was burned by spilling hot coffee on her lap, and sued Starbucks. Starbucks eventually lost the suit and was ordered to pay $75,000 to the woman. Starbucks decided not to appeal and now admits it is "probable" they will make payment to the woman. As a result, they must record a loss and a liability.

The effect on their accounting equation is

$$\overset{\uparrow\text{\$75K}}{\Delta A} \quad - \quad \Delta L \quad = \quad \Delta POE \quad + \quad \text{Rev} \quad - \quad \text{Exp} \quad + \quad \text{Gain} \quad - \quad \overset{\uparrow\text{\$75K}}{\text{Loss}}$$

In all of these cases, the resulting gains and losses are unlikely to be included on income statement line items for core revenue and expense. Rather, they are likely to be reported on a line for "other" gains and losses, or perhaps on their own separate line item if they are "material." In accounting "material" means that an amount is large enough or important enough that knowing the amount might make a difference in a decision that is being made by an investor or creditor. We discuss the concept of materiality in more detail in a later chapter.

Part II – Accounting in Practice

Chapter 7 – Starbucks' Balance Sheet

Overview of the Annual Report Form 10-K

The previous chapters discussed in some detail both the income statement and balance sheet, using hypothetical examples, both for an individual and for a company, Starbucks. In this and the following four chapters we survey Starbucks' five financial statements to see how the previously covered concepts lead to the financial statements that we see in practice.

As we discuss each line item in both the balance sheet and income statement, keep in mind that they are aggregations of many, in some cases very many, individual accounts. For example, on their balance sheet, Starbucks has only one line item for inventory, but this line is likely the summation of many separate accounts. Starbucks likely has separate accounts for coffee beans, dairy products, cups and lids, etc., and many of those are probably further subdivided, perhaps each type of coffee bean has its own account, and so forth.

On their income statement Starbucks has one line item for revenue from company-operated stores, but this is likely the summation of separate revenue accounts for each store, of which there are more than fifteen thousand. In each case they will have as many accounts as necessary to retrieve the information they need (e.g., how many tall lattes were sold at a certain store) in order to make the decisions they want to make.

Reporting the balances in all of Starbucks' (likely thousands of) individual accounts would be overwhelming to the average investor or creditor and would reveal proprietary information that Starbucks does not want to reveal. As a result, companies like Starbucks combine (often very many) similar accounts into single line items on their financial statements. While these line items are somewhat standardized across companies, managers have discretion over what to include in which line item and how much to aggregate or disaggregate, and these choices can vary from one company to another.

Publicly-traded companies that are under the jurisdiction of the Securities Exchange Commission (SEC) must file a document with the SEC every quarter that provides their financial statements and other required information. The document filed after the fourth quarter, i.e., the end of their fiscal year, is called a Form 10-K. The document that is filed after each of the first three quarters is called a Form 10-Q. The financial statements in the 10-K must be audited, but there is no requirement for the financial statements in the 10-Q to be audited.

The 10-Q is a reduced form of the 10-K, with much less required information. The length of 10-Ks can vary a great deal across companies, but most are 100 pages or more. Starbucks' 10-K for their fiscal year ending September 29, 2019, including all exhibits, has 139 pages.

In addition to the company's financial statements, 10-Ks provide a great deal of information about the company, including a description of its business, the property it owns, its competition, and the risks the company faces. One of the more important required disclosures in the 10-K is the Management Discussion and Analysis, which provides management's analysis of the company's performance over the last two years.

Another important element of the 10-K is the notes to the financial statements which provide information that directly supplements the financial statements, including

- Descriptions of the accounting methods used to prepare the financial statements
- Disaggregation of some line items that are highly aggregated in the financial statements
- Disclosure of some values not recognized in the financial statements
- Alternative measures of amounts recognized differently in the financial statements

In our discussion of the balance sheet below we will make reference to some of the information that Starbucks discloses in the notes to their financial statements.

Overview of Balance Sheets in General
A balance sheet presents a list of line items that are aggregations of the company's underlying accounts, divided into separate sections for assets, liabilities, and owners' equity.

The assets include cash, accounts receivable, which are obligations due from customers, and a variety of other assets. Those other assets are generally items that the company owns or controls that are waiting to be used to provide goods and services to customers at which time they will be expensed.

All of these assets other than cash are an important difference between cash accounting and accrual accounting. Cash accounting treats assets that have been paid for as outflows of cash, nothing more, and ignores assets that have not been paid for. Accrual accounting reports resources the company owns or controls and that will be used in the future to generate revenue as assets, regardless of whether they have been paid for or not. The company reports these assets on the balance sheet.

The liabilities include amounts that the company has explicitly borrowed from a bank or other lender, as well as obligations to suppliers for resources that have been or will be used to provide goods and services to customers. We cannot tell whether the related resources have been consumed, only that they have not yet been paid for. Another important liability for some companies, including Starbucks, is deferred revenue, which is the amount that has been collected from customers for goods and services that have not yet been provided.

These liabilities are also an important difference between cash accounting and accrual accounting. Cash accounting treats liabilities that have been explicitly borrowed as inflows of cash, nothing more, and ignores liabilities incurred to acquire an asset. Accrual accounting reports obligations the company owes, whether for cash that was explicitly borrowed or for acquisition of an asset, as a liability that reduces the company's wealth. The company reports these liabilities on the balance sheet.

Owners' equity line items represent the amounts that investors have invested in the company as well as the income earned previously that the investors have left in the company, as measured by the accountants. Under cash accounting this would be equal to the cash balance. Under accrual accounting this is equal to the difference between all of the recorded assets and the recorded liabilities. As a result, it must be the case that total assets on the balance sheet are equal to the sum of total liabilities and total owners' equity, i.e., that the balance sheet is in balance.

Overview of Starbucks' Balance Sheet

Starbucks' balance sheets as of September 29, 2019 and September 30, 2018 are presented below.

Consolidated – The top of the statement is titled "Starbucks Corporation Consolidated Balance Sheets." Another name for this statement used by some companies is Statement of Financial Position. The word "consolidated" tells us that Starbucks is not just one company, but is actually a family of corporations and this statement includes results for all of the "subsidiary" corporations that Starbucks "controls." Control is usually determined by the parent company owning more than fifty percent of the voting shares of the subsidiary company's stock.

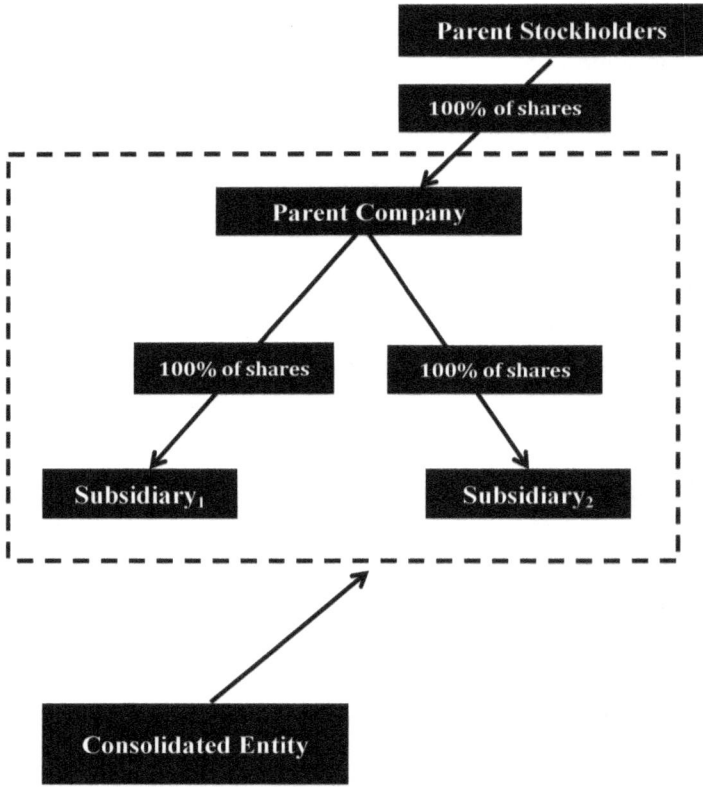

The picture above illustrates this concept of consolidated. Starting at the top, the shareholders of the parent own (by definition) 100 percent of the parent company. In this illustration, the parent company in turn owns 100

percent of each of two subsidiaries. The parent and each subsidiary are separate corporations that each must maintain its own accounting records. However, these separate accounting records are not publicly available.

The dashed box surrounding the parent and the two subsidiaries is the consolidated entity, the entity that reports financial statements. Thus, the balance sheet of the consolidated entity includes all of the cash, inventory, plant and equipment, and liabilities, etc., of each of the companies within the consolidated entity. Similarly, the income statement of the consolidated entity includes all of the revenue and expense of each of the companies within the consolidated entity. In the case of Starbucks, for example, the balance sheet not only includes the cash held by Starbucks the parent, but also the cash of its consolidated subsidiary companies.

Units – At the top of the statement Starbucks reports that all of the dollar amounts, except per share amounts, are reported in millions of dollars.

Accounting Period – This balance sheet reports results as of two dates, the end of two fiscal years, September 29, 2019 and September 30, 2018. In the United States companies can choose any date they wish for the end of their fiscal year. About two-thirds choose December 31, and the rest are scattered around the year. Some, like Starbucks, employ a rule rather than have a fixed date to end their fiscal year. In the notes to their financial statements Starbucks reports that their fiscal year ends on the Sunday closest to September 30th.

Current Assets
The first line in the statement is a heading for "current assets," which are assets that are expected to be used up or converted into cash within one year. The next five lines in the statement report results for each of these current asset categories.

Cash and cash equivalents – the term "cash" is self-explanatory and includes bank accounts without a maturity. The term "cash equivalents" refers to short-term investments that mature within 90 days.

Accounts receivable, net – These are amounts owed to Starbucks by customers who have not yet paid for goods or services provided by Starbucks. Starbucks "accrued" (recorded) the revenue at the time the goods or services were provided (control was transferred to the customer), but they have not yet collected the cash. In Starbucks' case these receivables are likely to be from corporate customers because Starbucks does not extend credit to individual customers like you and me. We will see who these corporate customers might be when we review their income statement in the next chapter and see the types of revenue Starbucks earns.

It is common for any company that some of their credit customers do not pay their bills. At the end of each accounting period, Starbucks recognizes that possibility by estimating the amount of that period's credit sales they expect not to collect and reducing accounts receivable and recording an expense for that amount. The term "net" in "accounts receivable, net" refers to the fact that Starbucks has reduced the amount reported here by the amount they expect not to collect.

In the notes to their financial statements Starbucks discloses that as of September 29, 2019 they estimate that $6.7 million of their receivables outstanding will not be collected. This disclosure, combined with the net amount of accounts receivable on the balance sheet of $879.2 million indicates that their gross receivables, i.e., the total amount owed by customers, is $885.9 million ($879.2 + $6.7). We discuss accounting for uncollectible accounts (bad debts) in more depth in chapter 13.

Inventories – In Starbucks' case, inventories include all of the ingredients necessary for the beverages they sell as well as all of the other items that are for sale in Starbucks' stores. This item also includes any items in warehouses that will eventually be for sale, or coffee beans in storage or in the process of being roasted. Starbucks will already have paid for some of this inventory and will still owe for some of this inventory.

As with most assets, inventories are valued at the amount that was or will be paid for them, but there are two general reasons why that amount might be reduced. First, items may be missing, broken, stolen or spoiled. Second, Starbucks may have some items in their inventory they now expect to sell for less than they paid for them. An example might be unsold Christmas mugs that they must deeply discount in order to sell them in January. Starbucks reduces its inventory on the balance sheet and increases cost of goods sold on the income statement for its estimate of both of these amounts at the end of the accounting period.

STARBUCKS CORPORATION
CONSOLIDATED BALANCE SHEETS
(in millions, except per share data)

	Sep 29, 2019	Sep 30, 2018
ASSETS		
Current assets:		
Cash and cash equivalents	$ 2,686.6	$ 8,756.3
Short-term investments	70.5	181.5
Accounts receivable, net	879.2	693.1
Inventories	1,529.4	1,400.5
Prepaid expenses and other current assets	488.2	1,462.8
Total current assets	5,653.9	12,494.2
Long-term investments	220.0	267.7
Equity investments	396.0	334.7
Property, plant and equipment, net	6,431.7	5,929.1
Deferred income taxes, net	1,765.8	134.7
Other long-term assets	479.6	412.2
Other intangible assets	781.8	1,042.2
Goodwill	3,490.8	3,541.6
TOTAL ASSETS	$ 19,219.6	$ 24,156.4
LIABILITIES AND SHAREHOLDERS' EQUITY/(DEFICIT)		
Current liabilities:		
Accounts payable	$ 1,189.7	$ 1,179.3
Accrued liabilities	1,753.7	1,752.5
Accrued payroll and benefits	664.6	656.8
Income taxes payable	1,291.7	102.8
Stored value card liability and current portion of deferred revenue	1,269.0	1,642.9
Current portion of long-term debt	—	349.9
Total current liabilities	6,168.7	5,684.2
Long-term debt	11,167.0	9,090.2
Deferred revenue	6,744.4	6,775.7
Other long-term liabilities	1,370.5	1,430.5
Total liabilities	25,450.6	22,980.6
Shareholders' equity/(deficit):		
Common stock ($0.001 par value) — authorized, 2,400.0 shares; issued and outstanding, 1,184.6 and 1,309.1 shares, respectively	1.2	1.3
Additional paid-in capital	41.1	41.1
Retained earnings/(deficit)	(5,771.2)	1,457.4
Accumulated other comprehensive loss	(503.3)	(330.3)
Total shareholders' equity/(deficit)	(6,232.2)	1,169.5
Noncontrolling interests	1.2	6.3
Total equity/(deficit)	(6,231.0)	1,175.8
TOTAL LIABILITIES AND SHAREHOLDERS' EQUITY/(DEFICIT)	$ 19,219.6	$ 24,156.4

Inventories are <u>never increased</u> in value before they are sold. Their higher value to the company is only recognized when they are sold.

In the notes to their financial statements Starbucks disaggregates the total cost of their inventory ($1,529.4 million) as of September 29, 2019 into the amounts related to unroasted coffee ($656.5 million), roasted coffee ($276.5 million), other merchandise held for sale ($288.0 million), and packaging and other supplies ($308.4 million).

Prepaid expenses and other current assets – This line includes items that Starbucks has paid for in advance, but has not yet consumed. Examples might include rent paid in advance, airline tickets paid for in advance, insurance paid in advance, office supplies, etc. It is likely that Starbucks has already paid for some of these assets and still owes for some of these assets.

The assets represented in this line item are also recorded initially at their purchase price. These values are then reduced as the items are used up. For some, using the asset is a discrete event, such as taking an airplane flight. For others, using the asset occurs over time, such as an insurance policy that expires slowly over the period being insured. In either case, when the asset is decreased an expense on the income statement is increased.

Total current assets – This is a subtotal that is the sum of the five preceding lines. As of September 29, 2019, Starbucks had $5,653.9 million of current assets.

Non-Current Assets
There is no heading for non-current assets, but all of the assets below the subtotal for current assets are non-current. These assets are expected to last for more than one year.

Long-term investments – These are investments that Starbucks has made in debt and equity securities whose value can be reasonably estimated. For equity investments (stock in another company), the investments reported on this line are for less than 20 percent of the outstanding stock of the company is which they are investing (the investee). Equity investments greater than 20 percent are accounted for differently and are included on the next line item. Equity investments of less than 20 percent in private companies whose value cannot be reasonably estimated are also included on the next line item.

These investments are initially recorded at what was paid for them. However, at the end of each accounting period, in many cases, they are written up or down to their fair market value. Permitting these assets to be written up in value is unique to these assets, and is permitted because it is relatively easy to objectively determine their fair value. For equity securities the resulting unrealized gain or loss is recorded on the income statement. For debt securities the resulting unrealized gain or loss may be (a) ignored, (b) recorded on the income statement, or (c) recorded on the statement of comprehensive income as a component of other comprehensive income, depending on the intent of management. This will be discussed in more detail below when we discuss the statement of comprehensive income.

Equity and cost investments – As the name indicates, "Equity investments" are accounted for using the "equity method." An "equity method investee" is a company that the parent company, Starbucks in this case, can "influence" but not "control." This generally means that the parent company owns between 20 percent and 50 percent of the outstanding stock of the other company. Fifty-fifty joint ventures are also considered to be equity method investees. In Starbucks' case, many of their equity method investees are international Starbucks operations, like Starbucks Korea, in which Starbucks owns between 20 and 50 percent of the company and local investors own the rest.

Equity method investments are initially valued at the amount that was paid for the investment. Subsequently, each accounting period, the investment is increased by the parent company's share of the investee's reported income. The balancing entry to this increase is income from equity method investees on the income statement. Also, each accounting period, the investment is decreased by the company's share of dividends paid by the equity method investee.

Thus, the balance in equity method investments can be viewed like the balance in a bank account, increasing when the investee earns income (like earning interest on a bank account) and decreasing when the investee pays a dividend (like making a withdrawal from a bank account). The market value of the investment is irrelevant for this method of accounting.

"Cost investments" are generally investments of less than a 20 percent interest (i.e., the parent does not have influence) in the stock of a private company that cannot be easily valued. These investments are initially valued at the amount paid, and remain at that amount on the balance sheet unless it is determined the investment has permanently fallen in value. In that case, the investment is reduced in value and a loss is recorded.

In the notes to their financial statements, Starbucks reports that as of September 29, 2019 the $396.0 million on this line consists of $336.1 million invested in equity method investees and $59.9 million invested in cost investments.

Property, Plant and Equipment, Net – This line includes all of Starbucks' physical assets such as land, buildings, machines, vehicles, office furniture and equipment, and coffee roasters. This item also includes "leasehold improvements" which refers to the cost incurred to modify unfinished retail space to make it look like a Starbucks store.

The term "net" refers to the fact that the initial amounts paid for these items have been reduced over time as Starbucks has used them and recorded depreciation. All of these items are subject to depreciation except land, which is assumed to maintain its value through time.

In the notes to their financial statements, Starbucks discloses that they use the straight-line method of depreciation. This means that the assets are reduced in value proportionately over their expected lives, which Starbucks discloses are 2 to 15 years for equipment, 30 to 40 years for buildings, and generally 10 years for leasehold improvements.

In the notes to their financial statements, Starbucks reports that as of September 29, 2019 the total original cost for these assets is $14,273.5 million, of which a little more than half is due to leasehold improvements. The accumulated depreciation on these items as of that date is $7,841.8 million, for a net book value of $6,431.7 million.

Starbucks also reports in the notes to their financial statements that in the year ended September 29, 2019 they recorded (realized) losses on disposal of property, plant and equipment of $64.6 million, and (unrealized) impairment losses of $43.4 million. An impairment loss is when an asset declines in value for some reason other than being used by the company. For example, Starbucks may have old roasters that have declined in value, not from use, but because new technology has made their old roasters worth less. We discuss accounting for property, plant, and equipment in more depth in chapter 14.

Deferred income taxes, net – This item arises because the financial accounting rules and the tax accounting rules are different in many ways that result in differences in the timing of when income is reported on the income statement and the tax return. The key to understanding deferred income taxes is to remember that income tax expense is based on reported income on the income statement following the rules of accounting, while income taxes currently payable is based on income reported on the tax return following tax rules.

Thus, these timing differences can result either in

- income reported on the income statement before it is reported on the tax return, which
    - results in tax expense greater than tax currently payable
    - and gives rise to a deferred tax liability

or

- income reported on the income statement after it is reported on the tax return, which
    - results in tax expense less than tax currently payable
    - and gives rise to a deferred tax asset

Most companies, including Starbucks, have both deferred tax assets and deferred tax liabilities. We discuss accounting for taxes in more depth in chapter 14.

Other long-term assets – As the name implies, this item includes any long-term assets (i.e., assets that are expected to last for more than a year) that are not included in other line items. Examples could be insurance premiums or rent that have been paid for more than one year in advance.

The accounting is the same as for other current assets: these assets are also initially recorded at their purchase price and subsequently reduced as they are used up or consumed. For some, using the asset is a discrete event, while for others, using the asset occurs over time.

Other Intangible Assets – The term "other" distinguishes this line item from the next line item, "goodwill," which is also an intangible asset. Intangible assets are assets that are not physical in nature. In the notes to their financial statements Starbucks reports amounts for the following categories of intangible assets: (a) acquired and reacquired rights, (b) acquired trade secrets and processes, (c) trade names, trademarks and patents, and (d) licensing agreements.

Under current accounting rules, intangible assets can only be recorded when they are purchased, either individually or in the context of acquiring another company. They cannot be recorded when they are developed internally by the company. For example, expenditures for employee training, research and development, and advertising, which can be thought of as developing intangible assets internally, must be expensed in the current period, with a few exceptions. This is because the uncertainty associated with the future benefits from these internally-developed assets is too great to warrant accounting for these expenditures as assets.

In contrast, when an intangible asset is acquired its value is established in an arms-length transaction, resolving much of the uncertainty. Once an intangible asset is acquired, the company must determine whether it has a finite expected life or whether the expected life is indefinite. If the asset has a finite life it will be amortized over that life. "Amortize" or "amortization" is the word used for the decline in the value of intangible assets, the same concept as depreciation for tangible assets.

If the asset is determined to have an indefinite life, it is not amortized, but remains on the balance sheet at its initial acquisition value as long as it has not permanently declined in value. If it is determined to have permanently declined in value, the asset is written down and an (unrealized) impairment loss is recorded on the income statement.

Goodwill – This item only arises in the context of acquiring another company. Consider an example in which Starbucks acquires one hundred percent of the outstanding stock of another company. After the acquisition, Starbucks' accountants examine the other company and allocate the purchase price to

- The fair value of the tangible assets acquired less the liabilities assumed

and

- The fair value of the identifiable intangible assets acquired. Identifiable intangible assets are items such as trademarks and patents, but can also include other intangible assets such as brand names and lists of loyal customers

After making these allocations,

- If any of the purchase price remains to be allocated it is then allocated to <u>goodwill</u>, which is a generic name to refer to other intangible assets that cannot be identified, but for which the acquiring company was willing to pay. Examples include a skilled workforce or a unique supplier relationship.

Goodwill is accounted for in the same way as indefinite-lived intangible assets. It is not amortized, but remains on the balance sheet at its initial acquisition value as long as it has not permanently declined in value. If it is determined to have permanently declined in value, the goodwill is written down and an (unrealized) impairment loss is recorded on the income statement.

In Starbucks' case, as of September 29, 2019 they have recorded $3,490.8 million of goodwill as a result of acquiring other companies in excess of the net fair value of the tangible and identifiable intangible assets acquired.

Total Assets – This is the total of all the assets listed above.

Current Liabilities
This is a heading for liabilities that are expected to be paid within one year. The next five lines in the statement report results for each of these current liability categories.

Accounts payable – This liability is generally to suppliers who have provided the company with inputs, most commonly inventory, and is usually paid within 30 to 60 days. In Starbucks' case this liability is likely to coffee suppliers and others. This liability increases when the company buys inventory and decreases when the company pays their supplier. Thus, much or all of this liability relates to inventory that Starbucks has not yet paid for.

Accrued liabilities – This liability is similar to accounts payable, but is for other items such as wages, taxes, utilities, etc. These are all items that have already been acquired or consumed, but not yet paid for. The expectation is that this amount will be paid in the near future (sooner than a year).

As with accounts payable, this liability increases when the company buys something, increasing an asset if it is something they have not yet consumed (e.g., office supplies or rent for next month) and increasing an expense if it is something they have already consumed (e.g., electricity for last month). The liability decreases when they pay cash.

In the notes to their financial statements, Starbucks disaggregates the total balance in accrued liabilities as of September 29, 2019 into amounts related to

- Accrued occupancy costs ($176.9 million) – essentially rent payable
- Accrued dividends payable ($485.7 million) – essentially dividends payable
- Accrued capital and other operating expenditures ($703.9 million) – essentially payments due for buying long-term (capital) assets and payments due for other operating expenses not included above (e.g., utilities)
- Self insurance reserves (210.5) – this is Starbucks' estimate of what they currently owe for insurance-like claims for events that have already happened and for which they do not carry insurance
- Accrued business taxes ($176.7 million) – essentially business taxes payable

Accrued payroll and benefits – This is the amount Starbucks owes its employees for work already performed in terms of wages and other benefits.

Income taxes payable – The amount Starbucks currently owes the government for income taxes.

Stored value card liability and current portion of deferred revenue – This item includes both

- Amounts that customers have on their stored value cards that have not yet been redeemed
- Other advance payments to Starbucks, perhaps by corporate customers, for services and products not yet received, but that Starbucks expects to provide within the next year.

In the case of stored value cards, when a customer adds $20 to their stored value card, Starbucks increases their cash holdings by $20 and also increases this liability by $20. Later, when the customer uses the stored value card to purchase a beverage for $5.00, Starbucks reduces this liability and records revenue for $5.00.

In the case of other advance payments that are not added to a stored value card, the process is very similar. When Starbucks receives the advance payment, they increase their cash holdings by the amount received and also increase this liability by the same amount. Later, when Starbucks provides this customer with the good or service ordered, Starbucks reduces this liability and records revenue.

As of September 29, 2019, Starbucks has received $1,269.0 million of payments in advance for which they have not yet provided goods or services, and for which they expect to provide goods or services within the next year.

Current portion of long-term debt – When it is initially issued (borrowed) long-term debt is not a current liability because at the time the borrowing takes place repayment is more than one year away. But as that repayment date draws nearer, eventually it will be within a year, and then the portion of the long-term debt that will be repaid within a year is moved into the current liability section of the balance sheet. As of September 29, 2019 Starbucks, has no long-term debt that will be paid within the next year. As of September 30, 2018, this amount was $349.9 million.

Total Current Liabilities – This is a subtotal that is the sum of the five preceding lines. As of September 29, 2019, Starbucks has $6,168.7 million in current liabilities.

Non-Current Liabilities
There is no heading for non-current liabilities, but all of the liabilities below the subtotal for current liabilities are non-current. These liabilities are expected to be paid more than one year from the balance sheet date.

Long-term debt – This is the amount of interest-bearing debt that Starbucks has outstanding that will be paid more than one year from the balance sheet date. As of September 29, 2019 this amount is $11,167.0 million.

Deferred Revenue – This is the same as deferred revenue reported in current liabilities except that this deferred revenue is not expected to be earned within the next year. As of September 29, 2019, this amount is

$6,744.4 million. Most of this amount is attributable to a transaction with Nestlé, the giant Swiss food company. In that transaction, Nestlé paid Starbucks $7,150 million in 2018 for the perpetual rights to market Starbucks' consumer packaged goods and foodservice products globally, outside of the company's coffee shops, with the exception of ready-to-drink products that are distributed under an agreement with Pepsico.

Starbucks deferred this revenue because they have not yet earned it. They will earn it by permitting Nestlé to distribute their products over time. However, because the agreement is "perpetual" Starbucks must choose some length of time over which to record the revenue. In the notes to their financial statements Starbucks discloses that they will record this revenue proportionately each year over forty years.

Other long-term liabilities – This line item includes any other long-term obligations that Starbucks has that will be paid more than one year from the balance sheet date. These could be due to deferred compensation for employees, or delayed rent payments to landlords, or other miscellaneous activities.

Total Liabilities – This is the total of all the liabilities listed above.

Shareholders' Equity
This heading indicates that the following line items are types of owners' equity.

Common Stock – The amount for which Starbucks originally sold their stock to investors is divided in the owners' equity section into two line items, this one and the following line, additional paid-in capital. The "par value" of the stock is assigned to this line, and the amount that was paid in excess of the par value is assigned to additional paid-in capital.

Par value is an arbitrary amount assigned to a stock when it is initially issued, often one dollar or less. The original intent of par value was that companies could not remove the par value from the company, forcing owners to keep some of their own money in the company to serve as security for creditors. However, par value is now mostly an historical anomaly that has no economic significance these days. In Starbucks' case, par value is one tenth of one cent ($0.001) per share, for a total of $1.2 million, which hardly provides protection to creditors any longer.

This line item increases when Starbucks issues stock and decreases when Starbucks repurchases its own stock.

Additional paid-in capital – As described above, this is the amount that was paid in excess of par value when Starbucks originally sold its stock to investors. This line item increases when Starbucks issues stock and decreases when Starbucks repurchases its own stock.

Retained earnings – This is the amount of earnings that Starbucks has earned over the life of the company AND retained in the company. This line item is increased when revenue and expense are closed to retained earnings each period, and is reduced when the company declares a dividend or when the company repurchases its own shares of stock.

During the fiscal year ended September 29, 2019 this balance changed from positive $1,457.4 million to negative $5,771.2 million, a decrease of a little more than $7 billion. This occurred because Starbucks repurchased a substantial amount of its own stock. We will see this on the Statement of Stockholders' Equity and the Statement of Cash Flows. These share repurchases are the equivalent of the investors withdrawing their investment from Starbucks just as you might withdraw money from a bank account, although your bank generally does not let your balance become negative.

Accumulated other comprehensive loss – This item is analogous to retained earnings, but for other income-like items that are reported on the statement of comprehensive income. We will discuss this item and that statement in detail in a later chapter.

Total Shareholders' Equity – This is the total of all the shareholders' equity items listed above. Thus, the value that Starbucks' shareholders have invested in Starbucks as of September 29, 2019, as measured by accountants, is negative $6,232.2 million.

Noncontrolling Interests – The concept of "noncontrolling interests"

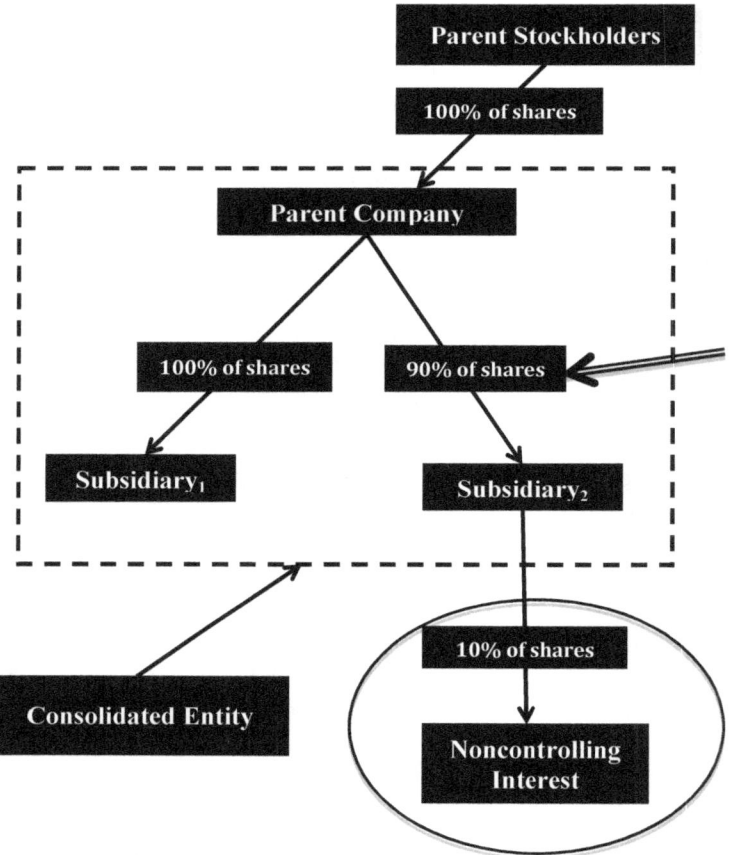

requires some explanation. Refer to the illustration above to see how this works.

We have already described how Starbucks' balance sheet is "consolidated," so that the assets and liabilities include not only those of the parent company, but also those of all of the subsidiary companies that the parent company controls. Earlier in this chapter we used a version of the picture above to illustrate the concept of consolidation.

The picture above has been modified to illustrate the concept of noncontrolling interests. First, the parent's ownership in one of its subsidiaries has been reduced from 100 percent to 90 percent (see double-lined arrow on the right). Second, the owner of the other ten percent has been added to the picture (see the circle at the bottom).

Starbucks "controls" both of these subsidiaries so <u>all</u> of the assets and liabilities of both subsidiaries are included on Starbucks' consolidated balance sheet. As in the earlier picture, the consolidated entity is shown by the dashed-line rectangle.

Starbucks shareholders own nearly all of the consolidated entity by virtue of owning 100 percent of the parent, who in turn owns all of subsidiary$_1$ and 90 percent of subsidiary$_2$. However, someone else, referred to as the noncontrolling interest, owns a small part of the consolidated entity by virtue of their ten percent ownership of subsidiary$_2$. The noncontrolling interest could be held by one person, such as the founder of a small company that Starbucks acquired, or by many people.

Returning to Starbucks' balance sheet, because they disclose some noncontrolling interest, it must be the case that Starbucks has one or more consolidating subsidiaries that they do not fully own. In the last three lines of the balance sheet, they report

- "Total shareholders' equity" of negative $6,232.2, which is the ownership of the parent shareholders in the consolidated entity.

- "Noncontrolling interest" of $1.2, which is the ownership of the noncontrolling interest in the consolidated entity

- "Total equity" of negative $6,231.0," which is the sum of the previous two lines and represents all outside ownership in the consolidated entity.

Total Equity – As discussed above, this item is the sum of the two previous lines, the interests of Starbucks shareholders and the interests claimed by others who own small shares of the Starbucks' subsidiaries that are less than 100 percent owned by Starbucks, and represents all outside ownership in the consolidated entity.

Total Liabilities and Equity – This item is the sum of all of Starbucks' liabilities and owners' equity. Notice that it is equal to total assets, such that the balance sheet is in fact in balance.

Authorized, Issued and Outstanding Shares

There is one more thing to discuss with respect to the balance sheet, and that is the share information in parentheses on the common stock line.

The first item is 2,400.0 million "authorized" shares. This is the number of shares the company is authorized to issue by its charter in the state in which it is incorporated (the state of Washington for Starbucks). This is not a binding constraint for the company and can generally be raised if necessary by filing some paperwork with the state.

The second item is 1,184.6 million shares that are issued and outstanding on September 29, 2019 and 1,309.1 million shares issued and outstanding on September 30, 2018. "Issued" shares refers to the number of authorized shares that have ever been issued to shareholders. From this information we can see that the number of shares that are issued and outstanding decreased by 116.4 million during the fiscal year ended September 29, 2019. This decrease is due to the shares of its own stock that Starbucks repurchased from its investors.

The term "outstanding" refers to shares that were previously issued and are still held by investors. The difference, if any, is shares the company has repurchased from investors and is still holding (has not retired).

For Starbucks the number of shares issued and outstanding are the same because Starbucks is not holding any repurchased shares. As we will discuss in a later chapter, when Starbucks repurchases its own shares it does not "hold" them, but retires them.

Finally, a term that is commonly used in the financial press is the market capitalization or market cap of a company. This is the market value of the company's shares that are outstanding and is computed as the product of the outstanding shares and the current market price of one share. In Starbucks case, as of their most recent balance sheet date, September 29, 2019, the market price of their shares was $88.42 per share, so that their market capitalization was about $104.7 billion ($88.42 x 1,184.6 million shares), which is obviously much greater than their reported owners' equity on the balance sheet of about negative 6.2 billion.

Why are these two measures of the owners' investment so different?

Remember in an earlier chapter when we discussed assets for individuals and for companies that were important, but too difficult to measure to be included in the accounting system? For companies these were intangible assets like an experienced workforce and loyal customers. The values for these items for Starbucks are not included on their balance sheet. Remember, owners' equity on the balance sheet is the stockholders' investment in the company <u>as measured by the accountants</u>.

In contrast, the market capitalization is the stockholders' investment in the company as measured by investors in the market. These investors are not restricted in assigning values to Starbucks' unrecorded intangible assets. In Starbucks' case, the investors in the market see a lot of value that is not captured by the accountants' measures on the balance sheet. Some argue that this makes accounting information less useful or even not useful at all. We will discuss some academic research on this issue in a later chapter.

Chapter 8 – Starbucks' Income Statement

This chapter discusses in detail each line item in Starbucks' income statement. Recall the basic principles that

- Revenue is recorded when control is transferred to the customer
- Expense is recorded in the same period as the revenue that the expense has generated
- Gains and losses are the <u>net</u> increase or decrease in owners' equity related to non-core activities and are either realized or unrealized
- All four types of temporary owners' equity accounts—revenue, expense, gains, and losses—are closed (transferred) to retained earnings at the end of the accounting period and reset to zero to begin counting in the next period.

Starbucks' income statements for the years ended September 29, 2019, September 30, 2018, and October 1, 2017, are presented below. As with the balance sheet, the income statements are "consolidated" income statements, which means that each line item is the sum across the parent Starbucks and its controlled subsidiaries for that line item.

An important difference from the balance sheet is that whereas the balance sheet values were amounts as of a point in time (stocks), midnight on the last day of the fiscal year, income statement amounts are changes in those stocks (flows) over a period of time, the fiscal year ending at midnight on the last day of the fiscal year.

Revenue and expense are very different on a cash basis versus an accrual basis. On a cash basis revenue is simply an inflow of cash and expense is simply an outflow of cash. In contrast, on an accrual basis, revenue is based on transfer of control of goods and services regardless of when the cash is received, which could be before, at the same time, or after the transfer of control. Similarly, expense is based on consumption of a good or service to generate revenue, regardless of when the cash is paid, which could be before, at the same time, or after the consumption occurs.

Net Revenue
The first line in Starbucks' income statement is a heading for the three line items on which Starbucks reports its "Net revenue."

Company-Operated Stores – Starbucks disaggregates their revenue into three line items. The first is for company-owned stores, the kind you might visit in a strip mall anywhere in the country. As of September 29, 2019, Starbucks had 15,834 company-owned stores world-wide, of which about two-thirds were in the United States. Starbucks had $21,544.4 million in revenue (about 81 percent of their total) from these stores in fiscal 2019. When you spend $5.00 on a beverage in one of these stores, that $5.00 appears on this revenue line. Starbucks is likely to have received all of this cash because they do not extend credit to customers like you and me.

Licensed Stores – This revenue line is for licensed stores, the Starbucks you might visit at an airport, bookstore, or university campus. As of September 29, 2019 Starbucks had 15,422 licensed stores world-wide, of which a little more than half were in the United States. Often it is difficult to determine whether you are in a company-owned store or a licensed store. If you spend $5.00 on a beverage in a licensed store, Starbucks receives a percentage of that amount as license revenue, as specified by the license agreement. Most of the revenue goes to the owner of the store who is operating the store under a license from Starbucks. About 11 percent of Starbucks total revenue is on this line. There is likely to be a lag between when Starbucks earns this revenue and when they collect this revenue. As a result, some of this revenue is likely to still be owed to Starbucks and is part of the accounts receivable reported on the balance sheet.

Other – This revenue line is for consumer packaged goods (CPG), foodservice and other. If you see Starbucks coffee beans in a grocery store, the amount the grocery store or distributor paid Starbucks appears as revenue on this line. About eight percent of Starbucks total revenue is on this line. Because the customers for this revenue are likely to be corporate customers, there is also likely to be a lag between when Starbucks earns this revenue and when they collect this revenue. As a result, some of this revenue is also likely to contribute to the accounts receivable reported on the balance sheet.

Total Net Revenues – The next line reports the sum of the three previous revenue line items. Starbucks had $26,508.6 million of revenue for the fiscal year ended September 29, 2019.

Expenses

The next six lines report operating expenses for Starbucks. Note that these line items are not explicitly indicated as negative, but are understood to be negative because they are expenses.

Cost of Sales –This item includes cost of goods sold for the coffee and other ingredients used to prepare their beverages, the coffee they sell as beans, and the other merchandise they sell in their stores. The amount for fiscal 2019 is $8,526.9 or about 32 percent of Starbucks' total revenue.

STARBUCKS CORPORATION
CONSOLIDATED STATEMENTS OF EARNINGS
(in millions, except per share data)

Fiscal Year Ended		Sep 29, 2019	Sep 30, 2018	Oct 1, 2017
Net revenues:				
Company-operated stores	$	21,544.4	$ 19,690.3	$ 17,650.7
Licensed stores		2,875.0	2,652.2	2,355.0
Other		2,089.2	2,377.0	2,381.1
Total net revenues		26,508.6	24,719.5	22,386.8
Cost of sales		8,526.9	7,930.7	7,065.8
Store operating expenses		10,493.6	9,472.2	8,486.4
Other operating expenses		371.0	554.9	518.0
Depreciation and amortization expenses		1,377.3	1,247.0	1,011.4
General and administrative expenses		1,824.1	1,708.2	1,408.4
Restructuring and impairments		135.8	224.4	153.5
Total operating expenses		22,728.7	21,137.4	18,643.5
Income from equity investees		298.0	301.2	391.4
Operating income		4,077.9	3,883.3	4,134.7
Gain resulting from acquisition of joint venture		—	1,376.4	—
Net gain resulting from divestiture of certain operations		622.8	499.2	93.5
Interest income and other, net		96.5	191.4	181.8
Interest expense		(331.0)	(170.3)	(92.5)
Earnings before income taxes		4,466.2	5,780.0	4,317.5
Income tax expense		871.6	1,262.0	1,432.6
Net earnings including noncontrolling interests		3,594.6	4,518.0	2,884.9
Net earnings/(loss) attributable to noncontrolling interests		(4.6)	(0.3)	0.2
Net earnings attributable to Starbucks	$	3,599.2	$ 4,518.3	$ 2,884.7
Earnings per share — basic	$	2.95	$ 3.27	$ 1.99
Earnings per share — diluted	$	2.92	$ 3.24	$ 1.97
Weighted average shares outstanding:				
Basic		1,221.2	1,382.7	1,449.5
Diluted		1,233.2	1,394.6	1,461.5

Store Operating Expenses – The amount for this line item for fiscal 2019 is 10,493.6 or almost 40 percent of Starbucks' total revenue. The notes to their financial statements do not specify which expenses are included in this line item, but most likely the largest items are wages for employees at company owned stores and the cost of rent for company owned stores. This item might also include utilities for the stores and janitorial services, among other expenses necessary to operate the stores.

Other Operating Expense – This item likely includes expense for the layer of management between the stores and corporate management. For example, this might include district offices and personnel that oversee the operations of stores, delivery and other vehicles, and perhaps roasting and storage activities.

Depreciation and Amortization Expenses – This relates to using up assets that are expected to last more than one year. "Depreciation" refers to using up physical assets like buildings and coffee roasters, and "amortization" refers to using up intangible assets, like patents on a coffee roasting process.

General and Administrative Expense – This line item contains most corporate level expenses, such as advertising, accounting, human resources, legal, etc.

Restructuring and Impairments – This item relates to two separate but related activities. A "restructuring" is a package of initiatives entered into by a company to improve its profitability. Most commonly restructurings include laying off employees, selling off assets that are no longer needed, and canceling leases. Each of these actions incurs an expense or loss that is reported on this line. Often when employees are laid off they are paid severance pay or provided with other benefits. When unneeded assets are sold off, it is frequently for a loss because they are no longer as valuable as the company had originally expected. Canceling leases usually requires paying a penalty to get out of the lease.

An "impairment" is when an asset is written down from its current book value to a lower value recognizing that it has fallen in value, not from use, but for some other reason. Examples of reasons for the loss of value include new technology or because the output from the asset no longer has value. The general rule is that when the fair value of the asset has fallen below its book value it must be written down to its fair value.

Notice that Starbucks recorded restructuring and impairments expenses for all three years. This suggests that for a company of this size some amount of disposing of or writing down under performing assets happens every year. For many companies restructuring activities occur occasionally, but not consistently. However, for some large companies such activities may be common nearly every year, as appears to be the case for Starbucks.

Total Operating Expenses – This line is the sum of the six lines above. For all of these expenses, Starbucks is likely to have paid most in cash, but still owe for some, and the amounts they owe will be reported on the balance sheet as accounts payable or accrued liabilities.

Income from Equity Investees – As we saw on the balance sheet, an "equity investee" is a company that the parent company, Starbucks in this case, can "influence" but not "control." This generally means that the company owns between 20 percent and 50 percent of the outstanding stock of the other company including fifty-fifty joint ventures. In Starbucks' case, many of their equity investees are international Starbucks operations, like Starbucks Korea.

Starbucks earns income from these investments in two general ways. First, as the equity investee earns profits, Starbucks records its share of those profits. Second, Starbucks may also sell coffee to the equity investee or have a license agreement with the equity investee that brings in revenue to Starbucks. Both of these sources of revenue from equity investees are included in this line item.

Operating Income – This line is a subtotal based on total revenue ($26,508.6) minus operating expenses ($22,728.7) plus income from equity investees ($298.0).

Other Income
The next four lines report non-operating activity for Starbucks, including gains and losses and interest income and interest expense. Because this section of the income statement may include either positive or negative items, these line items are explicitly indicated as positive or negative.

Gain Resulting from Acquisition of Joint Venture – This line only has a value recorded for fiscal year 2018. At the beginning of that year Starbucks owned 50 percent of a joint venture in East China. During that year they acquired the other 50 percent. Prior to this acquisition they accounted for their investment in East China as an equity method investment. Using this method, the value of this investment in their accounting records was (a) the original purchase price, plus (b) their share of income earned, minus (c) whatever earnings were paid to them as dividends by the East China joint venture.

After this acquisition, they consolidated the East China operations, including on their balance sheet all of East China's cash, receivables, equipment, etc. As a result of acquiring this additional fifty percent, the accounting rules required Starbucks to write up the value of their previous investment to the fair value of the East China assets less their liabilities. Doing so resulted in a gain of $1,376.4 million.

Net Gain Resulting from Divestiture of Certain Operations – In the notes to their financial statements Starbucks discloses that for fiscal year 2019 this line item primarily consists of a net gain from selling their company-owned operations in Thailand and converting them to a fully licensed market.

Interest Income and Other, Net – This line item clearly includes interest income earned on various investments. The word "other" indicates that other miscellaneous items are included here, such as relatively minor gains and losses on sales of investments. The word "net" indicates that some of these "other" items might be losses that offset some of their interest income.

Interest Expense – This line item is clearly interest expense they have incurred on interest-bearing debt. Notice that in contrast to other expenses listed above, this item is explicitly indicated as being negative by putting it in parentheses. The reason for this is that it is in a section of the income statement that includes both positive and negative amounts, so the company is explicit about the negative amounts to avoid confusion.

Earnings Before Income Taxes – This is a subtotal that begins with operating income and adds or subtracts as appropriate the previous four lines.

Income Taxes and Non-Controlling Interest
The remainder of the income statement, prior to the per share calculations, subtracts the expense for income taxes and divides the after-tax income between the amount due to the shareholders of Starbucks' common stock and the amount due to the non-controlling interest.

Income Tax Expense – This is the amount of income tax expense Starbucks incurred for the taxable income they reported on this statement of earnings. Note, this does not mean they will pay that amount to the government. The rules for financial reporting (the basis for the income statement) and the rules for taxation (the basis for their tax return) are different in many ways. These differences result in differences in the timing of when income is reported on the income statement and the tax return. This item is the amount of tax they will eventually pay for this period's reported accounting income that is taxable sometime, regardless of when they will pay it.

A common ratio related to income tax expense is the effective tax rate, which is the ratio of income tax expense to pre-tax income and measures the company's average tax rate. For Starbucks, this ratio in fiscal year 2019 was 19.5 percent (871.6/4,466.2), and in fiscal year 2018 this ratio was 21.8 percent (1,262/5,780). These values are substantially lower than the effective tax rate for fiscal year 2017, which was 33.2 percent (1,432.6/4,317.5). This reduction in the effective tax rate is due to the tax reform act that became effective in December of 2017, and which reduced the federal corporate statutory tax rate from 35 percent to 21 percent.

Net Earnings Including Noncontrolling Interests – This is a subtotal that is the difference between earnings before income taxes and income tax expense. The effect of "noncontrolling interests" will be discussed in the next line item.

Net Earnings/(Loss) Attributable to Noncontrolling Interests – As we discussed for the balance sheet in the previous chapter, when Starbucks owns less than 100 percent of a consolidating subsidiary, all of the subsidiaries assets and liabilities are included on the balance sheet. As a result, owners' equity must include all of the claims on those net assets, including the claims of the "others" who own the rest of the less-than-100-percent owned subsidiary. The claims of these "others" are referred to as noncontrolling interests.

In the same way, the income statement includes all of the revenue and expense of less-than-100-percent owned subsidiaries, so the earnings due to these "other" investors must also be reported. In this case, for fiscal year 2019, the noncontrolling interests had a loss of $4.6 million.

To help make this clear, assume that Starbucks has one subsidiary in which it owns 90 percent and some other entity or person owns the other ten percent. If that subsidiary incurred a loss of $46.0 million in fiscal year 2019, then the noncontrolling interest that year would be a loss of $4.6 million, ten percent of the subsidiary's loss. The idea would be the same if the subsidiary had earned a profit. Of course, Starbucks likely has more than one subsidiary with noncontrolling interest and the percentages may be different, but the idea is the same.

Net Earnings Attributable to Starbucks – This line reports the earnings for Starbucks shareholders ($3,599.2 million) after removing the earnings claimed by the noncontrolling interest reported in the previous line (a loss of $4.6 million).

Earnings per Share
This part of the income statement reports the net income that is due to Starbucks' shareholders, on a per share basis. This makes the net income (performance) of the company easier to compare with the current share price which is also on a per share basis.

Earnings per share – Basic – This item is the result of dividing the net earnings that is attributable to Starbucks by the weighted average of shares outstanding (disclosed further below). This provides investors with a measure of the earnings attributable to each of their shares, which can easily be compared with the current price per share in the market.

Earnings per share – Diluted – This item is the result of dividing the net earnings attributable to Starbucks by the weighted average of shares that would be outstanding if securities that Starbucks has outstanding that can be converted into common stock were converted into common stock. For current shareholders this provides a "worst case" scenario for how much their earnings per share would be reduced (diluted) if all convertible shares were converted. The most common example of a convertible security is employee stock options. Bonds and preferred stock that can be converted into common stock are other possibilities. The denominator for this calculation is discussed further below.

Weighted Average Shares Outstanding – This is a header that indicates the following two lines disclose shares outstanding on a weighted average basis. The term "weighted average" refers to weighting by time. For example if a firm with a December 31 fiscal year end began the period with 20 shares outstanding and issued 12 more shares on April 1, they would have had 20 shares outstanding for one quarter of the year and 32 shares for three quarters of the year, so the weighted average would be 29 shares (20 x 0.25 + 32 x 0.75 = 29).

Basic – This item discloses the weighted average of shares outstanding during the period.

Diluted – This item discloses the weighted average of shares that would have been outstanding during the period if the securities that are convertible into common stock had been converted into common stock.

This concludes our survey of Starbucks' income statement. As a final comment, it is essential that you see the connection between this statement and the balance sheet discussed in the previous chapter—the net income attributable to Starbucks reported on the income statement is added to the beginning balance of retained earnings on the balance sheet. As we will see later this is not the only change in retained earnings, but it is an important one.

Chapter 9 –
Starbucks Statement of Comprehensive Income

Overview of Comprehensive Income

As we discussed in chapter 6, many unrealized gains and losses are not reported on the income statement either because they are too uncertain or because managers (in the case of unrealized gains) may use them to inflate the company's performance. However, the accounting rule makers decided that many of these gains and losses should be reported somewhere so they created a second, supplementary income statement called the Statement of Comprehensive Income. This statement reports changes in value (unrealized holding gains and losses) of certain assets while they are held and certain liabilities while they are owed.

These particular unrealized gains and losses are recorded to temporary owners' equity accounts that are part of "other comprehensive income" and are reported on the statement of comprehensive income. At the end of the period these other comprehensive income gain and loss accounts are closed to a permanent owners' equity account called "accumulated other comprehensive income," in just the same way that gains and losses on the income statement are closed to retained earnings.

The effect of this on the accounting equation is shown below. To save space, gains and losses that are reported on the income statement are collapsed into one term (G/L) and a new term is added for the unrealized gains and losses that are recorded in other comprehensive income (OCI).

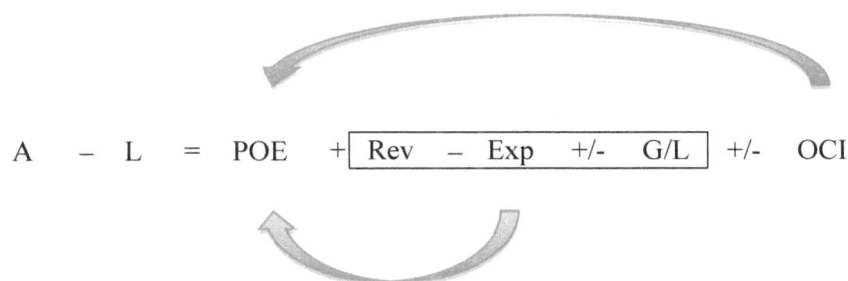

$$A \quad - \quad L \quad = \quad POE \quad + \boxed{Rev \quad - \quad Exp \quad +/- \quad G/L} \quad +/- \quad OCI$$

The arrow below the equation indicates that the components of net income (revenue, expense, gains, losses) are closed to Permanent Owners' Equity (retained earnings) at the end of the period. The arrow above the equation indicates that the components of other comprehensive income are also closed to a Permanent Owners' Equity account, but in this case they are closed to "accumulated other comprehensive income," (AOCI) at the end of each accounting period.

Thus, there are essentially two parallel income statements. The main income statement reports all revenue and expense, realized gains and losses, and many unrealized losses and few unrealized gains. All of this activity is closed to retained earnings at the end of the year.

The second income statement is the statement of comprehensive income, which reports changes in value, both unrealized gains and unrealized losses, for certain assets and liabilities (to be discussed below). At the end of the year, these gains and losses are closed to a Permanent Owners' Equity account that is called "accumulated other comprehensive income."

It is worth emphasizing here that we have just introduced two new accounts that are very different, but work together, and unfortunately have potentially confusing names. Accounts that are part of "other comprehensive income" (OCI) are <u>flow accounts</u> that are reported on the statement of comprehensive income and record the unrealized gains and losses that result from changes in the value of certain assets and liabilities. In contrast, the account "<u>accumulated</u> other comprehensive income" is a stock account reported in the owners' equity section of the balance sheet. As the name implies, this is the account to which all other comprehensive income accounts are closed at the end of the accounting period.

Finally, it is important to note that the unrealized gains and losses that are closed to accumulated other comprehensive income are there only temporarily. Over time, these gains and losses will either be reversed in the market, or they will be realized, i.e., the underlying asset will be sold or the underlying liability will be paid. If and when the gain or loss is realized it is backed out of other comprehensive income and reported on the income statement like any other realized gain or loss. Examples below will help to clarify the mechanics of how this works.

The Statement of Comprehensive Income
Companies have a choice of reporting the statement of comprehensive income in one of two alternative ways. The "two statement" alternative is

for a statement of comprehensive income that is separate from the income statement. In this case, the income statement is reported as before.

Income Statement
Revenue
- Expense
+ Gain
- Loss
Net Income

The statement of comprehensive income then begins with net income and adds one or more line items of other comprehensive income to produce a bottom line of comprehensive income, as follows.

Statement of
Comprehensive Income
Net Income
+/- Other Comprehensive Income
Comprehensive Income

The "single statement" alternative extends the income statement to be a statement of comprehensive income as follows

Statement of
Comprehensive Income
Revenue
- Expense
+ Gain
- Loss
Net Income
+/- Other Comprehensive Income
Comprehensive Income

There are four general categories of unrealized gains and losses that are included in other comprehensive income:

- Changes in value of available-for-sale marketable debt securities
- Changes in value of certain hedging instruments
- Changes in value for certain foreign currency translation adjustments

- • Changes in value of certain pension plan assets and liabilities

Each of these is complicated in its own way. The first, changes in value of available-for-sale marketable debt securities is the easiest to use as an example. The other three types of gains and losses are beyond the scope of this book and will be described only briefly below.

Accounting for Marketable Securities

Available-for-sale marketable debt securities are a subset of the more general category of marketable securities, which are investments in debt or equity securities that have an observable market price. In the case of equity securities, the investing company does not own enough to influence or control the company in which they are investing. This generally means that the investing company owns less than 20 percent of the investee.

Current accounting rules divide marketable securities into three groups.

The first group is "held-to-maturity securities," which can only be debt securities because equity securities have no maturity date. As the name implies, held-to-maturity securities are debt securities that the investing company has both the intent and ability to hold to maturity. For these securities, changes in value are ignored, i.e., not recorded on either the income statement or as part of other comprehensive income. The idea behind this is that since the company is committed to holding the security to maturity the intervening changes in market value are not relevant to anyone's decisions. Many companies, including Starbucks, have no securities in this category because they do not want to commit to holding debt securities to maturity. They would rather have the flexibility of selling them if the need arises.

The second group is "trading" securities. This group includes all equity securities and those debt securities that the company intends to actively trade in the short run to make a profit. Changes in the market prices of these securities and the resulting unrealized holding gains and losses may provide useful information to investors and creditors about how well the portfolio manager is performing. Thus, the accounting rules require that these unrealized holding gains and losses are recorded on the income statement as part of income just as though the securities had been sold and the gain or loss had been realized. In the notes to their financial statements, Starbucks discloses that they have $66.5 million of trading securities as of the end of fiscal year 2019, all classified as current assets.

The final group is "available-for-sale securities." This group includes debt securities that do not meet the criteria for the other two groups. In this case the accounting rules require that these securities are valued on the balance sheet at their current market value. That means that on the balance sheet they will be written up (holding gain) or down (holding loss) as the market price changes.

However, the offsetting gain or loss is not recognized on the income statement. Rather, it is recognized as a component of other comprehensive income.

In the notes to their financial statements, Starbucks discloses that they have $224.0 million of available-for-sale securities as of the end of fiscal year 2019. Nearly all of these are classified as non-current assets.

The allocations in Starbucks investment portfolio, in which there are no debt securities classified as held-to-maturity and relatively few equity securities overall, is fairly common. In general, companies use marketable securities to park excess cash. As a result, their investment decisions are passive not active (few or no trading securities), low risk (mainly debt securities), and designed to maintain flexibility (no or few held-to-maturity securities). This results in portfolios that are made up mostly of debt securities classified as available-for-sale.

To see how available-for-sale debt securities are accounted for in practice, let's consider a simple two-period example in which a company purchases an available-for-sale debt security in the first period and sells it in the second period. Assume the investment was purchased for $100, and at the end of the first period its value has risen to $110. In the second period the company sold the security for $110.

At the time the investment was purchased the effect on the equation was

↑$100
A   –   L   =   POE   + Rev   –   Exp   +/-   G/L   +/-   OCI
↓$100

At the end of the period the company recognized that the value of the investment had risen from $100 to $110 by recording an unrealized holding gain in other comprehensive income.

↑$10   ↑$10

A   –   L   =   POE   +   Rev   –   Exp   +/-   G/L   +/-   OCI

As part of the closing process, the gain in other comprehensive income, which is a temporary owners' equity account, was closed to the Permanent Owners' Equity account, accumulated other comprehensive income. This is analogous to closing gains and losses on the income statement into retained earnings.

                        ↑$10

A   –   L   =   POE   +   Rev   –   Exp   +/-   G/L   +/-   OCI
                                                                        ↓$10

This concludes the accounting for the first period. The income statement for that year shows no gain or loss on this investment. Rather the unrealized holding gain of $10 is shown as a component of other comprehensive income on the statement of comprehensive income.

On the balance sheet the investment has been written up to its current market value as of the end of the period of $110 and the owners' equity account accumulated other comprehensive income has a balance of $10 due to this investment.

In the next period the security was sold for $110. It is critical to understand that gains and losses that are recorded in other comprehensive income and closed to accumulated other comprehensive income are only kept in accumulated other comprehensive income <u>temporarily</u> until the gain or loss is realized when the security is sold.

When the security is sold, the gain or loss is reversed out of other comprehensive income and recorded as part of net income.

Let's take this a step at a time. The first step, at the time of sale, is to reverse the previously recorded gain in other comprehensive income. This reversal of an unrealized gain or loss previously recorded in other comprehensive income is referred to as a "reclassification" of the gain or loss because (as we will see) it is being reclassified (moved) from other comprehensive income to net income. The effect of the reclassification entry to reverse the previously recorded unrealized gain is

A   –   L   =   POE   +   Rev   –   Exp   +/-   G/L   +/-   OCI
↓$10   ↓$10

After the reclassification entry, the value of the security on the balance sheet has been reset to its original cost of $100.

Now, we record the sale for $110 and the realized gain of $10 just as we would any other gain or loss.

↑$110   ↑$10

A   –   L   =   POE   + Rev   –   Exp   +/-   G/L   +/-   OCI

↓$100

This realized gain is reported on the income statement and closed to retained earnings at the end of the period.

                      ↑$10

A   –   L   =   POE   + Rev   –   Exp   +/-   G/L   +/-   OCI

                                               ↓$10

In addition, the reclassification "loss" (reversal of a previous gain) is closed to accumulated other comprehensive income at the end of the period.

                                                        ↑$10

A   –   L   =   POE   + Rev   –   Exp   +/-   G/L   +/-   OCI

                    ↓$10

This concludes the accounting for the second period. The income statement for that year shows a realized gain of $10. Other comprehensive income shows a reclassification loss of $10. Since both are included in comprehensive income, there is no net gain or loss on the statement of comprehensive income for this investment.

On the balance sheet the investment has been eliminated, and the $10 realized gain has been closed to retained earnings. Finally, by closing the reclassification loss in other comprehensive income to accumulated other comprehensive income the balance in that account related to this investment has been reset to zero.

To recap the accounting for available-for-sale debt securities

- When the security is purchased it is recorded at the purchase price
- At the end of a period when the security is still being held, its value is written up or down to its current market value and the unrealized gain or loss is recorded in other comprehensive income (OCI), which is then closed to accumulated other comprehensive income (AOCI)

- When the security is sold, the cumulative previously recorded gain or loss is reversed out of OCI, which resets the value of the security to its original cost, and this reversal (reclassification) is closed to (AOCI)
- Then, as a second step, the proceeds received for the sale of the security are recorded, the original cost is removed, and the difference is recorded as a realized gain or loss, which is reported on the income statement and closed to retained earnings

In summary, notice

- Unrealized gains and losses on available-for-sale marketable debt securities are recorded in other comprehensive income in the year in which they occur, and therefore affect comprehensive income in that year
- Realized gains and losses on available-for-sale marketable debt securities are recorded on the income statement in the year in which they are realized (i.e., when the security is sold)
- Reclassification gains and losses in other comprehensive income offset the realized gains and losses on the income statement in the year in which the securities are sold, so that there is no effect on comprehensive income that year

This is summarized for the numerical example above in the following table. Notice that comprehensive income records (unrealized) gains and losses as they occur (year 1 in this case). In contrast, net income reports (realized) gains and losses when the securities are sold (year 2 in this case).

	Year 1	Year 2
Net Income	0	10
Other Comprehensive Income	10	-10
Comprehensive Income	10	0

This accounting probably seems complicated and it is not without its critics. The reason for this accounting is that many argued that including these unrealized gains and losses in net income would distort net income in two ways. First, they argued, these investments are not part of the core business of the investing company and including them in net income could obscure the performance of the core business. Second, the holding gains and losses on these securities may reverse as market prices go up and down, and the resulting volatility would mislead investors about the volatility of the core business.

The accounting rule makers accepted these arguments, and essentially decided on a compromise by requiring companies to record these changes in value on the balance sheet, but not on the income statement. To accomplish this, they invented new temporary and Permanent Owners' Equity accounts that operate parallel to existing revenue, expense, gain, loss and retained earnings accounts, and a new statement on which to report this activity, the statement of comprehensive income.

Later, once this new statement had been created, they found it a convenient temporary dumping ground for other unrealized holding gains and losses waiting to be realized or reversed in the market. As was stated above, these included gains and losses on certain hedging activities, certain pension assets and liabilities, and certain foreign exchange activity.

Starbucks' Statement of Comprehensive Income
Let's apply these concepts to Starbucks with a line-by-line review of their statement of comprehensive income (presented below). Starbucks uses the "two statement" alternative presentation, i.e., a statement of comprehensive income that is separate from the income statement.

Net Earnings Including Noncontrolling Interests – This is directly from the income statement and is always the starting point for computing comprehensive income, which is the sum of net income and other comprehensive income. Confirm that this line is the same amount as the line on the income statement with the same label.

Other Comprehensive Income/(Loss), Net of Tax – This header indicates that the following lines are components of other comprehensive income. As the caption indicates, and as is required by the accounting rules, the amounts reported will be adjusted to an after-tax (net-of-tax) basis. For example, if there is a gain of $100, and the tax rate is 30 percent, then the tax on that gain will be $30, and the net-of-tax gain will be $70 ($100, - $30 = $70). The company may not actually pay this tax now, depending on the tax rules, but they must account for it according to the accounting rules and record a deferred tax liability.

Unrealized Holding Gains/(losses) on Available-for-Sale Securities – This is the item that we used above as our example of other comprehensive income, gains and losses on available-for-sale debt securities. Note that this number includes only changes in value that occurred this period for securities that Starbucks is still holding, and not the reversal (reclassification) of previously recognized gains and losses for securities that Starbucks sold during the period. We know this because several lines below there is a line that reports such "reclassifications." Also note that this line is on a pre-tax basis. We know this because the tax effect is given in the next line.

Tax (Expense)/Benefit – This item is the tax effect of the gain reported on the previous line. For fiscal year 2019, the pre-tax gain is $10.5 million, and the tax expense is $2.3 million so the net-of-tax gain is $8.2 million ($10.5 - $2.3 = $8.2). Starbucks will not pay this tax now because the tax rules generally do not require taxes on unrealized gains. But following the rules of accounting they must account for the tax expense now and record a deferred tax liability.

STARBUCKS CORPORATION
CONSOLIDATED STATEMENTS OF COMPREHENSIVE INCOME
(in millions)

Fiscal Year Ended	Sep 29, 2019	Sep 30, 2018	Oct 1, 2017
Net earnings including noncontrolling interests	$ 3,594.6	$ 4,518.0	$ 2,884.9
Other comprehensive income/(loss), net of tax:			
Unrealized holding gains/(losses) on available-for-sale securities	10.5	(7.0)	(9.5)
Tax (expense)/benefit	(2.3)	1.9	2.9
Unrealized gains/(losses) on cash flow hedging instruments	(14.1)	24.4	53.2
Tax (expense)/benefit	3.4	(6.5)	(12.6)
Unrealized gains/(losses) on net investment hedging instruments	(39.8)	7.8	20.1
Tax (expense)/benefit	10.1	(2.2)	(7.4)
Translation adjustment and other	(146.2)	(220.0)	(38.3)
Tax (expense)/benefit	2.5	3.4	(2.4)
Reclassification adjustment for net (gains)/losses realized in net earnings for available-for-sale securities, hedging instruments, and translation adjustment	1.3	24.7	(67.2)
Tax expense/(benefit)	1.6	(1.2)	14.0
Other comprehensive income/(loss)	(173.0)	(174.7)	(47.2)
Comprehensive income including noncontrolling interests	3,421.6	4,343.3	2,837.7
Comprehensive income/(loss) attributable to noncontrolling interests	(4.6)	(0.3)	0.2
Comprehensive income attributable to Starbucks	$ 3,426.2	$ 4,343.6	$ 2,837.5

Unrealized Gains/(Losses) on Cash Flow Hedging – Accounting for hedging activities is beyond the scope of this book, so only a brief explanation for this item is presented here. Assume that a U.S. company expects to receive some cash flows next year that are in a foreign currency. This could be from making sales in another country, or a financial investment in another country. Because the expected cash flows are in a foreign currency the company is exposed to the risk that the exchange rate between the foreign currency and the U.S. dollar will change before they receive the cash flows. If this happens, the cash flows they receive next year will be worth more or less in terms of U.S. dollars.

To avoid this risk the company can invest in another financial instrument whose value will move in exactly the opposite direction of the changes in value of the expected foreign currency cash flows should the exchange rate change. This instrument is referred to as a "hedging instrument," and the foreign currency cash flows are referred to as the "hedged item."

Hedge accounting rules permit the company to (temporarily) record the change in value of the hedging instrument in other comprehensive income, waiting until the cash flows of the hedged item are realized. This line item is for those changes in value on a pre-tax basis.

Tax (Expense) Benefit – This item is the tax effect of the loss reported on the previous line. For fiscal year 2019, the pre-tax loss is $14.1 million, and the tax benefit is $3.4 million so the net-of-tax loss is $10.7 million (-$14.1 + $3.4 = -$10.7).

Unrealized Gains/(Losses) on Net Investment Hedging Instruments – This item is similar to the cash flow hedges described above, but relates to the hedging the risk of foreign currency exchange rate changes on investments in foreign countries rather than future cash flows.

Tax (Expense)/Benefit – This item is the tax effect of the gain or loss reported on the previous line. For fiscal year 2019, the pre-tax loss is $39.8 million, and the tax benefit is $10.1 million so the net-of-tax loss is $29.7 million (-$39.8 + $10.1 = -$29.7).

Translation Adjustment and Other – This item is also beyond the scope of this book so only a brief explanation is provided. A translation adjustment arises when a company has a foreign subsidiary whose accounting is denominated in a foreign currency. Before consolidating the subsidiary, its accounts must be converted into dollars at the current exchange rate. For example, assume a company has land in France that has a value of one million euros on the French subsidiary's balance sheet, and further assume that the exchange rate was 1.2 dollars to the euro at the beginning of the year and 1.3 dollars to the euro at the end of the year. Without changing the value of the land in euros, the value in dollars has risen from $1.2 million to $1.3 million during the year and the company has experienced an unrealized gain of $100,000 in terms of dollars. Following the rules of accounting, the land is written up by $100,000 on the balance sheet and this unrealized gain is reported on this line in other comprehensive income.

Tax (Expense)/Benefit – This item is the tax effect of the gain or loss reported on the previous line. For fiscal year 2019, the pre-tax loss is $146.2 million and the tax benefit from the loss is $2.5 million so the net-of-tax loss is $143.7 million (-$146.2 + $2.5 = -$143.7).

Reclassification Adjustment for Net (Gains)/Losses Realized in Net Earnings for Available-for-Sale Securities, Hedging Instruments, and Translation Adjustment – The term "reclassification" refers to the reversal of unrealized gains and losses previously recorded in other comprehensive income that have now been realized and are being transferred to the income statement. Starbucks has chosen to combine all of their reclassification gains and losses into one line.

Reclassification for available-for-sale securities occurs when they sell the security and realize the gain or loss. From this line item we cannot determine the effect of reclassifications for available-for-sale securities sold during the year because those effects are combined with the reclassification gains and losses for the other components of other comprehensive income.

Tax (Expense)/Benefit – This item is the tax effect of the total reclassifications reported on the previous line. For fiscal year 2019 the pre-tax reclassification loss for all items is $1.3 million, and the related tax expense is $1.6 million so the net-of-tax loss is $2.9 million (-$1.3 - $1.6 = -$2.9).

Other Comprehensive Income (Loss) – This item is the total of all of the other comprehensive income lines above.

Comprehensive Income Including Noncontrolling Interests – This item is the sum of the previous line, other comprehensive income, and the first line in the statement, net earnings including noncontrolling interests.

Comprehensive Income (Loss) Attributable to Noncontrolling Interests – This item is the portion of comprehensive income that is due to consolidated subsidiaries that are less than 100 percent owned by Starbucks, and that is claimed by the noncontrolling owners of those subsidiaries. Note that net income attributable to noncontrolling interests (from the income statement) and comprehensive income attributable to noncontrolling interests (from the statement of comprehensive income) are both a loss of $4.6 million, indicating that there is no other comprehensive income attributable to noncontrolling interests.

Comprehensive Income attributable to Starbucks – This item is the portion of comprehensive income that is claimed by Starbucks' shareholders.

The unrealized gains and losses reported on the statement of comprehensive income were determined to be important enough by the accounting rule makers to invent this reporting technology that disclosed these gains and losses without incorporating them into the measure of net income. On the other hand, many view these unrealized gains and losses as not very informative because they are less likely to recur in the future than most components of net income. As a result, these unrealized gains and losses are less likely to be useful in predicting the future performance of the company, something that investors and creditors are trying to do as they make decisions about their relationship with the company.

Chapter 10 –
Starbucks' Statement of Owners' Equity

Overview of the Statement of Owners' Equity
The statement of owners' equity is the fourth of the five financial statements that all publicly-traded companies are required to provide. This statement provides more detailed information about changes in owners' equity during the year.

To begin, refer to Starbucks' balance sheet where the owners' equity section includes the following line items

- Common stock
- Additional paid-in capital
- Retained earnings
- Accumulated other comprehensive income
- Stockholders' equity
- Noncontrolling interest
- Total equity

The main sources of changes in these items are

- Net income or loss, which increases or decreases retained earnings
- Other comprehensive income, which increases or decreases accumulated other comprehensive income
- Issuances of common stock, which increase common stock and additional paid-in capital and can occur from selling stock to the public or by employees exercising their employee stock options
- Declarations of dividends, which decreases retained earnings
- Repurchases of common stock, which decrease common stock and additional paid-in capital, and often also reduce retained earnings

Let's review Starbucks' 2019 statement of owners' equity to see the specific reconciling items for Starbucks.

Starbucks' Statement of Equity
There are three parts to the statement, corresponding to the most recent three years. We will focus on the bottom third (the only part shown

below) that begins with the row "Balance, September 30, 2018." This row has the balances for the owners' equity line items on the fiscal year 2018 balance sheet, the beginning balances for fiscal year 2019.

This panel ends with the row "Balance, September 29, 2019." This row has the balances for the owners' equity line items on the fiscal year 2019 balance sheet, the ending balances for fiscal year 2019.

Take a moment to verify that the numbers in the owners' equity section of the Starbucks' balance sheets and these two rows from the Starbucks statement of owners' equity provided below are the same.

Now, we proceed through this part of the statement line by line.

Cumulative effect of adoption of new accounting guidance – As disclosed in the notes to Starbucks' financial statements, this line reports the cumulative effect of two changes in the accounting rules that were recorded directly to retained earnings, bypassing the income statement. The first change related to a rather technical issue, when to record the tax effects of transfers of assets other than inventory between entities within the consolidated entity. The new rule requires that the tax effects be recorded at the time of the intracompany transfer, not at the time of sale to an outside party. The catch-up credit to retained earnings for this change was $227.6 million. The second change is related to recognizing revenue from stored value cards. Previously revenue from stored value cards was recognized either as goods and services were provided or when it was deemed that the value would never be used. Under the new rule, revenue for value expected to never be used is to be recognized proportionately as the cards are used. The catch-up credit to retained earnings for this change was $268.0 million. This type of catch-up adjustment to retained earnings for a change in accounting rules is relatively rare. Together, these two changes account for the $495.6 reported on the statement of equity.

Net earnings/(loss) – On this line retained earnings and shareholders' equity are increased by $3,599.2 million, which is net earnings attributable to Starbucks reported on the income statement. Noncontrolling interests is decreased by $4.6 million, which is the net loss attributable to noncontrolling interests reported on the income statement. The net of these two increases total equity.

Other comprehensive income/(loss) – This line is negative $173.0 million, which is total other comprehensive income from the statement of comprehensive income, and reduces (because it is a loss) accumulated other comprehensive income/(loss).

We can clearly see from this line and the previous line that net income increases or decreases (are closed to) retained earnings and other comprehensive income increases or decreases (are closed to) accumulated other comprehensive income/(loss). In this case the noncontrolling interests had no other comprehensive income, but they could have.

Stock-based compensation expense – This line reports the amount of stock-based compensation earned by employees in the current year, $311.3 million. Less than ten percent of this amount was due to employee stock options and the remainder was due to restricted stock units (RSUs). In both cases, stock-based compensation is recorded as an expense as employees earn the rights to the options or RSUs in the same way that an expense is recorded as employees earn their wages. The difference is that in the case of stock-based compensation the offset to the expense is not cash or a liability as in the case of wages. Rather the offset for stock-based compensation is additional paid-in capital (a Permanent Owners' Equity account), because this is "paid" by the company granting a form of owners' equity to its employees.

Exercise of stock options/vesting of RSUs – Employees can only exercise their stock options after they have earned the rights to the stock options. This is referred to as "vesting" in the options, and usually takes several years, depending on the details of the options. When the employees exercise the options, they give the option back to the company and pay an amount to the company (called the exercise price) in exchange for a share of stock. Also, when employees vest (earn) an RSU, they receive a share of stock. This line reports the dollar increase in owners' equity as a result of all of these actions, which included the issue of 14.7 million shares that increased owners' equity by $264.9 million. The increase in the dollar amount for common stock is too small to report (14.7 million shares times par value of $0.001 equals $0.0147 million), so the entire $264.9 million is reported as an increase in additional paid-in capital.

STARBUCKS CORPORATION
CONSOLIDATED STATEMENTS OF EQUITY
(in millions, except per share data)

	Common Stock		Additional Paid-in Capital	Retained Earnings/(Deficit)	Accumulated Other Comprehensive Income/(Loss)	Shareholders' Equity/(Deficit)	Noncontrolling Interests	Total
	Shares	Amount						
Balance, September 30, 2018	1,309.1	$ 1.3	$ 41.1	$ 1,457.4	$ (330.3)	$ 1,169.5	$ 6.3	$ 1,175.8
Cumulative effect of adoption of new accounting guidance	—	—	—	495.6	—	495.6	—	495.6
Net earnings/(loss)	—	—	—	3,599.2	—	3,599.2	(4.6)	3,594.6
Other comprehensive income/(loss)	—	—	—	—	(173.0)	(173.0)	—	(173.0)
Stock-based compensation expense	—	—	311.3	—	—	311.3	—	311.3
Exercise of stock options/vesting of RSUs	14.7	—	264.9	—	—	264.9	—	264.9
Sale of common stock	0.4	—	33.4	—	—	33.4	—	33.4
Repurchase of common stock	(139.6)	(0.1)	(609.6)	(9,521.8)	—	(10,131.5)	—	(10,131.5)
Cash dividends declared, $1.49 per share	—	—	—	(1,801.6)	—	(1,801.6)	—	(1,801.6)
Net distributions to noncontrolling interests	—	—	—	—	—	—	(0.5)	(0.5)
Balance, September 29, 2019	1,184.6	$ 1.2	$ 41.1	$ (5,771.2)	$ (503.3)	$ (6,232.2)	$ 1.2	$ (6,231.0)

Sale of common stock – This line reports that Starbucks issued (sold) 0.4 million shares of common stock for $33.4 million, consistent with an average share price of $83.50 (33.4/0.4). As reference points, at the beginning of fiscal year 2018 Starbucks' stock was selling for about $57.00, and at the end of the year it was selling for $88.00. During the year, Starbucks' share price rose as high as about $99.00. As with the previous line, the increase in the dollar amount for common stock is too small to report (0.4 million shares times par value of $0.001 equals $0.0004 million), so the entire $33.4 million is reported as an increase in additional paid-in capital.

Repurchase of common stock – During the year Starbucks repurchased 139.6 million shares of their own stock for $10,131.5 million, consistent with an average share price of $74.17 (10,131.5/139.6). This is a common way for a company to return cash to shareholders that the company does not need to finance its growth. In general, repurchases are accounted for by reversing the original issue of the stock, reducing common stock and additional paid-in capital, and then reducing retained earnings for the remainder. We can see that in this case the reduction in retained earnings was $9,521.8, which was primarily responsible for the negative ending balances in both retained earnings and shareholders' equity.

Cash dividends declared, $1.49 per share – During the year Starbucks declared dividends of $1,801.6 million. This is the second common way for a company to return cash to shareholders that the company does not need to finance its growth. The full amount of cash dividends reduces retained earnings.

Net distribution to noncontrolling interest – This line indicates that one or more of the consolidating subsidiaries in which Starbucks does not own 100 percent paid a dividend, and the noncontrolling interest received $0.5 million.

Balance, September 29, 2019 – This line reports the ending balances for the owners' equity line items on the fiscal year 2019 balance sheet. Take a moment to compare these numbers with those on the balance sheet.

As was stated earlier, owners' equity is the measure of the owners' investment in the company as measured by the accountants. This measure is much more conservative than the measure in the market where investors are not restricted to ignore the company's many intangible assets. As such, the main usefulness of this statement to investors and creditors is to clearly disclose the transactions that took place during the year between the company and its owners in terms of new stock issues, stock repurchases, and dividends. This statement also provides information about equity transactions between the company and its employees in terms of employee stock options and restricted stock units earned and issued.

Chapter 11 – Starbucks' Statement of Cash Flows

Overview of the Statement of Cash Flows

The fifth and final financial statement is the statement of cash flows. The purpose of this statement is to explain how the company's cash balance changed from the beginning of the accounting period to the end. Recall that the cash line on the balance sheet also includes cash equivalents, which are investments that mature within 90 days, so the statement actually explains why the sum of cash and cash equivalents changed during the period.

The statement of cash flows is important for several reasons. First, as we have seen, the computation of net income depends on estimates, such as for bad debts and depreciation, and there are many more as well. The operating section of the statement of cash flows reverses these estimated amounts and focuses on how the company has performed in terms of cash in and cash out. This is thought by many to be a more objective measure of performance.

Second, the statement of cash flows provides information about the company's ability to generate cash, which is important for creditors thinking of lending to the company.

Third, the statement of cash flows also provides information that is easily digested about assets the company bought and sold, about borrowing and debt that was repaid, and about transactions with stockholders.

The statement of cash flows presents this information in three sections, operations, investing and financing. We'll discuss them in reverse order, beginning with financing.

The <u>financing section</u> reports the cash effects of transactions between the company and both creditors and stockholders. In terms of transactions with creditors, the company may borrow money, receiving cash, and the company may use cash to repay past borrowings. In terms of stockholders, the company may issue stock, receiving cash, or the company may use cash to repurchase shares or to pay dividends.

Moving up the statement, the <u>investing section</u> reports the cash effects of buying and selling assets. These assets can include financial investments, property, plant and equipment, intangible assets, and whole companies (corporate acquisitions). These assets do not include current assets needed to operate the company like inventory or pre-paid current assets. The information reported in this section is the cash received from selling these assets and the cash paid for purchasing these assets.

Finally, the operating section reports the cash effects of everything else. These cash flows are primarily the receipt of cash from customers (whether earned that period or not) and the payment of cash to suppliers, employees, the government, etc. (whether for expenses incurred that period or not).

Amounts reported in the financing and investing sections are explicitly cash flows, positive for inflows and negative for outflows. However, the amounts reported in the operating section are not cash flows. **They are adjustments**. This requires further explanation. We begin with a simple example.

A Simple Example of the Operating Section

Assume that a company has net income of $25 that consists of $100 of cash revenue, $60 of cash expenses and $15 dollars of depreciation expense. The company's income statement looks like this

Revenue	$100
- Cash Expense	(60)
- Depreciation Expense	(15)
Net Income	$25

Focusing on cash transactions, the company's cash from operations is

Cash from Customers	$100
- Cash to Suppliers, etc.	(60)
Cash from Operations	$40

This presentation of cash from operations is called the "direct method."

An alternative presentation starts with net income ($250), and adjusts out operating items that are in income that did not involve cash and adjusts in operating items that are not in income but did involve cash. In this case depreciation is the only item requiring adjustment. This version of the statement would look like this

Net Income	$25
Depreciation Expense	+15
Cash from Operations	$40

Depreciation expense is in net income as a negative item (expense), but it is not a cash outflow, so to compute cash from operations we have to add it back to net income to <u>remove</u> it.

We get the same cash from operations either way. The difference is not in the amount of cash from operations, but in how it is presented.

This alternative method of presenting cash from operations is referred to as the "indirect method." This method is used by nearly all companies, so it is important that we understand it.

Let's complicate the previous example a little by saying that the company also sold investments with a recorded value of $20 for $25 in cash, recording a gain of $5. As a result, the company's net income is now $30, and their income statement looks like this

Revenue	$100
- Cash Expense	(60)
- Depreciation Expense	(15)
+ Gain	5
Net Income	$30

The sale of these investments is an investing transaction, not an operating transaction. The cash inflow of $25 has no effect on cash from operations. The direct method of reporting cash from operations is still

Cash from Customers	$100
- Cash to Suppliers, etc.	(60)
Cash from Operations	$40

However, the indirect method of reporting cash from operations changes. Now we not only need to adjust net income for non-cash depreciation expense, but also for the non-cash, non-operating loss, as follows

Net Income	$30
+ Depreciation Expense	15
- Gain on Sale of Investment	(5)
Cash from Operations	$40

The gain on the sale of the investment is in net income as a positive item, but it is not the cash inflow from this transaction so it must be <u>removed</u> by subtracting it out. The cash flow from this transaction is the $25 inflow, but this is an investing transaction, not an operating transaction, so it will appear in the investing section.

Finally, let's complicate this example one more time by assuming that accounts receivable increased by $7 during the period. Ignore the possibility of bad debts.

After adding this assumption, the income statement is the same as in the previous example because whether the revenue was collected or not has no effect on measuring net income. But the company's collections from customers would have been $7 less (the increase in accounts receivable). As a result, the direct method cash from operations would be

Cash from Customers	$93
- Cash to Suppliers, etc.	(60)
Cash from Operations	$33

Notice that cash from customers is only $93, the $100 of revenue less the $7 they did not collect (the increase in accounts receivable).

For the indirect method we now need an additional adjustment to net income for the increase in accounts receivable which is revenue that has not yet been collected. We now have

Net Income	$30
+ Depreciation Expense	15
- Gain on Sale of Investment	(5)
- Increase in Accounts Receivable	(7)
Cash from Operations	$33

The increase in accounts receivable represents revenue that is included as a positive item in net income, but that is not a cash inflow, so using the indirect method we subtract the increase in accounts receivable from net income to <u>remove</u> it.

These examples demonstrate that there are two ways to present cash from operations, the direct method and the indirect method. In practice companies are allowed to choose between these two methods, but more than 99 percent choose the indirect method so we focus on that one. This choice between the direct and indirect method only affects the operating section. This choice has no effect on the investing and financing sections.

The final version of the example above using the indirect method demonstrates the three general types of adjustments made to net income to compute cash from operations.

The first adjustment is to add back non-cash expenses because they are included in net income but do not involve cash. Depreciation is the most common example.

The second adjustment is to add back losses and subtract gains. Transactions that give rise to gains and losses are most commonly investing transactions, and occasionally financing transactions, but not operating transactions, and the amounts of the gain or loss are not the cash amount of the transaction. And yet these gain and loss amounts are in net income, so they must be removed. We remove a gain by subtracting it and we remove a loss by adding it back.

The third adjustment is for changes in current asset and liability accounts. In each case, by adjusting for the change in these accounts, we are effectively replacing the recorded revenue or expense with the cash revenue or expense. This final adjustment is often the most difficult to understand, so several examples may help.

Examples of Adjusting for Changes in Current Assets and Liabilities
We begin with more detail about the accounts receivable example above. Assume that the beginning balance for accounts receivable was $42, and the ending balance was $49, and that during the period the company had revenue of $100 and cash collections of $93. This can be summarized by the following equation

$$\text{Beginning} + \text{Revenue} - \text{Collections} = \text{Ending}$$

Which can be restated as

$$\text{Revenue} - \text{Collections} = \text{Ending} - \text{Beginning}$$

Which in this case is

$$100 - 93 = 49 - 42$$

This equation demonstrates that the increase in the accounts receivable balance during the period (right-hand side of equation) is equal to the difference between the revenue that was earned and the revenue that was collected (left-hand side of equation). In this case they are equal to seven.

Recall that the indirect operating section of the statement of cash flows begins with net income and then this amount is adjusted to get to cash. In this example, revenue of $100 is included in net income, but this amount overstates the cash inflow from customers by $7. To adjust for this we need to subtract the increase in accounts receivable of $7, reducing the $100 of revenue that is included in income to the $93 that was actually collected from customers.

We can change this example to a decrease in accounts receivable and see that we add back that decrease. Assume that the beginning balance for accounts receivable was $42, and the ending balance was $37, and that during the period they had revenue of $100 and cash collections of $105. This can be summarized by the following equation

$$\text{Revenue} - \text{Collections} = \text{Ending} - \text{Beginning}$$

Which in this case is

$$100 - 105 = 37 - 42$$

Again, the decrease in the accounts receivable balance during the period (right-hand side of equation) is equal to the difference between the revenue that was earned and the revenue that was collected (left-hand side of equation), and the two are equal to negative five.

In this case, the first line in the indirect operating section of the statement of cash flows is net income, which includes revenue of $100, but this amount understates the cash inflow from customers by $5. To adjust for this we need to add the decrease in accounts receivable of $5, increasing the $100 of revenue that is included in income to the $105 that was actually collected from customers.

All current asset accounts behave this way. To adjust income to cash from operations we subtract increases in current asset accounts and add decreases in current asset accounts.

Now let's consider a current liability example, wages payable. Assume that the beginning balance for wages payable was $25, and the ending balance was $35, and that during the period the company had wage expense of $75 and wages actually paid of $65. This can be summarized by the following equation

$$\text{Beginning} + \text{Expense} - \text{Payments} = \text{Ending}$$

Which can be restated as

$$\text{Expense} - \text{Payments} = \text{Ending} - \text{Beginning}$$

Which in this case is

$$75 - 65 = 35 - 25$$

We can see from this that the increase in the wages payable balance during the period (right-hand side of equation) is equal to the difference between the expense incurred and the expense that was paid (left-hand side of equation), and the two are equal, in this case to $10.

In this case, the first line of the indirect operating section of the statement of cash flows (net income) includes an expense for wages of negative $75. However this amount overstates the cash outflow for wages by $10. To adjust for this we need to add back the increase in wages payable of $10, reducing the negative wage expense of $75 that is included in income to the $65 that was actually paid for wages.

If we change this example to a decrease in wages payable, we subtract out the decrease. To see this, assume that the beginning balance for wages payable was $25, and the ending balance was $17, and that during the period they had expense of $75 and cash payments for wages of $83. This can be summarized by the following equation

$$\text{Expense} - \text{Payments} = \text{Ending} - \text{Beginning}$$

Which in this case is

$$75 - 83 = 17 - 25$$

In this case, the decrease in the wages payable balance during the period (right-hand side of equation) is equal to the difference between the expense incurred and the expense paid (left-hand side of equation), and the two are equal to negative $8.

The first line in the indirect operating section of the statement of cash flows (net income) includes negative $75 for wage expense, but this amount understates the cash outflow for wages by $8. To adjust for this, we need to subtract the decrease in wages payable of $8, increasing the negative wage expense of $75 that is included in income to the cash outflow of $83 that was actually paid for wages.

All current liability accounts behave this way. To adjust income to cash from operations we add increases in current liability accounts and subtract decreases in current liability accounts.

To summarize, to adjust net income to cash in the indirect operating section of the statement of cash flows we

- Add back non-cash expenses
- Subtract gains and add losses
- Adjust for changes in current asset and liability balances

When we adjust for current asset and liability balances, we

- Add decreases in current asset accounts
- Subtract increases in current asset accounts
- Subtract decreases in current liability accounts
- Add increases in current liability accounts

Starbucks' Statement of Cash Flows – The Operating Section
Now that we have a general understanding of the statement of cash flows, we review each line item in Starbucks' statement (presented below).

Net Earnings Including Noncontrolling Interest – This item is taken directly from the income statement (take a moment to confirm this) and is a clear indication that this is an indirect method operating section.

Adjustments to reconcile net earnings to net cash provided by operating activities – This is a header that indicates that all that follows in the operating section are adjustments that are intended to convert net earnings to cash from operations.

Depreciation and Amortization – This item adds back these non-cash expenses in order to remove them from earnings because they are not cash. Note that this amount, $1,449.3, is different from the amount reported on the income statement for depreciation and amortization expenses, which is $1,377.3. The notes to the financial statements explain that the line item on the income statement for depreciation expense does not include all of Starbucks' depreciation expense. Depreciation expense related to production and distribution facilities (e.g., coffee roasters and warehouses) is included in the line item for cost of sales.

Deferred income taxes, net – This item is another expense that does not use cash and represents income tax expense that was not paid because of timing differences between reported income and taxable income.

STARBUCKS CORPORATION
CONSOLIDATED STATEMENTS OF CASH FLOWS
(in millions)

Fiscal Year Ended	Sep 29, 2019	Sep 30, 2018	Oct 1, 2017
OPERATING ACTIVITIES:			
Net earnings including noncontrolling interests	$ 3,594.6	$ 4,518.0	$ 2,884.9
Adjustments to reconcile net earnings to net cash provided by operating activities:			
Depreciation and amortization	1,449.3	1,305.9	1,067.1
Deferred income taxes, net	(1,495.4)	714.9	95.1
Income earned from equity method investees	(250.6)	(242.8)	(310.2)
Distributions received from equity method investees	216.8	226.8	186.6
Gain resulting from acquisition of joint venture	—	(1,376.4)	—
Net gain resulting from divestiture of certain retail operations	(622.8)	(499.2)	(93.5)
Stock-based compensation	308.0	250.3	176.0
Goodwill impairments	10.5	37.6	87.2
Other	187.9	89.0	68.9
Cash provided by changes in operating assets and liabilities:			
Accounts receivable	(197.7)	131.0	(96.8)
Inventories	(173.0)	(41.2)	14.0
Prepaid expenses and other current assets	922.0	(839.5)	(20.0)
Income taxes payable	1,237.1	146.0	(91.9)
Accounts payable	31.9	391.6	46.4
Deferred revenue	(30.5)	7,109.4	130.8
Other operating assets and liabilities	(141.1)	16.4	107.2
Net cash provided by operating activities	5,047.0	11,937.8	4,251.8
INVESTING ACTIVITIES:			
Purchases of investments	(190.4)	(191.9)	(674.4)
Sales of investments	298.3	459.0	1,054.5
Maturities and calls of investments	59.8	45.3	149.6
Acquisitions, net of cash acquired	—	(1,311.3)	—
Additions to property, plant and equipment	(1,806.6)	(1,976.4)	(1,519.4)
Net proceeds from the divestiture of certain operations	684.3	608.2	85.4
Other	(56.2)	5.6	54.3
Net cash used by investing activities	(1,010.8)	(2,361.5)	(850.0)
FINANCING ACTIVITIES:			
Proceeds from issuance of long-term debt	1,996.0	5,584.1	750.2
Repayments of long-term debt	(350.0)	—	(400.0)
Proceeds from issuance of common stock	409.8	153.9	150.8
Cash dividends paid	(1,761.3)	(1,743.4)	(1,450.4)
Repurchase of common stock	(10,222.3)	(7,133.5)	(2,042.5)
Minimum tax withholdings on share-based awards	(111.6)	(62.7)	(82.8)
Other	(17.5)	(41.2)	(4.4)
Net cash used by financing activities	(10,056.9)	(3,242.8)	(3,079.1)
Effect of exchange rate changes on cash and cash equivalents	(49.0)	(39.5)	10.8
Net increase/(decrease) in cash and cash equivalents	(6,069.7)	6,294.0	333.5
CASH AND CASH EQUIVALENTS:			
Beginning of period	8,756.3	2,462.3	2,128.8
End of period	$ 2,686.6	$ 8,756.3	$ 2,462.3
SUPPLEMENTAL DISCLOSURE OF CASH FLOW INFORMATION:			
Cash paid during the period for:			
Interest, net of capitalized interest	$ 299.5	$ 137.1	$ 96.6
Income taxes, net of refunds	$ 470.1	$ 1,176.9	$ 1,389.1

Income earned from equity method investees – This is Starbucks' share of the income earned by their investees for which they use the equity method of accounting. This is generally for investees in which Starbucks owns between 20 and 50 percent. For these investments Starbucks records their share of the investees' income as their income even though they have received no cash. Here they are subtracting out that income (revenue) as though none of it was received in cash.

Compare this amount, $250.6 million, with the amount on the income statement for income from equity investees, which is $298.0 million. Recall that the amount on the income statement not only includes Starbucks' share of the income of their equity method investees, but also profit earned from transactions with those investees (e.g., license revenue and income from selling them coffee beans). Thus, the extra $47.4 million on the income statement is likely due to profit earned on these transactions between Starbucks and the equity method investees.

Distributions received from equity method investees – The first line of the indirect operating section of the statement of cash flows is net income, which includes Starbucks' share of income earned by their equity method investees. The previous line subtracted out <u>all</u> of this income, removing it from the operating section. This line adds back as a cash inflow the dividends Starbucks' received from those investees, $216.8 million. Some companies collapse these two lines into one line item, the net income earned from equity method investees in excess of dividends received, while other companies, like Starbucks, report the gross amounts on two separate lines.

Gain resulting from acquisition of joint venture – Recall from a similar line item on the income statement that during fiscal year 2018 Starbucks acquired the remaining 50 percent of a joint venture in East China that they did not already own at the beginning of the year. As a result of this acquisition, the accounting rules required Starbucks to write up the value of their previous investment to the fair value of the East China assets less their liabilities, and this resulted in a gain of $1,376.4 million. This item is a gain that is included in net income, but is not cash and is not operations, so it is removed by subtracting it out.

Net gain resulting from divestiture of certain retail operations – The income statement included a similar line item that primarily related to a gain from the sale of their Thailand operations and other sales. This total net gain of $622.8 million is included in net income, but is not cash and not operations, so it is removed by subtracting it out.

Stock-Based Compensation – Many companies give employee stock options to some or all of their employees as part of their compensation. The option gives the employee the right to buy a share of the company's stock for a certain price. If the price of the stock in the market goes up, the employee can exercise the option, buy the stock at a lower price, sell it in the market at a higher price, and pocket the profit. Employees usually need to work for several more years after receiving the options to earn the right to exercise them (this is called the vesting period). The company must record an expense for the value of the options given to the employees, spreading that expense over the vesting period. This line item is the amount ($308.0 million) that Starbucks recorded as an (non-cash) expense in 2019. As an expense, this item is included in net income as a negative amount, but as a non-cash expense it is added back to remove it, just like depreciation. This item differs from the $311.3 million reported on the statement of equity for stock-based compensation expense. The difference of $3.3 million was recorded as an asset rather than an expense and so does not need to be added back here because it did not reduce income.

Goodwill impairments – This adjustment is for the write-down of the intangible asset goodwill by $10.5 million dollars during fiscal year 2019. As an expense, this item is included in net income as a negative amount, but as a non-cash expense it is added back to remove it, just like depreciation.

Other – It is not possible to determine exactly what this relates to, but because the sign is positive the net amount must be either a cash inflow that was not also a positive component of net income, or a negative component of net income that was not a cash outflow.

Cash provided by changes in operating assets and liabilities – This is a header that indicates that the following items relate to changes in non-cash current assets and liabilities.

Accounts receivable – This negative amount indicates that accounts receivable increased by $197.7 million from operating the company. This means that cash collections were less than revenues earned during the year, so income overstated cash, and this line item is subtracting that additional revenue.

We would like to be able to look at the balance sheet and see that accounts receivable increased by this amount, $197.7 million. However, making that calculation we see that accounts receivable on the balance sheet actually increased by $186.1 million ($879.2 - $693.1 = $186.1), which is $11.6 less than the increase on the statement of cash flows. This failure to perfectly reconcile is quite common, and there are several potential explanations.

The first potential explanation is that Starbucks may have sold one or more other companies, and those companies had $11.6 million of receivables, so that receivables on the balance sheet increased by $186.1, which is a combination of an increase of $197.7 from operating the company (reported in the operating section of the statement of cash flows) and a decrease of $11.6 from selling one or more of their subsidiaries (reported in the investing section).

Another possibility is that Starbucks has some receivables in a foreign currency, and the value of those receivables decreased during the year in terms of U.S. dollars because of changes in the exchange rate between the U.S. dollar and that currency. In this case, the receivables increase on the balance sheet of $186.1 is a combination of an increase of $197.7 million from operating the company (reported in the operating section of the statement of cash flows) and a decrease of $11.6 million from foreign exchange rate changes (reported in a line item toward the bottom of the statement of cash flows for the effect of exchange rate changes on cash and cash equivalents, discussed below).

It is likely that both of these explanations (and perhaps others that are less common) combine to explain the difference between the amount on the statement of cash flows and the change reported on the balance sheet.

Inventories – This line item indicates that inventories increased by $173.0 million from operating the company. This item is negative because the company would have used cash to increase their inventory (or accounts payable, which is the next adjustment). On the balance sheet the increase is $128.9 million ($1,529.4 - $1,400.5 = $128.9). The difference is $44.1 million. As with accounts receivable, this difference could be due to either selling a company with $44.1 million of inventory (which would be reported in investing) or changes in the value of inventory held by subsidiaries in foreign countries (which would be reported in the line item for effect of exchange rate changes on cash and cash equivalents) or a combination.

Prepaid expenses and other current assets - This line item indicates that prepaid expenses and other current assets decreased by $922.0 million from operating the company. This item is positive because the company consumed more of this asset than it paid for in cash. This represents a non-cash expense that is being added back. On the balance sheet the decrease is $974.6 million ($488.2 - $1,462.8 = -$974.6). The additional decrease is $52.6 million, and could be due to either selling a company with $52.6 million of prepaid expenses and other current assets (which would be reported in investing) or changes in the value of this asset held by subsidiaries in foreign countries (which would be reported in the line item for effect of exchange rate changes on cash and cash equivalents) or a combination.

Income taxes payable - This line item indicates that income taxes payable increased by $1,237.1 million from operating the company. This item is positive, indicating that they saved cash by not paying all of the taxes payable incurred during the year. On the balance sheet we see that the increase is $1,188.9 million ($1,291.7 - $102.8 = $1,189.9). The difference is $48.2 million. This difference could be due to either selling a company with $48.2 million of taxes payable (which would be reported in investing) or changes in the value of accounts payable held by subsidiaries in foreign countries (which would be reported in the line item for effect of exchange rate changes on cash and cash equivalents) or a combination.

Accounts payable - This line item indicates that accounts payable increased by $31.9 million from operating the company. This item is positive, indicating that they saved cash by not paying all of the payables incurred during the year. On the balance sheet we see that the increase is $10.4 million ($1,189.7 - $1,179.3 = $10.4). The difference is $21.5 million. This difference could be due to either selling a company with $21.5 million of accounts payable (which would be reported in investing) or changes in the value of accounts payable held by subsidiaries in foreign countries (which would be reported in the line item for effect of exchange rate changes on cash and cash equivalents) or a combination.

Deferred revenue - This line item indicates that deferred revenue decreased by $30.5 million from operating the company. This item is negative because the decrease in deferred revenue is revenue that was not received as cash and therefore must be subtracted.

This amount likely relates to two line items on the balance sheet, the current liability for stored value card liability and current portion of deferred revenue, and the noncurrent liability for deferred revenue. The change on the balance sheet for stored value card liability and current portion of deferred revenue is -$373.9 million (= $1,269.0 - $1,642.9). The change on the balance sheet for noncurrent deferred revenue is -$31.3 million (= $6,744.4 - $6,775.7). The combined change in the two line items is -$405.2, which is $374.7 million more negative than the amount reported on the statement of cash flows.

This difference could be due to either selling a company with $374.7 million of deferred revenue (which would be reported in investing) or changes in the value of deferred revenue held by subsidiaries in foreign countries (which would be reported in the line item for effect of exchange rate changes on cash and cash equivalents) or a combination.

Other operating assets and liabilities – This is a miscellaneous item to account for other changes in current assets and liabilities not otherwise accounted for and cannot be easily compared with changes reported on the balance sheet. The line item indicates that there was an additional cash outflow of $141.1 million for these items beyond the effect of these items on net income. This could be due to a net increase in other assets or decreases in other liabilities, or a combination.

Net cash provided by operating activities – This is the subtotal of cash from operations and is the sum of all of the preceding line items. In 2019 Starbucks generated $5,047.0 million, about $5.0 billion, in cash from operations. The next two sections, investing and financing, tell us what they did with that cash.

Starbucks' Statement of Cash Flows – The Investing Section
The investing section of the statement of cash flows presents the cash flow results from purchases and sales of long-term assets, primarily, property, plant and equipment, investments in debt and equity securities, and purchases of the stock of other companies. The amounts reported are

the actual cash flow amounts. In that sense, this part of the statement is "direct," in contrast to the indirect presentation in the operating section.

Purchase of investments – This item reports that during fiscal year 2019 Starbucks spent $190.4 million to purchase financial investments such as stocks and bonds.

Sale of investments – This item reports that during fiscal year 2019 Starbucks sold financial investments such as stocks and bonds for $298.3 in cash.

Maturities and calls of investments – This item reports a $59.8 million cash inflow either from investments that matured during the year, or from investments that were "called" by the borrower, which means that Starbucks had to pay the money back early, before the bond matured. This item, together with the previous two line items, accounts for the turnover in Starbucks' investment portfolio. Netting these three items in 2019, Starbucks decreased their investment portfolio by $167.7 million ($190.4 - $298.3 - $59.8 = -$167.7).

Acquisitions, net of cash acquired – Apparently Starbucks made no acquisitions in fiscal year 2019. In 2018 Starbucks spent $1,311.3 million of cash, net of cash acquired, to acquire other companies. If as part of the acquisition Starbucks acquired receivables, inventory or payables, etc., those increases are included here, not in operations.

Additions to property, plant and equipment – This item reports that Starbucks spent $1,806.6 million of cash on property, plant and equipment. This does not include property, plant and equipment acquired by purchasing another company, which is included in the previous line item.

Net proceeds from divestiture of certain operations – This item reports that Starbucks received a cash inflow of $684.3 million from selling certain businesses. This item is likely to be primarily related to the sale of their Thailand operations. We saw on the income statement that the sale of these businesses resulted in a net gain of $622.8 million that was adjusted out in the operating section of the statement of cash flows. If we assume that the gain of $622.8 million and this cash inflow of $684.3 million relate to the same transactions, then the combined book value of the businesses sold was $61.5 million ($684.3 - $622.8).

Other – This item reports that Starbucks had an additional cash outflow of $56.2 million for miscellaneous investing transactions not otherwise reported above.

Net Cash Used By Investing Activities – This is the subtotal of cash from investing and is the sum of all of the preceding line items in this section of the statement of cash flows. In 2019 Starbucks had a net cash outflow of $1,010.8 million, or about $1.0 billion for investing activities, mainly to add to property, plant and equipment. Subtracting this from the $5.0 billion of cash from operations, leaves about $4.0 billion that was used either for financing activities or to increase their cash balance.

Starbucks' Statement of Cash Flows – The Financing Section
The financing section of the statement of cash flows presents the cash flow results from borrowing and repaying interest-bearing debt, and from transactions with shareholders, which include cash inflows from issuing stock and cash outflows from paying dividends or repurchasing the company's own stock. As with the investing section, the amounts reported are the actual cash flow amounts.

Proceeds From Issuance of Long-Term Debt – This item reports that Starbucks had a cash inflow of $1,996.0 million from borrowing on a long-term basis.

Repayments of Long-Term Debt – This item reports the cash outflow from repaying $350.0 million of long-term debt in fiscal year 2019.

Proceeds from Issuance of Common Stock – This item reports the cash inflow of $409.8 million from issuing common stock in fiscal year 2019. This includes cash received from employees exercising their stock options.

Cash Dividends Paid – This item reports that Starbucks paid $1,761.3 million in cash dividends to shareholders. This is one of the two primary means by which the company returns to shareholders part of their investment in the company.

Repurchase of Common Stock – This item reports that Starbucks paid $10,222.3 million to buy the company's stock back from shareholders. This is the second primary means by which the company returns to shareholders part of their investment in the company.

Notice that Starbucks repurchased much more stock in fiscal years 2018 and 2019 than in 2017. This is likely due to large infusions of cash from the sale of distribution rights to Nestlé and the tax reform act adopted in late 2017.

Minimum Tax Withholdings on Share-Based Awards – This item reports the cash outflow from transferring to the government withholding tax on the exercise of employee stock-based compensation (stock options and restricted stock units).

Other – This item is for miscellaneous financing transactions not otherwise reported above. The net effect of these transactions was a cash outflow of $17.5 million.

Net Cash Used By Financing Activities – This is the subtotal of the net cash outflow of $10,056.9 million from financing and is the sum of all of the preceding line items in this section of the statement of cash flows. The biggest item was about $12 billion returned to shareholders, $1.8 billion in cash dividends and $10.2 billion in share repurchases.

The Rest of Starbucks' Statement of Cash Flows

The remainder of the statement of cash flows reports the effect on cash of changes in exchange rates and reconciles the overall change in cash (from operations, investing, financing, and foreign exchange) with the change reported on the balance sheet. At the bottom there are two more required disclosures, the cash paid for interest and the cash paid for income taxes.

Effect of Exchange Rate Changes on Cash and Cash Equivalents – This item reports the net effect of changes in exchange rates between the U.S. dollar and foreign currencies used to account for Starbucks' foreign subsidiaries, which reduced their cash balance in fiscal year 2019 in terms of dollars by $49.0 million.

Net Increase (Decrease) in Cash and Cash Equivalents – This item reports the net effect of negative $6.1 billion on Starbucks cash balance, which as we have seen is due to (rounding) (a) cash from operations (positive $5.0 billion); (b) cash from investing (negative $1.0 billion); (c) cash from financing (negative $10.0 billion); and (d) exchange rate changes (negative $0.049 billion).

Cash and Cash Equivalents – This is a header to indicate that the following two lines relate to cash and cash equivalents.

Beginning of Period – This is the balance for cash and cash equivalents at the beginning of the period, $8,756.3 million, as on the balance sheet.

End of Period – This is the balance for cash and cash equivalents at the end of the period, $2,686.6, as on the balance sheet. Take a moment to confirm that this number and the number on the previous line are the same amounts reported on the balance sheet.

This number is also the sum of the previous two line items, the net increase (decrease) in cash and cash equivalents and the beginning of period balance. This demonstrates that the statement of cash flows explains the change in cash and cash equivalents during the period.

Supplemental Disclosure of Cash Flow Information – The previous line ends the statement of cash flows. This line is a header that indicates there is some additional supplementary information added at the bottom of the statement.

Cash Paid During the Period For – This is a header for the next two lines, indicating that they are both cash outflows for particular purposes.

Interest, Net of Capitalized Interest – This item reports that Starbucks paid $299.5 million dollars during fiscal year 2019 for interest expense. This amount excludes interest paid that was capitalized, which is the portion of interest that was recorded as an asset (capitalized) rather than an expense. This is permitted under certain circumstances when outstanding debt is used to finance the construction of an asset such as a warehouse or office building.

Income Taxes, Net of Refunds – This item reports that Starbucks paid $470.1 million dollars during fiscal year 2019 for income taxes, net of any cash refunds received from a taxing authority. Notice that this amount is much less than in the previous two years, probably at least in part due to the benefit of the tax reform act adopted in late 2017.

Summary of Starbucks' Statement of Cash Flows
Fiscal years 2018 and 2019 were somewhat unusual for Starbucks from a statement of cash flows perspective for several reasons. To better see this, let's review in broad terms their statement of cash flows for fiscal year 2017, a more normal year.

In fiscal year 2017, Starbucks generated $4.3 billion in cash from operations. They used $0.9 billion for investing, of which the $1.5 billion outflow for property, plant and equipment was offset by net cash collected from reducing their investment portfolio by $0.5 billion. They used $3.1 billion for financing, principally returning $3.5 billion to shareholders, offset by net long-term borrowing of about $0.4 billion.

The net effect of all of this on their cash balance was to increase cash and cash equivalents by $0.3 billion (4.3 − 0.9 − 3.1).

In contrast, in fiscal year 2018 Starbucks generated $11.9 billion in cash from operations, about $7.6 billion more than in fiscal year 2017. This increase was mainly due to the more than $7 billion they received from Nestlé for distribution rights.

They used $2.4 billion for investing, about $1.5 billion more than in fiscal year 2017. This increase was mainly due to $0.5 billion more outflow for property, plant and equipment and acquisitions of $1.3 billion, offset by proceeds from divestitures of $0.6 billion and a $0.3 billion smaller reduction in their investment portfolio.

They had a net cash outflow of $3.2 billion for financing activities, which is only about $0.1 billion more than in fiscal year 2017, but the composition is very different. In fiscal year 2018 they returned about $8.9 billion to shareholders, about $5.4 billion more than in fiscal year 2017. They financed this by borrowing long-term about $5.6 billion, which is about $5.1 billion more than their net long-term borrowing in fiscal year 2017.

Fiscal year 2019 was also somewhat unusual. The operating and investing sections were not that different from fiscal year 2017, but in the financing section they had a $10.0 billion outflow, primarily due to share repurchases, compared with an outflow of $3.1 billion in 2017.

This concludes our review of Starbucks statement of cash flows. As a parting comment it is important to remember the purpose of this statement—to explain the change in the balance of cash and cash equivalents that occurred during the year. The statement also provides a more objective measure of performance, cash from operations. However, this measure is incomplete in the sense that revenue earned but not collected, and expense incurred but not yet paid are not included. At the same time, it includes cash collections that have not been earned and cash payments for items not yet consumed. So, although cash from operations may be more objective (and some argue with this), these inclusions and exclusions are likely to make it less useful as a source of information about the performance of the company that is useful for investors and creditors, and substantial academic research supports this conclusion.

Part III – Bookkeeping

Chapter 12 – Debits and Credits and T-Accounts

Introduction
In the previous chapters I have purposefully avoided the details of bookkeeping. Those chapters focused on the concepts of accounting, including <u>when</u> to record the financial statement elements (assets, liabilities, owners' equity, revenue, expense, gains, and losses) and <u>how to measure</u> them.

In contrast to accounting, bookkeeping is the process of keeping track of those measurements once the accountants have decided what they should be. This chapter covers that bookkeeping system, which is usually associated with debits and credits, journal entries, and T-accounts.

Becoming familiar with the bookkeeping process has several benefits. First, understanding bookkeeping provides an organizing device to help think through how more complex transactions affect the financial statements. Debits and credits, journal entries and T-accounts are used by practicing accountants every day to help them think and communicate. This brings us to the second benefit of familiarity with bookkeeping. Such familiarity will allow you to communicate more effectively with the accountants in your current or future organization.

Debits and Credits
Let's return to our basic accounting equation

$$\text{Assets} \quad - \quad \text{Liabilities} \quad = \quad \text{Owners' Equity}$$

To make the explanations below easier to follow, we eliminate minus signs in the equation by moving liabilities to the right-hand side of the equals sign.

$$\text{Assets} \quad = \quad \text{Liabilities} \quad + \quad \text{Owners' Equity}$$

This equation must always remain in balance (i.e., the equality must be maintained). There is a finite set of operations that do this. For example, an increase to the left-hand side of the equation matched by an increase to the right-hand side will keep the equation in balance. Similarly, a decrease to the left-hand side matched by a decrease to the right-hand side will keep the equation in balance. We might arbitrarily label these increases and decreases using the letters A and B, where A is an increase in an asset or a decrease in a liability or owners' equity and B is the opposite, as follows

$$\begin{array}{ccccc}
\uparrow\textbf{A} & & \uparrow\textbf{B} & & \uparrow\textbf{B} \\
\text{Assets} & = & \text{Liabilities} & + & \text{Owners' Equity} \\
\downarrow\textbf{B} & & \downarrow\textbf{A} & & \downarrow\textbf{A}
\end{array}$$

If we require that A = B for every transaction, that is, if every operation A is matched by an operation B, then as we account for each transaction the equation will remain in balance. This is how we showed the effects of various transactions on the accounting equation in the preceding chapters.

Consider two simple examples. If the company buys inventory for $10 in cash, increasing one asset by $10 and decreasing another asset by $10, we have

$$\begin{array}{lll}
\uparrow\textbf{10 (A)} & & \\
\text{Assets} & = & \text{Liabilities} \quad + \quad \text{Owners' Equity} \\
\downarrow\textbf{10 (B)} & &
\end{array}$$

If the company buys inventory on account (paying later), increasing an asset by $10 and increasing a liability by $10, we have

$$\begin{array}{lll}
\uparrow\textbf{10 (A)} & \uparrow\textbf{10 (B)} & \\
\text{Assets} & = \quad \text{Liabilities} & + \quad \text{Owners' Equity}
\end{array}$$

Take a few minutes to verify for yourself that if we account for every transaction such that A = B, the equation will remain in balance.

However, in the language of accounting we do not call these operations A and B. Rather we call them debits and credits.

The operations labeled "A" are "debits." A "debit" is (refer to the equation at the top of the page)

- an increase in an asset
- a decrease in a liability
- a decrease in owners' equity

The operations labeled "B" are "credits." A "credit" is (refer to the equation at the top of the page)

- a decrease in an asset or
- an increase in a liability or
- an increase in owners' equity.

Thus, if we account for each transaction such that the debits equal the credits (A = B) the accounting equation will remain in balance.

I am not a believer in memorizing. I think it is much more important to understand. But when it comes to debits and credits there is nothing to understand. They are only labels for operations on the accounting equation. Do not try to rationalize these labels by thinking that a debit is a "bad" thing that makes owners' equity go down, also a bad thing. Just memorize that debits increase assets and decrease liabilities and owners' equity, and credits do the opposite.

The standard abbreviations for debit and credit are Dr and Cr. Thus, our rule from above that the equation will remain in balance if A = B is now that the equation will remain in balance if Dr = Cr. (The abbreviations Dr and Cr probably have their roots in the Latin origins of accounting in what is now Italy more than 500 years ago.)

If we replace A and B in the equation above with Dr and Cr, we have the following

$$
\begin{array}{ccc}
\uparrow\text{Dr} & \uparrow\text{Cr} & \uparrow\text{Cr} \\
\text{Assets} \;=\; & \text{Liabilities} \;+\; & \text{Owners' Equity} \\
\downarrow\text{Cr} & \downarrow\text{Dr} & \downarrow\text{Dr}
\end{array}
$$

Because there are three elements in this (balance sheet) equation, and each element can either increase or decrease, there are only nine possible pair-wise combinations of increases and decreases in these three elements that can keep the equation in balance. The nine cells in the following matrix represent those nine possibilities, each of which represents a transaction in which the debits equal the credits.

		Debits (Dr)		
		A↑	L↓	OE↓
Credits (Cr)	A↓	x	x	x
	L↑	x	x	x
	OE↑	x	x	x

Spend a few minutes getting familiar with this matrix using these examples

- When a company pays cash to buy a truck, they will increase (Dr) the asset Truck and decrease (Cr) the asset Cash (see cell in first row and column)

- When a company borrows from a bank they will increase (Dr) the asset Cash and increase (Cr) the liability Bank Loan (see cell in second row and first column)

Journal Entries

Now that we have the idea of what debits and credits are, we need to discuss how they are used to record transactions in the accounting system.

So far, we have used arrows on the accounting equation to "record" the effects of various transactions on the three balance sheet elements (assets, liabilities, and owners' equity). Obviously, this is not an efficient way to either (a) record a single transaction or (b) to keep track of the cumulative effect of many transactions.

Imagine the number of transactions that occur each year for a large corporation like Starbucks, or Walmart, or Apple. These organizations have millions of transactions in a year and keeping track of all of that activity requires a very systematic accounting system. This is where bookkeeping comes in.

The first step for businesses to record transactions in a simple and efficient way is to record each transaction using a "journal entry."

Let's begin with a simple example. Assume the company buys $100 of inventory on account. This transaction is represented by the equation as follows:

$$\uparrow\textbf{100 (Dr)} \qquad \uparrow\textbf{100 (Cr)}$$
$$\text{Assets} \quad = \quad \text{Liabilities} \quad + \quad \text{Owners' Equity}$$

The journal entry for this transaction is:

Inventory (A)	100	
Accounts Payable (L)		100

All journal entries follow this format, so let's discuss it in detail.

First, to say the journal entry out loud we say, "Debit inventory, credit accounts payable for $100." Notice that we are not debiting and crediting "Assets" and "Owners' Equity," but we are debiting and crediting accounts within those categories.

Each business has a list of accounts that is called their "chart of accounts." The business will decide on the number of accounts that are necessary to be able to retrieve the information they want. In this example, inventory is debited because inventory (an asset) is increased and a debit increases an asset account. Accounts payable, the common account title for obligations to suppliers, is credited because accounts payable (a liability) is increased and a credit increases a liability account.

To write the journal entry, the debit is written first. The credit is written second and is indented relative to the debit. The numbers are written to the right, as though they are in two columns, with the debit in the left column and the credit in the right column. In the "old days" journal entries were written on ledger paper that had columns for the numbers. Today we still write the numbers as though the columns were there.

In the journal entry above, after each of the accounts, a letter in parentheses indicates the type of account (A for asset, L for liability, and OE for owners' equity). These letters are not used in conventional accounting systems, but are used here as a learning aid. In a conventional accounting system, accounts are numbered to indicate what kind of an account it is (e.g., assets might begin with a 1 and liabilities with a 2). Here, we replace that with a simple letter indicator.

Finally, note that <u>every</u> transaction and economic event the company accounts for <u>must</u> be recorded as a journal entry. That's how it gets into the accounting system. There is no other way.

Before computers, these journal entries were made in a book called the General Journal. These days, the General Journal is more likely to be a virtual book on a computer. The technology has changed, but the idea is the same.

Three Balance Sheet Transactions
At the end of chapter three we presented a list of ten common types of transactions that companies enter into. Now we want to integrate that list with the concepts of debits and credits and journal entries, and represent them on the matrix above.

We begin with the three common balance sheet transactions. Recall that these transactions do not affect owners' equity, but only affect assets and liabilities.

The three common balance sheet transactions are:

1. An increase in an asset (Dr) and a decrease in an asset (Cr) – when the company purchases an asset for cash
2. An increase in an asset (Dr) and a liability (Cr) – when the company borrows money or purchases an asset on credit
3. A decrease in an asset (Cr) and a liability (Dr) – when the company repays a loan, that resulted either from borrowing cash or from purchasing an asset on credit

These are transactions companies engage in to prepare to operate and make money: Raising cash from creditors, acquiring assets for cash and credit, and paying back creditors. These three common balance sheet transactions can be represented in the matrix as follows:

		Debits (Dr)		
		A↑	L↓	OE↓
Credits (Cr)	A↓	1	3	x
	L↑	2	x	x
	OE↑	x	x	x

Let's consider an example for each of these transactions. In each case, we both repeat the equation representation for the transaction and supply a representative journal entry.

As we go through these examples, compare the equations with the corresponding journal entries to become comfortable with this way of recording transactions.

1. Buying an asset for cash. The effect on the equation is

$$\overset{\uparrow}{\underset{\downarrow}{Assets_{Beg}}} \quad - \quad Liab_{Beg} \quad = \quad POE_{Beg} \quad + \quad Revenue \quad - \quad Expense$$

As a more specific example, assume the company purchased a truck for $25,000 in cash. The journal entry would be

Truck (A)	25,000	
Cash (A)		25,000

2. Buying an asset on credit or borrowing cash. The effect on the equation is

$$\text{Assets}_{Beg} \uparrow \quad - \quad \text{Liab}_{Beg} \uparrow \quad = \quad \text{POE}_{Beg} \quad + \quad \text{Revenue} \quad - \quad \text{Expense}$$

Modify the previous example to assume the company took out a loan for $25,000 and used the resulting cash to buy the truck. The journal entry for taking out the loan would be

Cash (A)	25,000	
Loan (L)		25,000

Alternatively, if the company had purchased inventory on account for $4,000, the journal entry would be

Inventory (A)	4,000	
Accounts Payable (L)		4,000

3. Paying a liability. The effect on the equation is

$$\text{Assets}_{Beg} \downarrow \quad - \quad \text{Liab}_{Beg} \downarrow \quad = \quad \text{POE}_{Beg} \quad + \quad \text{Revenue} \quad - \quad \text{Expense}$$

Assume the company paid back the loan from the previous example in one lump payment (ignore interest to keep it simple). The journal entry would be

Loan (L)	25,000	
Cash (A)		25,000

If the company paid the accounts payable from the previous example the journal entry would be

Accounts Payable (L)	4,000	
Cash (A)		4,000

Three Transactions With Owners

The three transactions between the company and its owners are:

4. An increase in an asset (Dr) and an increase in owners' equity (Cr) – when the company issues (sells) stock to owners for cash

5. An increase in a liability (Cr) and a decrease in owners' equity (Dr) – when the company declares a dividend to shareholders

6. A decrease in an asset (Cr) and a decrease in owners' equity (Dr) – when the company repurchases some of its own common stock from investors for cash

To see how debits and credits and journal entries work with these transactions with owners, we first have to expand the accounting equation to divide owners' equity into Permanent Owners' Equity (POE) and temporary owners' equity represented by revenue (Rev) and expense (Exp), indicating the debits and credits for each

$$\begin{array}{ccccc}
\uparrow\textbf{Dr} & \uparrow\textbf{Cr} & \uparrow\textbf{Cr} & \uparrow\textbf{Cr} & \uparrow\textbf{Dr} \\
\text{Assets}_{\text{Beg}} - & \text{Liab}_{\text{Beg}} = & \text{POE}_{\text{Beg}} + & \text{Revenue} - & \text{Expense} \\
\downarrow\textbf{Cr} & \downarrow\textbf{Dr} & \downarrow\textbf{Dr} & \downarrow\textbf{Dr} & \downarrow\textbf{Cr}
\end{array}$$

Recall that the three transactions with owners do not affect income and are recorded to Permanent Owners' Equity, where a credit increases owners' equity and a debit decreases owners' equity. We will discuss the effect of debits and credits on revenue and expense further below. These three transactions can be represented as transactions 4 – 6 in the matrix as follows:

		Debits (Dr)		
		A↑	L↓	OE↓
Credits (Cr)	A↓	1	3	6
	L↑	2	x	5
	OE↑	4	x	x

Here is an example for each of these transactions.

4. The company sells (issues) its own stock to investors for cash

$$\begin{array}{ccccc}
 & & \uparrow & & \\
\text{Assets}_{\text{Beg}} - & \text{Liab}_{\text{Beg}} = & \text{POE}_{\text{Beg}} + & \text{Revenue} - & \text{Expense}
\end{array}$$

Assume the company sold 1,000 shares of stock for $15 each in cash and that the company records the full amount to an account called Common Stock. The journal entry would be

Cash (A)   15,000
    Common Stock (OE)   15,000

5. The company declares a cash dividend for its investors, which is a legal liability on the part of the company

$$\text{Assets}_{\text{Beg}} \quad - \quad \overset{\uparrow}{\text{Liab}_{\text{Beg}}} \quad = \quad \underset{\downarrow}{\text{POE}_{\text{Beg}}} \quad + \quad \text{Revenue} \quad - \quad \text{Expense}$$

Assume the company declared a cash dividend for each of its 1,000 outstanding shares of $0.25 per share. The journal entry would be

> Retained Earnings (OE)   250
>   Dividends Payable (L)   250

6. The company repurchases from its investors some of its own stock

$$\underset{\downarrow}{\text{Assets}_{\text{Beg}}} \quad - \quad \text{Liab}_{\text{Beg}} \quad = \quad \underset{\downarrow}{\text{POE}_{\text{Beg}}} \quad + \quad \text{Revenue} \quad - \quad \text{Expense}$$

Assume the company repurchased 100 of the 1,000 shares they had previously issued when (to keep it simple) the share price was still $15.00. The journal entry would be

> Common Stock (OE)   1500
>   Cash (A)   1500

Four Income Statement Transactions

Now we expand the transactions under consideration to include those that affect both the balance sheet and the income statement. While the previous transactions prepare the company to operate and make money, the following income statement transactions are those that the company enters into in order to make money. These are transactions between the company and its non-owners, and they affect the temporary owners' equity accounts, revenue and expense, and thereby affect both income and owners' equity.

To see how debits and credits affect revenue and expense accounts we repeat the expanded accounting equation from above

$$\overset{\uparrow \textbf{Dr}}{\underset{\downarrow \textbf{Cr}}{\text{Assets}_{\text{Beg}}}} \quad - \quad \overset{\uparrow \textbf{Cr}}{\underset{\downarrow \textbf{Dr}}{\text{Liab}_{\text{Beg}}}} \quad = \quad \overset{\uparrow \textbf{Cr}}{\underset{\downarrow \textbf{Dr}}{\text{POE}_{\text{Beg}}}} \quad + \quad \overset{\uparrow \textbf{Cr}}{\underset{\downarrow \textbf{Dr}}{\text{Revenue}}} \quad - \quad \overset{\uparrow \textbf{Dr}}{\underset{\downarrow \textbf{Cr}}{\text{Expense}}}$$

The effect of debits and credits on revenue and expense are directly related to the effect of debits and credits on owner's equity. A credit increases owners' equity, and since revenue is a positive (temporary) owners' equity account, a credit also increases revenue. Correspondingly, a debit decreases revenue.

Similarly, a debit decreases owners' equity, but increases an expense because an expense is negative (temporary) owners' equity. Correspondingly, a credit decreases expense.

To summarize

A "debit" is also
- an increase in an expense
- a decrease in a revenue

A "credit" is also
- a decrease in an expense
- an increase in a revenue

When we expand the matrix from above to incorporate revenue and expense, it grows from nine cells to 25 cells. However, among the 16 cells that have been added, there are only four income statement transactions that are common in the sense that most companies have all of these transactions in most accounting periods.

Below, numbers 7 – 10 are added to the matrix to indicate these four income statement transactions. The matrix now has labels for all ten of the common transactions introduced in chapter three. The other fifteen cells are described briefly below, but they rarely or never occur.

		Debits (Dr)				
		A↑	L↓	OE↓	R↓	E↑
	A↓	1	3	6	x	9
	L↑	2	x	5	x	10
Credits (Cr)	OE↑	4	x	x	x	x
	R↑	7	8	x	x	x
	E↓	x	x	x	x	x

The four common income statement transactions are (from the list at the end of chapter 3):

7. Recording a revenue (Cr) and increasing an asset (Dr) – when the company transfers control of a good or service to a customer who has not paid in advance

8. Recording a revenue (Cr) and decreasing a liability (Dr) – when the company transfers control of a good or service to a customer who has paid in advance

9. Recording an expense (Dr) and decreasing an asset (Cr) – when the company consumes a resource that was paid for previously

10. Recording an expense (Dr) and increasing a liability (Cr) – when a company consumes a resource that was not paid for previously

Here are examples for these four income statement transactions. Again, as you go through these examples, take your time and compare the equations with the corresponding journal entries. This will help you to become comfortable with this shorthand way of recording transactions.

In the journal entries below, after each of the accounts, a letter in parentheses indicates the type of account. As above, A is for asset, L for liability, and OE for owners' equity. In addition, we now have R for revenue and E for expense.

7. The company provides goods and services that are either paid for upon delivery or later

$$\text{Assets}_{Beg} \quad - \quad \text{Liab}_{Beg} \quad = \quad \text{POE}_{Beg} \quad + \quad \overset{\uparrow}{\text{Revenue}} \quad - \quad \text{Expense}$$

(with $\uparrow$ over Assets)

Assume the company sold inventory for $300 in cash. The journal entry would be

Cash (A)	300	
Revenue (R)		300

On the other hand, assume the company sold inventory for $400 on account. The journal entry would be

Accounts Receivable (A)	400	
Revenue (R)		400

8. The company provides goods and services that were paid for in advance

$$\text{Assets}_{Beg} \quad - \quad \text{Liab}_{Beg} \quad = \quad \text{POE}_{Beg} \quad + \quad \overset{\uparrow}{\text{Revenue}} \quad - \quad \text{Expense}$$

(with $\downarrow$ under Liab)

Let's first assume that the company collected $150 in advance for the purchase of some goods to be delivered in the future. This is an example of transaction #2 above, an increase in an asset and a liability, and the journal entry would be

Cash (A)   150
    Deferred Revenue (L)   150

Later, when the company provides the goods, they reduce the liability and record revenue. This is the example of transaction #8 and the journal entry would be

Deferred Revenue (L)   150
    Revenue (R)   150

9. The company consumes (uses up) a good or service that is paid for at that time or earlier

$$\text{Assets}_{Beg} \quad - \quad \text{Liab}_{Beg} \quad = \quad \text{POE}_{Beg} \quad + \quad \text{Revenue} \quad - \quad \overset{\uparrow}{\text{Expense}}$$
$$\underset{\downarrow}{}$$

Assume a company hired a day laborer for one day and paid him $50 cash at the end of the day. The journal entry would be

Wage Expense (E)   50
    Cash (A)   50

As another example, assume a company purchased $225 of office supplies and later used them. The transaction at the time of the purchase is an example of transactions #1, and the journal entry would be

Office Supplies (A)   225
    Cash (A)   225

Using the office supplies is an example of transaction #9, and the journal entry would be

Office Supplies Expense (E) 225
    Office Supplies (A)   225

10. The company consumes (uses up) a good or service that will be paid for later

$$\overset{\uparrow}{\text{Assets}_{Beg}} \quad - \quad \text{Liab}_{Beg} \quad = \quad \text{POE}_{Beg} \quad + \quad \text{Revenue} \quad - \quad \overset{\uparrow}{\text{Expense}}$$

Assume an employee works during the day, earning $80 that will be paid later. The journal entry would be

Wage Expense (E)	80	
Wages Payable (L)		80

To this point I have said little about account titles. The reason for that is that account titles are not important.

When a company develops its chart of accounts, the list of all the accounts it intends to use, the company can determine the number of accounts and the names for those accounts. For example, an account title "miscellaneous expense" might include many expenses of different types such as office supplies, janitorial services, electricity, etc. Or the company might have different accounts for each of those. They might have an account dedicated to entertainment, or one dedicated just to meals.

The number and names for the accounts is up to the company and the amount of detailed information they want to retrieve from their accounting system. Just remember that the more details they want in the accounting system, i.e., the more accounts they will have, the more expensive the system will be to maintain. So, each company has to balance the costs of the accounting system with the benefits of having that more detailed information.

This might suggest that there is no uniformity in company accounts. That is not true. While the detailed accounts are likely to vary from one company to another depending on their information needs, what we see in the published financial statements across companies is quite similar, though not perfectly similar. Many financial statement line items such as cash, accounts receivable, inventory, accounts payable, etc., are used by virtually every company, though the level of detail in the accounts that are aggregated to form those line items may differ.

Adjusting Entries
The examples provided above for the four income statement transactions were all transactions that occurred during the accounting period. However, companies also record journal entries for events that have the same effects on the accounting equations as transactions #7 through #10 discussed above, but that are not triggered by transactions that occur during the period. Rather, they are journal entries that are made at the

end of the period to record certain economic events that do not involve transactions.

The journal entries to record these economic events are referred to as "adjusting" entries. Recording these adjusting entries is necessary to ensure that the accounting records are as accurate as possible.

There are four types of adjusting entries that correspond to the four types of income statement entries just discussed. Here is a summary of the four types of adjusting entries with examples:

a. Record revenue that is earned as of the end of the accounting period that was not previously recorded and was not previously paid (**transaction #7**) –

    This occurs when the company provides goods and services in advance of payment but the revenue has not been recorded as of the end of the accounting period. This is often for services that are provided over time. For example, a landlord provides rental services that as of the end of the accounting period have not been paid. The journal entry would be.

    Rent Receivable (A)   500
        Rent Revenue (R)   500

    Another example is a bank that has a loan outstanding on which the bank is earning interest. At the end of the period, even though the borrower is not obligated to pay the interest right now, the bank has earned the interest revenue and can record the following journal entry

    Interest Receivable (A)   40
        Interest Revenue (R)   40

    If these journal entries were not recorded at the end of the period, revenue and income would be understated for the period and assets would be understated at the end of the period.

b. Record revenue that is earned as of the end of the accounting period that was previously paid but was not previously recorded (**transaction #8**) –

    This occurs when the company provides goods and services that were paid for in advance but the revenue has not been recorded as of the end of the accounting period. An example is rent that was paid in advance that now (later) has been earned. When the rent was received in advance, the landlord recorded

Cash (A)   250
     Deferred Revenue (L)   250

Later, at the end of the accounting period, time has passed and the landlord has earned some of the rent that was paid in advance. The landlord records

Deferred Revenue (L)   100
     Revenue (R)   100

Another example is an insurance premium paid in advance. When the insurance company receives the premium, they defer revenue because they have not yet provided the service. The insurance company records the following journal entry

Cash (A)   125
     Deferred Revenue (L)   125

Later, at the end of the accounting period, time has passed and the insurance company has provided service (standing ready to pay any claims that arise). At that time, the company has earned some of the revenue they were paid in advance and records

Deferred Revenue (L)   100
     Revenue (R)   100

If these adjusting entries were not recorded at the end of the period, revenue and income would be understated for the period and liabilities would be overstated at the end of the period.

c. Record an expense that was incurred as of the end of the period that was paid previously but that was not previously recorded **(transaction #9)**

This occurs when the company consumes a good or service that was paid for previously but the expense has not been recorded as of the end of the accounting period. An example is using up pre-paid rent from the renter's point of view. When the renter pays rent in advance, she records

Prepaid rent (A)   300
     Cash (A)   300

Later, at the end of the accounting period, when the renter has consumed some of the rental services, she records the following journal entry for the amount of rental services consumed

Rent Expense (E)	100	
Prepaid Rent (A)		100

If this adjusting entry was not recorded at the end of the period, expense would be understated and income would be overstated for the period and assets would be overstated at the end of the period.

d. Record an expense that was incurred as of the end of the period that was not previously paid and was not previously recorded (**transaction #10**)

This occurs when the company consumes a good or service that was not paid for previously and the expense has not been recorded as of the end of the accounting period. An example is when a renter consumes rental services that were not paid for in advance. At the end of the period the renter must record the expense and liability for using those services

Rent Expense (E)	100	
Rent Payable (L)		100

As another example, at the end of the accounting period a borrower must record the expense and liability for interest incurred up to the end of the period

Interest Expense (E)	100	
Interest Payable (L)		100

If these adjusting entries were not recorded at the end of the period, expense would be understated and income would be overstated for the period and liabilities would be understated at the end of the period.

Closing Entry

The last journal entry made at the end of the accounting period is to "close" the temporary owners' equity accounts (revenue, expense, gain, loss) into the Permanent Owners' Equity account, retained earnings. This returns the balances in the temporary accounts to zero, preparing them to accumulate revenue, expense, gains and losses in the next period.

To "close" these accounts, those with a credit balance (revenues and gains) are debited for their entire balance, and those with a debit balance (expenses and losses) are credited for their entire balance. This entry is then balanced by crediting retained earnings (if the company has positive net income) or by debiting retained earnings (if the company has negative net income).

As a simple example, assume that a company had only the following revenue and expense account balances at the end of the accounting period, after all of the adjusting entries have been recorded: $2,100 in revenue and $1,945 in expense, which consists of $1,020 for cost of goods sold, $800 for wages expense, and $125 for utilities expense.

The effect on the equation of closing these revenue and expense accounts to retained earnings is

$$
\begin{array}{ccccccc}
 & & & \uparrow 155 \text{ (Cr)} & & & \\
\text{Assets} & - & \text{Liab} & = & \text{Perm OE} & + & \text{Rev} & - & \text{Exp} \\
 & & & & & & \downarrow 2,100 \text{ (Cr)} & & \downarrow 1,945 \text{ (Cr)}
\end{array}
$$

The "closing" journal entry for closing these revenue and expense accounts to retained earnings is

Revenue (R)	2,100	
Cost of Goods Sold (E)		1,020
Wage Expense (E)		800
Utilities Expense (E)		125
Retained Earnings (OE)		155

This concludes the first step in the bookkeeping process, recording a journal entry for each economic event that is to be recorded in the accounting system, including both journal entries for transactions during the period and adjusting journal entries for other events at the end of the period. The journal entries provide the company with a record of each event that affected their accounting system and both (or all of the) accounts that were affected.

However, journal entries alone are not useful for answering questions such as how much cash is on hand? How much inventory do we have? How much revenue did the company earn during the year? To answer these questions, the company needs a way to keep a running total of the balance in each account. This leads us to the second step in the bookkeeping process, posting the journal entries to the General Ledger, which is commonly represented by T-accounts.

T-Accounts

Journal entries are recorded in the General Journal, and provide a chronological listing of all of the company's economic activity, showing all of the accounts that are affected by each event. The General Ledger in contrast has a separate listing for each account, maintaining a running total for that account.

The second step for businesses to record transactions is to "post" each journal entry to its respective General Ledger accounts.

To "post" each journal entry to the General Ledger, we break apart the journal entry and record its effect in each account that was affected. The shorthand that is commonly used to represent the General Ledger in practice is with a T-Account, which looks like this.

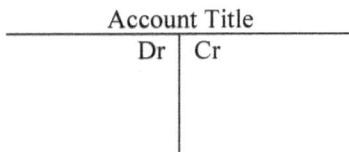

The T-account has the account name written on top. Debits are recorded in the left column and credits are recorded in the right column.

To see how this works let's post the following journal entries to the T-Accounts provided below, each of which begins the period with a balance of zero.

(A) The company sells $1,500 of common stock to investors

Cash (A)	1,500	
Common Stock (OE)		1,500

(B) The company buys $900 of inventory on account

Inventory (A)	900	
Accounts Payable (L)		900

(C) The company sells inventory for $1,200 on account

Accounts Receivable (A)	1,200	
Revenue (R)		1,200

(D) The inventory just sold cost the company $750

Cost of Goods Sold (E)	750	
Inventory (A)		750

(E) The company pays wages of $300 in cash

Wage Expense (E)	300	
Cash (A)		300

(F) The company pays $400 of Accounts Payable

Accounts Payable (L)	400	
Cash (A)		400

(G) The company closes revenue and expense accounts

Revenue (R)	1,200	
Cost of Goods Sold (E)		750
Wage Expense (E)		300
Retained Earnings (OE)		150

Each journal entry above was labeled with a letter A through G. Those letters are used below to identify where each part of the journal entry is "posted" to its respective T-account.

Take a moment to track these journal entries in the T-accounts below. For example, the journal entry for transaction A is posted to the left (debit) side of the Cash T-account and to the right (credit) side of the Common Stock T-account.

Cash				Accounts Payable				Revenue	
Beg 0					0 Beg				0 Beg
(A) 1,500					900 (B)				1,200 (C)
	300 (E)		(F) 400						
	400 (F)								1,200
								(G) 1,200	
End 800					500 End				0 End

Accounts Receivable			Common Stock			Cost of Goods Sold	
Beg 0				0 Beg		Beg 0	
(C) 1,200				1,500 (A)		(D) 750	
						750	
							750 (G)
End 1,200				1,500 End		End 0	

Inventory			Retained Earnings			Wage Expense	
Beg 0				0 Beg		Beg 0	
(B) 900				150 (G)		(E) 300	
	750 (D)					300	
							300 (G)
End 150				150 End		End 0	

Finally, notice that at the bottom of each account is a horizontal line and the account balance is below that line.

The next chapter presents a comprehensive example of the full accounting cycle from recording journal entries to posting to T-accounts to preparing financial statements. Carefully following this example will help you to internalize the bookkeeping process discussed in this chapter.

The Rest of the Matrix

In the last version of the matrix above there were still 15 cells that were not yet labeled. Below is the final version of the matrix with these remaining cells labeled A through O. These transactions are much less common than those previously discussed, and in some cases do not occur at all. They are only briefly discussed below for completeness.

		Debits (Dr)				
		A↑	L↓	OE↓	R↓	E↑
Credits (Cr)	A↓	3	4	10	H	7
	L↑	2	B	9	I	8
	OE↑	1	C	E	J	M
	R↑	5	6	F	K	N
	E↓	A	D	G	L	O

Here are examples for these remaining 15 transactions.

A. Reversing an expense previously recorded – one example is when a customer returns a good that originally cost $100 and the company puts it back into their inventory. The journal entry would be

Inventory (A)   100
    Cost of Goods Sold (E)   100

B. Refinancing debt, paying off one liability with the proceeds from another liability – one example is using a bank loan to pay off accounts payable. If the bank paid the money directly to the creditor so that the company never held the cash, this would be recorded as

Accounts Payable (L)   100
    Bank Loan (L)   100

C. Issuing common stock for a liability – an example is when a creditor holds a $10,000 bond that is convertible into common stock and they decide to convert it. The journal entry would be

      Bond Payable (L)   10,000
            Common Stock (OE)   10,000

D. Reversing an expense previously recorded that had never been paid – the main example here would be correcting an error when an expense had erroneously been recorded. If the error was for $40 for utilities expense the journal entry would be

      Utilities Payable (L)   40
           Utilities Expense (E)   40

E. Issuing common stock for another form of owners' equity – an example is when an investor exchanges preferred stock for common stock or when an investor exchanges stock options for common stock. In the case of convertible preferred stock, if the preferred stock has a value of $100 the journal entry would be

      Preferred Stock (OE)   100
           Common Stock (OE)   100

In the case of stock options, if the stock option had a fair value of $5.00 when granted and an exercise price of $20, the journal entry would be

      Stock Options (OE)   5
      Cash (A)   20
           Common Stock (OE)   25

F. There is no reasonable example for this transaction

G. There is no reasonable example for this transaction

H. Reversing revenue previously recorded that was not paid in advance – one example is when a customer returns a good that was originally purchased for $150 and the company gives the customer cash or a credit on their account receivable. If they give a cash refund, the journal entry would be

      Revenue (R)   150
          Cash (A)   150

If the customer had not previously paid and the seller reduces their account receivable, the journal entry would be

Revenue (R)	150	
Account Receivable (A)		150

I.   Reversing revenue previously recorded that was paid in advance – one example is when a customer returns a good that was originally purchased for $150. If the company continues to hold the customer's advance payment, the journal entry would be

Revenue (R)	150	
Deferred Revenue (L)		150

J.   There is no reasonable example for this transaction

K.   There is no reasonable example for this transaction

L.   There is no reasonable example for this transaction

M. Recording an expense when employees earn stock-based compensation – When companies grant stock options to their employees as part of their compensation, the employees earn the right to these options during the option's vesting period. As an example, assume a company grants one option with a fair value at the time of grant of $20 that will vest (be earned by the employee) over the next four years. During each of the next four years the employee earns one quarter of the option, which is a form of owners' equity, and each year the company records the following journal entry

Compensation Expense (E)	5	
Stock Options (OE)		5

N. There is no reasonable example for this transaction

O. There is no reasonable example for this transaction

Finally, to keep the discussion and the size of the matrix manageable, we have not included gains and losses. Gains behave just the same as revenue, they are increased by a credit and decreased by a debit, though they will only be decreased to correct an error. Losses behave just the same as expense, they are increased by a debit and decreased by a credit, though they will only be decreased to correct an error.

Chapter 13 – A Comprehensive Example

The Accounting Cycle

This chapter presents an annotated comprehensive example of the full accounting cycle from recording journal entries to preparing financial statements. The accounting cycle is often represented as a series of seven steps that are repeated every accounting period. Those steps are

- Record journal entries for every transaction and event that affects the financial statements
- Post every journal entry to the general ledger (T-Accounts)
- Prepare an unadjusted trial balance (described below)
- Record and post adjusting entries to the general ledger
- Prepare an adjusted trial balance (described below)
- Record and post closing entries to the general ledger
- Prepare financial statements

We will use a small business that is just getting started, Clay's Coffee Services (CCS), as our example. CCS provides daily coffee service to business customers. Customers pay an annual membership fee in advance and a monthly fee by the fifth day of the following month that depends on how much coffee their employees drank the previous month. CCS began business on July 1, 20x1, and closed their books and prepared financial statements on December 31, 20x1.

Journal Entries for Transactions

Here are CCS's transactions for the first six months of business, along with the journal entries for each transaction.

Clay started the business by investing $10,000 of his own money.

(A)	Cash (A)	10,000	
	Common Stock (OE)		10,000

Note, by crediting Common Stock we assume Clay's Coffee Service is a corporation and that Clay issued stock (certificates of ownership) to himself when he invested the $10,000. Note also that Clay (the person) and Clay's Coffee Services (the company) are separate economic entities and in this example, we are only accounting for Clay's Coffee Services.

CCS borrowed $4,000 from a bank on July 1, 20x1. CCS is to pay six percent interest every twelve months (i.e., $240), and repay the balance on July 1, 20x5.

| (B) | Cash (A) | 4,000 | |
| | Bank Loan (L) | | 4,000 |

CCS purchased coffee brewing equipment on July 1, 20x1 for $4,500. The equipment is expected to last for five years, at which time Clay expects it to be worthless. Debit equipment for the full amount because as of July 1, 20x1 when the money is paid CCS has not consumed any of the equipment.

| (C) | Equipment (A) | 4,500 | |
| | Cash (A) | | 4,500 |

CCS paid $500 for business insurance for one year on July 1, 20x1. Debit pre-paid insurance because as of July 1, 20x1 when the money is paid CCS has not consumed any of the insurance services.

| (D) | Pre-paid Insurance (A) | 500 | |
| | Cash (A) | | 500 |

CCS sold 25 one-year coffee memberships for $100 each in cash. For simplicity assume the memberships were all sold on July 1, 20x1. Credit deferred revenue because as of July 1, 20x1 when the money is received, CCS has not provided any goods or services.

| (E) | Cash (A) | 2,500 | |
| | Deferred Revenue (R) | | 2,500 |

CCS purchased $4,600 of coffee beans and other supplies on account during the remainder of 20x1.

| (F) | Inventory (A) | 4,600 | |
| | Accounts Payable (L) | | 4,600 |

During the remainder of 20x1, CCS collected $9,500 in monthly payments from coffee members. These payments were for July through November and were collected in August through December. Payment for December will be made in January. Credit revenue because as of the collection of these payments, which were for services the previous month, CCS had provided the service to the customers.

(G)	Cash (A)	9,500	
	Revenue (R)		9,500

During the remainder of 20x1, CCS consumed $3,800 of coffee beans and other supplies providing coffee for its customers.

(H)	Cost of Goods Sold (E)	3,800	
	Inventory (A)		3,800

During the remainder of 20x1, CCS paid $4,100 toward accounts payable for previously purchased coffee beans and other supplies.

(I)	Accounts Payable (L)	4,100	
	Cash (A)		4,100

During the remainder of 20x1, CCS paid Clay a salary of $1,200 per month on the first day of the month following the month in which he worked. By the end of the year on December 31, Clay had received five payments in August through December for work done in July through November. The journal entry that represents all of these payments is

(J)	Wage Expense (E)	6,000	
	Cash (A)		6,000

CCS invested $5,000 of extra cash in a certificate of deposit on October 1, 20x1. The certificate matures in one year and pays an annual interest rate of 4 percent, with all interest and principle to be paid on October 1, 20x2.

(K)	CD Investment (A)	5,000	
	Cash (A)		5,000

Posting Journal Entries for Transactions to T-Accounts

In this step the journal entries recorded above are posted to their respective T-Accounts (General Ledger accounts).

Cash			
Beg	0		
(A)	10,000		
(B)	4,000		
		4,500	(C)
		500	(D)
(E)	2,500		
(G)	9,500		
		4,100	(I)
		6,000	(J)
		5,000	(K)
End	5,900		

Accounts Payable		
	0	Beg
	4,600	(F)
(I) 4,100		
	500	End

Revenue	
	9,500 (G)
	9,500

Accounts Receivable		
Beg	0	
End	0	

Wages Payable	
	0 Beg
	0 End

Interest Revenue

Interest Receivable		
Beg	0	
End	0	

Interest Payable	
	0 Beg
	0 End

Cost of Goods Sold	
(H) 3,800	
3,800	

Inventory		
Beg	0	
(F)	4,600	
		3,800 (H)
End	800	

Deferred Revenue	
	0 Beg
	2,500 (E)
	2,500 End

Wages Expense	
(J) 6,000	
6,000	

Pre-Paid Insurance		
Beg	0	
(D)	500	
End	500	

Loan Payable	
	0 Beg
	4,000 (B)
	4,000 End

Interest Expense

Equipment		
Beg	0	
(C)	4,500	
End	4,500	

Common Stock	
	0 Beg
	10,000 (A)
	10,000 End

Depreciation Expense

CD Investment		
Beg	0	
(K)	5,000	
End	5,000	

Retained Earnings	
	0 Beg
	0 End

Insurance Expense

The Unadjusted Trial Balance

An unadjusted trial balance is a list of all of the company's accounts with their respective debit or credit balances. The idea is very simple, to verify that at this stage in the accounting cycle the debits still equal the credits. If the debits do not equal the credits then an error was made somewhere in recording the journal entries or in posting the journal entries to the T-Accounts.

Here is CCS's unadjusted trial balance as of December 31, 20x1.

Clay's Coffee Service
Unadjusted Trial Balance as of December 31, 20x1

	Dr	Cr
Cash	$5,900	
Accounts Receivable	0	
Interest Receivable	0	
Inventory	800	
Pre-Paid Insurance	500	
Equipment	4,500	0
Certificate of Deposit	5,000	0
Accounts Payable		$500
Wages Payable		0
Interest Payable		0
Deferred Revenue		2,500
Loan Payable		4,000
Common Stock		10,000
Retained Earnings		0
Revenue		9,500
Interest Revenue		0
Cost of Goods Sold	3,800	
Wages Expense	6,000	
Interest Expense	0	
Depreciation Expense	0	
Insurance Expense	0	
Total	$26,500	$26,500

Record and Post Adjusting Entries

The next step in the accounting cycle after preparing the unadjusted trial balance is to record the necessary adjusting entries. Here are CCS's adjusting entries at the end of the accounting period (December 31, 20x1) prior to preparing financial statements.

At the end of the year, CCS must recognize that they have incurred six months of interest expense on the $4,000 loan they borrowed on July 1,

20x1. The interest rate on the loan is six percent, so the interest expense for six months is $120 ($4,000 x 0.06 x 0.5). The adjusting journal entry is

(L)	Interest Expense (E)	120	
	Interest Payable (L)		120

At the end of the year CCS must recognize that the coffee equipment has declined in value. They expected the equipment to last for five years with no value at the end of five years. So far, they have used the equipment for one half of a year, so they have consumed ten percent of the equipment's life. Depreciation expense for this one-half year is $4,500/10 = $450. The adjusting journal entry is

(M)	Depreciation Expense (E)	450	
	Equipment (A)		450

(For simplicity here we make the credit to the equipment account. As is explained in the next chapter the credit is actually made to a contra asset account called accumulated depreciation.)

At the end of the year, CCS must recognize that they have incurred six months of insurance expense, consuming half of the $500 they paid on July 1, 20x1 for a one-year insurance policy. This insurance expense is $250 ($500 x 6/12) and the adjusting journal entry is

(N)	Insurance Expense (E)	250	
	Prepaid Insurance (A)		250

At the end of the year, CCS must recognize that they have earned six months of the one-year membership fees paid on July 1 (for the months of July through December). The revenue for these months is $1,250 ($2,500 x 6/12) and the adjusting journal entry is

(O)	Deferred Revenue (L)	1,250	
	Revenue (R)		1,250

At the end of the year, CCS must recognize that they earned $1,900 of revenue in December for coffee services provided that month that their members will pay in January. The adjusting journal entry is

(P)	Accounts Receivable (A)	1,900	
	Revenue (R)		1,900

At the end of the year, CCS must recognize that the company benefited from Clay's work in December and owes Clay his salary of $1,200 for that month that will be paid in early January. The adjusting journal entry is

(Q)   Wage Expense (E)   1,200
                Wages Payable (L)   1,200

At the end of the year, CCS must recognize that they are owed $50 for three months (October through December) of interest on the CD investment they have earned (5,000 x 0.04 x 3/12). The adjusting journal entry is

(R)   Interest Receivable (A)   50
                Interest Revenue (R)   50

These adjusting journal entries have been posted to the T-Accounts below.

Cash			
Beg 0			
(A) 10,000			
(B) 4,000			
	4,500	(C)	
	500	(D)	
(E) 2,500			
(G) 9,500			
	4,100	(I)	
	6,000	(J)	
	5,000	(K)	
End 5,900			

Accounts Payable	
	0 Beg
	4,600 (F)
(I) 4,100	
	500 End

Revenue		
	9,500	(G)
	1,250	(O)
	1,900	(P)
	12,650	

Accounts Receivable	
Beg 0	
(P) 1,900	
End 1,900	

Wages Payable	
	0 Beg
	1,200 (Q)
	1,200 End

Interest Revenue	
	50 (R)
	50

Interest Receivable	
Beg 0	
(R) 50	
End 50	

Interest Payable	
	0 Beg
	120 (L)
	120 End

Cost of Goods Sold	
(H) 3,800	
3,800	

Inventory	
Beg 0	
(F) 4,600	
	3,800 (H)
End 800	

Deferred Revenue	
	0 Beg
	2,500 (E)
(O) 1,250	
	1,250 End

Wages Expense	
(J) 6,000	
(Q) 1,200	
7,200	

Pre-Paid Insurance	
Beg 0	
(D) 500	
	250 (N)
End 250	

Loan Payable	
	0 Beg
	4,000 (B)
	4,000 End

Interest Expense	
(L) 120	
120	

Equipment	
Beg 0	
(C) 4,500	
	450 (M)
End 4,050	

Common Stock	
	0 Beg
	10,000 (A)
	10,000 End

Depreciation Expense	
(M) 450	
450	

CD Investment	
Beg 0	
(K) 5,000	
End 5,000	

Retained Earnings	
	0 Beg
	0 End

Insurance Expense	
(N) 250	
250	

The Adjusted Trial Balance

The adjusted trial balance is similar to the unadjusted trial balance, but constructed after the adjusting entries have been recorded.

Here is CCS's adjusted trial balance as of December 31, 20x1.

Clay's Coffee Service
Adjusted Trial Balance as of December 31, 20x1

	Dr	Cr
Cash	$5,900	
Accounts Receivable	1,900	
Interest Receivable	50	
Inventory	800	
Pre-Paid Insurance	250	
Equipment	4,050	
Certificate of Deposit	5,000	
Accounts Payable		$500
Wages Payable		1,200
Interest Payable		120
Deferred Revenue		1,250
Loan Payable		4,000
Common Stock		10,000
Retained Earnings		0
Revenue		12,650
Interest Revenue		50
Cost of Goods Sold	3,800	
Wages Expense	7,200	
Interest Expense	120	
Depreciation Expense	450	
Insurance Expense	250	0
Total	$29,770	$29,770

Record and Post the Closing Entry

Here is CCS's <u>closing entry</u>, transferring revenue and expense to retained earnings.

(S)	Revenue (R)	12,650	
	Interest Revenue (R)	50	
	Cost of Goods Sold (E)		3,800
	Wage Expense (E)		7,200
	Depreciation Expense (E)		450
	Insurance Expense (E)		250
	Interest Expense (E)		120
	Retained Earnings (OE)		880

Notice that the effect of "closing" the revenue and expense accounts is to return them to a zero balance so they can begin collecting the next period's revenue and expense. The difference of $880 is net income for the period and is added to owners' equity. The entries in the closing entry are also the information for CCS's income statement

Here are the final T-Accounts after the closing entry has been posted.

Cash			
Beg	0		
(A)	10,000		
(B)	4,000		
		4,500	(C)
		500	(D)
(E)	2,500		
(G)	9,500		
		4,100	(I)
		6,000	(J)
		5,000	(K)
End	5,900		

Accounts Payable			
		0	Beg
		4,600	(F)
(I)	4,100		
		500	End

Revenue			
		9,500	(G)
		1,250	(O)
		1,900	(P)
(S)	12,650	12,650	
		0	

Accounts Receivable		
Beg	0	
(P)	1,900	
End	1,900	

Wages Payable		
	0	Beg
	1,200	(Q)
	1,200	End

Interest Revenue		
	50	(R)
(S)	50	50
	0	

Interest Receivable		
Beg	0	
(R)	50	
End	50	

Interest Payable		
	0	Beg
	120	(L)
	120	End

Cost of Goods Sold		
(H)	3,800	
	3,800	3,800 (S)
	0	

Inventory		
Beg	0	
(F)	4,600	
		3,800
		(H)
End	800	

Deferred Revenue		
	0	Beg
	2,500	(E)
(O)		
1,250		
	1,250	End

Wages Expense		
(J)	6,000	
(Q)	1,200	
	7,200	7,200 (S)
	0	

Pre-Paid Insurance		
Beg	0	
(D)	500	
		250 (N)
End	250	

Loan Payable		
	0	Beg
	4,000	(B)
	4,000	End

Interest Expense		
(L)	120	
	120	120 (S)
	0	

Equipment		
Beg		
0		
(C)		
4,500		
		450 (M)
End		
4,050		

Common Stock		
	0	Beg
	10,000	(A)
	10,000	End

Depreciation Expense		
(M)		
450		
	450	450 (S)
	0	

CD Investment		
Beg	0	
(K)	5,000	
End	5,000	

Retained Earnings		
	0	Beg
	880	(S)
	880	End

Insurance Expense		
(N)	250	
	250	250 (S)
	0	

Prepare Financial Statements

Here is the balance sheet. The account balances are taken directly from the final balances in the T-Accounts on the previous page.

Clay's Coffee Service
Balance Sheet as of December 31, 20x1

		20x1
Cash		$5,900
Accounts Receivable		1,900
Interest Receivable		50
Inventory		800
Prepaid Insurance		250
Equipment		4,050
Certificate of Deposit		5,000
Total Assets		$17,950
Accounts Payable		$500
Wages Payable		1,200
Interest Payable		120
Deferred Revenue		1,250
Loan Payable		4,000
Total Liabilities		$7,070
Common Stock		$10,000
Retained Earnings		880
Total Liab and Owners' Equity		$17,950

Here is the income statement. The amounts are taken directly from the pre-closing T-Account balances, which are the same as those in the closing journal entry.

Clay's Coffee Service
Income Statement
for the year ending December 31, 20x1

		20x1
Revenue		$12,650
Cost of Goods Sold	$3,800	
Wages Expense	7,200	
Interest Expense	120	
Depreciation Expense	450	
Insurance Expense	250	
Total Expense		$11,820
Interest Income		50
Net Income		$880

Here is the statement of stockholders' equity, which reflects the changes in owners' equity from issuing stock and earning income.

Clay's Coffee Service
Statement of Stockholders' Equity
for the year ending December 31, 20x1

	Common Stock	Retained Earnings	Total
Beginning balance, July 1, 20x1	0	0	0
Net Income		$880	880
Issue Common Stock	10,000		10,000
Ending balance, December 31, 20x1	10,000	880	10,880

Here is the statement of cash flows. Details for preparing the statement of cash flows are presented in the next section.

Clay's Coffee Service
Statement of Cash Flows
for the year ending December 31, 20x1

		20x1
Operations		
Net Income	$880	
Depreciation Expense	450	
Changes in current assets and liabilities		
Change in accounts receivable	(1,900)	
Change in interest receivable	(50)	
Change in inventory	(800)	
Change in prepaid insurance	(250)	
Change in accounts payable	500	
Change in wages payable	1,200	
Change in interest payable	120	
Change in deferred revenue	1,250	
Cash from operations		$1,400
Investing		
Purchase Equipment	(4,500)	
Purchase Certificate of Deposit	(5,000)	
Cash from investing		(9,500)
Financing		
Issue Common Stock	$10,000	
Borrow from Bank	4,000	
Cash from financing		14,000
Change in Cash		$5,900

Preparing a Statement of Cash Flows

As we just saw, the balance sheet and the income statement can be taken directly from the T-Accounts. The statement of comprehensive income does not apply to CCS, and preparation of the statement of stockholders' equity is relatively simple. The same cannot be said of the statement of cash flows, especially the indirect operating section.

This section guides you through the preparation of a statement of cash flows, using data from Clay's Coffee Service. Being able to prepare a statement of cash flows is not necessary to understanding the statement, but working your way through the preparation at least once can deepen your understanding of the statement.

Refer to the financial statements for Clay's Coffee Service for 20x1 presented above as we prepare a statement of cash flows for that year. To begin, since this is Clay's first year of operation the beginning cash balance was zero, so the ending balance of $5,900 is also the change for the year. This is the number that the statement of cash flows will explain.

Net income for the period as reported on the income statement is $880. This is our starting point in the indirect operating section of the statement of cash flows provided on the previous page.

The first adjustment we make to net income is to remove the non-cash depreciation expense of $450 by adding it back.

The rest of the line items in the indirect operating section of the statement of cash flows are adjustments for changes in current assets and liabilities.

The first current asset adjustment is for the increase in accounts receivable from zero to $1,900 when CCS recorded $1,900 of revenue that is included in income for which the company received no cash. Thus, income overstates cash received by $1,900 and this $1,900 must be removed by subtracting it.

Interest receivable also increased, from zero to $50. This means that CCS recorded $50 of interest revenue that is included in income for which the company received no cash. Thus, income overstates cash received by $50 and this $50 must be removed by subtracting it.

Next, we subtract the increase in inventory of $800. This might be easiest to think about if we assume for the moment that CCS pays cash for all inventory. In this case, an increase in inventory of $800 means that CCS spent $800 more on inventory than they recorded as cost of goods sold. **Pause here and make sure you see that this is the case.** Thus, cost of goods sold that is included in net income understates the cash (outflow) spent on inventory by $800 so we must adjust this amount to make it $800 more negative by subtracting $800.

We make a similar adjustment for pre-paid insurance. The $250 increase in this account means that CCS spent more cash for insurance than they recorded as expense, so we subtract this additional cash expenditure that was not expensed.

The remaining adjustments are for changes in current liabilities.

The first is for the increase in accounts payable of $250. If we assume (to keep this simple) that all inventory is sold and expensed and that accounts payable was only to purchase inventory, then this increase means that CCS had $250 of expense for inventory that it has not yet paid. **Pause here and make sure you see that this is the case.** So, this additional $250 is a non-cash expense that needs to be added back to remove it from net income.

To be clear on the interaction between inventory and accounts payable, let's consider them together. CCS began the year with no inventory and no accounts payable. During the year they acquired $4,600 in inventory, but they only sold $3,800 (refer to the T-accounts). If they had paid cash for all of that increase in inventory, cost of goods sold would understate the cash outflow for inventory by $800, and $800 should be subtracted, as we did above. But they did not pay cash for all of that increase in inventory. Accounts payable increased by $250, indicating that they did not pay cash for $250 of the $800 increase in inventory, and cost of goods sold understates the cash outflow for inventory by $550, not $800. When we add back the $250 that they have not yet paid, the net of the two adjustments, negative $800 for the increase in inventory and positive $250 for the increase in accounts payable, adjusts cost of goods sold for the additional cash outflow of $550 for inventory.

Returning to the adjustments for changes in current assets and liabilities, the next item that requires an adjustment is wages payable. In this case, CCS recorded an expense of $1,200 at the end of the year as an adjusting entry that has not been paid. As a result, wage expense of $7,200 on the income statement overstates the cash outflow for wages by $1,200. This amount must be added back to reduce the negative $7,200 included in net income to the $6,000 cash outflow that actually occurred.

The next item requiring adjustment is interest payable. In this case, CCS recorded an expense of $120 that has not been paid. As a result, interest expense of $120 on the income statement overstates the cash outflow for wages by the full amount of $120. This amount must be added back to eliminate the negative $120 included in net income that was not paid.

The final item requiring adjustment is deferred revenue, which increased during the year from zero to $1,250. CCS received $2,500 in advance payments from customers, half of which was earned during the period and is included in revenue and net income. However, the other half is a cash inflow that is not included in income, so this amount of $1,250 must be added to account for this cash inflow.

Next, we move to the investing section. There are two transactions that affect this section of the statement of cash flows, the purchase of equipment and the purchase of a certificate of deposit. Each of these is represented by its direct cash flow effect, a $5,000 cash outflow for the equipment, and a $4,500 cash outflow for the certificate of deposit.

Finally, in the financing section there are also two transactions, an issue of common stock and a loan from a bank. Each of these is represented by its direct cash flow effect, a $10,000 cash inflow for the issue of common stock and a $4,000 cash inflow for the bank loan.

Overall, CCS's statement of cash flows looks like that of an early stage company, which of course it is. The company generated $1,400 from operations, but used $9,000 of cash for investing. This excess investing was financed by $14,000 from an issue of stock and a bank loan. It appears that they obtained more funds than currently necessary from these two financing sources, possibly preparing for future expansion. The "extra" cash at the end of the period was invested in a certificate of deposit.

This might be a good time to refer back to chapter 11 to see if Starbucks' statement of cash flows makes even more sense now.

Chapter 14 – Selected Accounting Rules

This chapter explains in more detail the accounting for selected financial statement items that are often covered in introductory financial accounting classes, including:

- Accounts receivable and bad debts
- Depreciation of property, plant and equipment
- Deferred income taxes
- Product warranties
- Extended warranties
- Declaration and payment of dividends
- Repurchases of common stock

The accounting for these items is a little more involved than the accounting explained in the preceding chapters. As a result, you are more likely to have to "study" rather than "read" this chapter to fully understand the accounting being explained.

Accounts Receivable and Bad Debts

In an earlier chapter we noted that the line item for accounts receivable on Starbucks' balance sheet included the term "net." This was because the receivables reported on the balance sheet had been reduced from the original amount by an estimate of the amount of receivables Starbucks expects to never collect, leaving the amount they expect to collect as the "net" amount.

Many companies make credit sales, expecting to collect the revenue in 30 to 60 days (typically), depending on their credit policy. However, it is virtually always the case, regardless of the care the company takes in extending credit to customers, that some of the customers will not pay.

Because the revenue from credit customers has been recorded, and because some of them will not pay, the company must record an expense for the amount of revenue recorded that period that they expect not to collect. It is important to record the expense in the same period in which the revenue is recorded in order to have as accurate a measure of income as possible. Because the company does not yet know this amount, it must be estimated at the end of the period and recorded as an adjusting entry. The effect on the accounting equation is

							↑**Bad Debt**
							Expense
Assets	–	Liab	=	Perm OE	+ Rev	–	Exp
↓**Account**							
Receivable							

The bookkeeping for this is a bit more involved. When the estimate is recorded, the company debits (increases) an expense account called bad debt expense, but they do not credit (reduce) accounts receivable directly. The reason for this is that the company does not yet know <u>who</u> will not pay, and they want the accounts receivables account to sum to the amounts that are currently owed by their customers. So, rather than credit accounts receivable directly, the company credits an associated "contra asset" account that collects these credits until the company identifies who will not pay. (Contra assets are indicated by "CA" in the journal entries below.)

We can think of a "contra" asset as a negative asset account that has a pair-wise association with an asset account. When the asset account is to be reduced, rather than recording that reduction directly to the asset account itself, the reduction is recorded to the associated contra asset account.

In the language of debits and credits, rather than crediting the asset account directly, the credit is made to the contra asset account, which preserves the gross value in the asset account and produces the "net" (reduced) value when the two accounts are combined.

In the case of accounting for bad debts, the contra asset account is usually referred to as the allowance for uncollectibles or allowance for doubtful accounts. At the end of each period, to recognize the revenue recorded that period that is not likely to be collected, the company records (debits) bad debt expense and increases (credits) the contra asset account allowance for uncollectibles.

The ending accounts receivable balance has the gross amount that is owed by customers, the ending allowance for uncollectibles account has the amount owed by customers that the company expects not to collect, and the difference between the two is the net receivables reported on the balance sheet, the amount the company expects to collect.

Later, when the company identifies the customer who will not pay, they (a) remove (write-off) the customer's receivable from the accounts receivable account (by crediting the account), and (b) use up (reduce by debiting) that amount in the allowance for uncollectibles account. Notice that this "write-off" entry has no effect on net accounts receivable because both gross accounts receivables and the allowance for uncollectibles are reduced by the amount of the write-off.

Here is a simple example.

Assume at the beginning of the year there is a debit balance in accounts receivable of $100 and a credit balance in allowance for uncollectibles of $15.

Accounts Receivable	Allow for Uncollectibles	Bad Debt Expense
Beg 100	15 Beg	

The balance sheet at the end of the previous year reported an accounts receivable balance as the net of these two, or $85. This is the amount of their $100 of outstanding accounts receivable at that time that the company expected to collect.

Assume that during the next year the company sells $1,000 on account and collects $980, so that the resulting balance in accounts receivable is $120 ($100 + $1,000 - $980). After recording these transactions, net accounts receivable is $105 ($120 – 15) and the accounts look like this

Accounts Receivable	Allow for Uncollectibles	Bad Debt Expense
Beg 100	15	
Rev 1,000 — 980 Collect		
120	15	

Now, assume that during the year the company identifies $7 of receivables that they have given up trying to collect and will "write off." Since they have given up trying to collect these receivables, they are going to remove them from their accounts receivable account. But recall that they had already lowered their net receivables amount when they recorded bad debt expense in prior periods. At that time, they increased their allowance for uncollectibles account, waiting to be used when they identified the customers who would not pay. Now that they have identified some of those customers who will not pay, they "use" some of the allowance for uncollectibles account with the following journal entry.

Allowance for Uncollectibles (CA)   15
Accounts Receivable (A)   15

Notice that after making this entry the net accounts receivable balance is still $105. Accounts receivable has been reduced to $113 ($120 - $7), and allowance for uncollectibles has been reduced to $8 ($15 - $7), so the net is still $105 and the accounts look like this (W/O means write-off).

Accounts Receivable		Allow for Uncollectibles		Bad Debt Expense	
Beg 100			15	Exp 20	
Rev 1,000	980 Collect	W/O 7			
	7 W/O			20	20 closing
End 113		8 End		0	

We can think of the preceding journal entry as "housekeeping." We are only eliminating receivables that the company has given up collecting, and since the expense for these uncollected receivables was recorded in a prior period, this entry has no effect on the income statement or the net value on the balance sheet.

Finally, assume that at the end of the year the company estimates that $22 of that year's $1,000 of credit sales will never be collected. To record the estimated bad debts for the year the company makes the following adjusting journal entry at the end of the year

Bad Debt Expense (E)   22
Allowance for Uncollectibles (CA)   22

After making this entry the balance in the allowance for uncollectibles account is $30 ($8 + $22) and net accounts receivable is $83 ($113 - $30). Here are the completed T-accounts.

Accounts Receivable		Allow for Uncollectibles		Bad Debt Expense	
Beg 100			15	Exp 20	
Rev 1,000	980 Collect	W/O 7			
	7 W/O		Exp 22	20	20 closing
End 113		30 End		0	

We can see that the allowance for uncollectibles is a running total of current receivables outstanding the company does not expect to collect. As such, there is no "settling up." As long as the company extends credit to customers, they will have a balance in the allowance for uncollectibles. At the end of each period the company should assess whether the balance in that account is sufficient for their expected bad debts. If the balance seems too high or too low, the company would dial down or up their bad debt expense estimation algorithm to decrease or increase the allowance for uncollectibles going forward.

Finally, it is worth emphasizing that the topic of bad debts is included in this chapter not only because nearly all companies have bad debts, but because the topic illustrates one method of recognizing expense in the same period as the revenue the expense helped to produce. This is important in order to have an accurate measure of income per period. In this case, the company estimates the expense before it actually happens (at the time of write off of the uncollectible receivable) in order to record the expense in the same period as the revenue.

Depreciation of Property, Plant and Equipment

In the case of property, plant and equipment, use of the term "net" on Starbucks' balance sheet indicates that the amount originally paid to acquire these assets has been reduced by the amount the company has recorded as depreciation expense since acquisition. Depreciation is recorded each period to recognize that the asset's value is decreasing because the company is consuming part of the asset each period. The effect on the accounting equation is

$$\text{Assets} \ - \ \text{Liab} \ = \ \text{Perm OE} \ + \ \text{Rev} \ - \ \overset{\uparrow \text{Depreciation} \atop \textbf{Expense}}{\text{Exp}}$$
$$\downarrow \textbf{Property,} \atop \textbf{Plant \&} \atop \textbf{Equipment}$$

Similar to what we just discussed for accounts receivable, the bookkeeping for this is also a bit more involved. When the company records depreciation expense they do not reduce (credit) the relevant property, plant and equipment account directly, but rather record an increase (credit) in an associated "contra asset" account that collects these reductions in the depreciable asset. In the case of depreciable assets, the contra asset account is called accumulated depreciation.

As we saw with accounting for bad debts and the allowance for uncollectibles, we can think of the "contra" asset accumulated depreciation as a negative asset account that has a pair-wise association with the account of a depreciable asset.

At the end of each period the company records (debits) depreciation expense for the period and also increases (credits) the contra asset account accumulated depreciation. The ending depreciable asset balance is equal to (a) the original cost of the asset minus (b) the ending accumulated depreciation account balance. i.e., the part of the asset that has been used up. The difference between these two is the net book value of the depreciable asset reported on the balance sheet, the amount of the asset that remains to be used.

The accumulated depreciation account is only reduced when the asset is sold or otherwise disposed of, at which time both the original cost of the asset and its accumulated depreciation are removed from the accounting records (zeroed out).

Here is a simple example.

Assume that at the beginning of the year the company buys a new machine for $75,000. They expect the machine will last five years and be worthless at the end of five years. For the acquisition they record

Machine (A)	75,000
Cash (A)	75,000

At the end of the first year they record $15,000 of depreciation ($75,000/5 = $15,000) as follows

Depreciation Expense (E)	15,000
Accum Depr – Machine (CA)	15,000

At the end of the period the T-accounts for this asset are (in thousands)

Property, Plant & Equipment		Accumulated Depreciation		Depreciation Expense	
Beg 0		0			
Acquire 75		15 Exp		Exp 15	
				15	15 closing
End 75		15 End		0	

On the balance sheet at the end of the first year the company reports $60,000 of property, plant and equipment, net (75,000 – 15,000).

Now assume that the company sells the machine for $55,000 at the beginning of the next year. In this case they must record the cash inflow of $55,000, and they must eliminate the asset from the accounting records by eliminating both its original cost and its accumulated depreciation. Any difference between the cash the company received and the net book value of the asset they gave up is recorded as a gain or loss.

In this case, they received $55,000 for an asset that has a value of $60,000 in the accounting records, so the company has a loss of $5,000 (55,000 – 60,000 = -5,000). The company records the following journal entry ("Lo" indicates a loss account).

Cash (A)	55,000	
Accumulated Depreciation (CA)	15,000	
Loss on Sale of Machine (Lo)	5,000	
Machine (A)		75,000

Here are the relevant T-Accounts for this particular asset, which has now been removed from the accounting records.

Property, Plant & Equipment				Accumulated Depreciation				Loss on Sale of PPE		
Beg 0					0					
Acquire 75	75	Sale		Sale 15	15	Exp		Loss 5		
									5	5 closing
End 0					0	End		End 0		

The topic of depreciation is included in this chapter not only because nearly all companies have depreciable assets, but because the topic illustrates another method of recognizing expense in order to produce an accurate measure of income. In this case, the company allocates the cost of an asset that benefits multiple periods to align with the revenue that benefits from use of that asset.

Deferred Income Taxes

In the United States there are separate rules for financial reporting and taxation. The rules for financial reporting are mainly set by the Financial Accounting Standards Board, and are intended to result in financial statements that provide useful information for investors, creditors and others making decisions. The U.S. Congress establishes the rules for taxation with multiple goals in mind such as raising revenue, stimulating the economy, and redistributing income. As a result of these differing objectives, the rules are different.

Some of these differences are "permanent" differences, items that appear on the financial accounting income statement but are either never taxable or never deductible for tax purposes. For example, interest income on municipal bonds is reported on the income statement but is never taxable.

However, most of the differences between the financial accounting rules and the tax rules result in "temporary" or "timing" differences. In these cases, the same total amount of revenue or expense will be reported eventually for both taxes and financial reporting, but <u>when</u> the revenue or expense is reported for tax and financial reporting is different. Revenue and expense may be reported on the income statement first and the tax return later, or the opposite, they may be reported on the tax return first and the income statement later.

This difference is important because tax expense is based on income reported on the income statement, and tax currently payable to the government is based on that year's tax return.

The following table summarizes how reported income and income on the tax return are related to each other

Reported Income				
+/- Permanent Differences				
= Taxable Sometime Income	X	Tax Rate	=	Tax Expense
<u>+/- Timing Differences</u>	X	Tax Rate	=	Deferred Tax Asset or Liability
= Tax Return Income	X	Tax Rate	=	Taxes Currently Payable

The first line in the table is Reported Income as it appears on the income statement. Reported Income is then adjusted for "Permanent Differences" between reported income and income on the tax return. These are components of reported income that will <u>never</u> appear on a tax return, in the current year or any other year.

After adjusting Reported Income for Permanent Differences, we are left with what I call "Taxable Sometime Income," which is the basis for income tax expense. This is income that was reported on the income statement in the current year that will also be included on some year's tax return, though not necessarily the tax return for the current year.

The next line adjusts for "Timing Differences." There are two gross types of adjustments here.

The first is to add income components that (a) were or will be included in reported income in a year other than the current year, <u>and</u> (b) are included on the tax return this year.

The second is to subtract income components that (a) were included in reported income this year, but (b) were or will be included on the tax return in a year other than the current year.

After adjusting for these timing differences, we are left with income as reported on the tax return for the current year, which is the basis for taxes currently payable.

Thus, these "timing differences" are the basis for the difference between tax expense on the income statement (based on taxable sometime income) and taxes payable (based on income on the tax return). The difference is recorded as a deferred tax asset or deferred tax liability.

If income on the tax return is greater than income on the income statement, taxes payable will be greater than tax expense, and the difference will be recorded as a deferred tax asset. The effect on the accounting equation is

↑Deferred Tax Asset		↑Tax Payable						↑Tax Expense
Assets	–	Liab	=	Perm OE	+	Rev	–	Exp

And the journal entry is

Tax Expense (E)	xxx	
Deferred Tax Asset (A)	xxx	
Taxes Payable (L)		xxx

As we will see in the examples below, the timing difference that gave rise to this deferred tax asset must reverse later. When that happens the effect on the accounting equation is

		↑Tax Payable						↑Tax Expense
Assets	–	Liab	=	Perm OE	+	Rev	–	Exp
↓ Deferred Tax Asset								

And the journal entry is

Tax Expense (E)	xxx	
Deferred Tax Asset (A)		xxx
Taxes Payable (L)		xxx

On the other hand, if income on the tax return is less than income on the income statement, taxes payable will be less than tax expense, and the difference will be recorded as a deferred tax liability. The effect on the accounting equation is

$$\underset{\substack{\uparrow\text{Tax} \\ \text{Payable} \\ \text{and} \\ \uparrow\text{Deferred} \\ \text{Tax} \\ \text{Liability}}}{\text{Assets} \quad - \quad \text{Liab}} \;=\; \text{Perm OE} \;+\; \text{Rev} \;-\; \underset{\substack{\uparrow\text{Tax} \\ \text{Expense} \\ \text{Exp}}}{}$$

And the journal entry is

Tax Expense (E)	xxx	
Deferred Tax Liability (L)		xxx
Taxes Payable (L)		xxx

Again, the timing difference that gave rise to this deferred tax liability was only a timing difference that will be reversed over time. When that happens, the effect on the accounting equation is

$$\underset{\substack{\uparrow\text{Tax} \\ \text{Payable} \\ \text{Liab} \\ \downarrow\text{Deferred} \\ \text{Tax} \\ \text{Liability}}}{\text{Assets} \quad - \quad} \;=\; \text{Perm OE} \;+\; \text{Rev} \;-\; \underset{\substack{\uparrow\text{Tax} \\ \text{Expense} \\ \text{Exp}}}{}$$

And the journal entry is

Tax Expense (E)	xxx	
Deferred Tax Liability (L)	xxx	
Taxes Payable (L)		xxx

Most companies, including Starbucks, have both deferred tax liabilities and deferred tax assets. In all cases, the deferred tax asset or liability will be eliminated over time when the item that gave rise to the deferred tax asset or liability has appeared on both the income statement and the tax return. How much of either the company has, and for which items, depends on the interaction between their business activities and the tax rules.

Here are two examples. The first is based on accounting for bad debt expense, which often gives rise to a deferred tax asset. The second is based on accounting for depreciation expense, which often gives rise to a deferred tax liability.

Deferred Tax Asset Example – Bad Debt Expense
As discussed earlier in this chapter, companies must estimate and record bad debt expense in the year in which the associated revenue was recorded. On the other hand, companies are not permitted to deduct bad debt expense for tax purposes until the receivables have been deemed worthless and written off, which will frequently be in a subsequent period. This creates a timing difference between financial reporting and tax reporting for bad debt expense.

Assume a company begins the period with $150 in the allowance for uncollectibles and that during the year they record bad debt expense of $450 and write off receivables of $370. The ending balance in the allowance for uncollectibles would then be $230 (150 + 450 − 370). Also assume the company's reported income for the year (which includes $450 of bad debt expense) is $2,000 million, so that taxable income on their tax return (which includes only $370 of bad debt expense) is $2,080 (2,000 + 450 − 370).

With a tax rate of 21 per cent, tax expense would be $420 million ($2,000 x 0.21), and taxes payable would be $436.8 million ($2,080 x 0.21). The journal entry for tax expense would be

Tax Expense (E)	420.0	
Deferred Tax Asset (A)	16.8	
Taxes Payable (L)		436.8

If the company's allowance for uncollectibles continues to increase over time, their deferred tax asset balance related to bad debt expense will also increase over time. However, if in any particular year their allowance for uncollectibles declines, the deferred tax asset will reverse.

To see how this works, assume that in the following year the company recorded bad debt expense of $350 and wrote off receivables of $390. During the year the ending balance in the allowance for uncollectibles would have declined from $230 to $190 (230 + 350 − 390 = 190). Also assume the company's reported income for the year (which includes $350 of bad debt expense) was $2,000 million, so that taxable income on their tax return (which includes $390 of bad debt expense) was $1,960 (2,000 + 350 − 390 = 1,960).

With a tax rate of 21 per cent, tax expense would be $420 million ($2,000 x 0.21), and taxes payable would be $411.6 million ($1,960 x 0.21). The journal entry for tax expense would be

Tax Expense (E)	420.0	
Deferred Tax Asset (A)		8.4
Taxes Payable (L)		411.6

This journal entry illustrates that when the balance in allowance for uncollectibles is decreasing, tax expense is higher than taxes payable, and the company is consuming some of their deferred tax asset (pre-paid tax) by paying the government the lesser amount that is due this year.

Of course, over the life of the company total bad debts expensed for reporting purposes and total bad debts written off for tax purposes will be equal, i.e., the allowance for uncollectibles account will be zero. But this will only occur if the company stops giving credit to their customers or (unrealistically) all of their credit customers pay them. The more likely scenario is that the company continues to extend credit to customers, that some of these customers do not pay, and that the balances in the allowance for uncollectibles and the related deferred tax asset continue to grow over time.

Deferred Tax Liability Example – Depreciation Expense
In the case of depreciation, the accounting rules require companies to allocate the cost of their property, plant and equipment over the useful life of the asset. The tax rules often permit much faster depreciation in order to provide companies with an incentive to invest more in plant and equipment to help grow the economy. This creates a timing difference between financial reporting and tax reporting for depreciation expense.

Assume that in a particular year a company has depreciation for tax purposes that is $200 million more than depreciation for reporting purposes, and that this is the only difference between reported income and taxable income. Also assume that reported income for the year was $2,000 million, so that taxable income on their tax return was $1,800.

With a tax rate of 21 per cent, tax expense would be $420 million ($2,000 x 0.21), and taxes payable would be $378 million ($1,800 x 0.21). The journal entry for tax expense would be

Tax Expense (E)	420.0	
Taxes Payable (L)		378.0
Deferred Tax Liability (L)		42.0

To see how this will reverse over time, assume that the next year the company's depreciation for tax purposes was $60 million less than depreciation for reporting purposes, and this was the only difference between reported and taxable income. Assume reported income for the year was $2,000 million, so their tax return income was $2,060.

With a tax rate of 21 per cent, their tax expense would be $420 million ($2,000 x 0.21), and their taxes payable would be $432.6 million ($2,060 x 0.21). The journal entry for tax expense would be

Tax Expense (E)	420.0	
Deferred Tax Liability (L)	12.6	
Taxes Payable (L)		432.6

Of course, total depreciation over the life of any particular asset must be equal for both tax and reporting purposes. Thus, in the early years of the asset's life, when tax depreciation is greater than reported depreciation, the deferred tax liability increases, as in the first journal entry above. In contrast, in the later years of the asset's life, when tax depreciation is less than reported depreciation, the deferred tax liability decreases, as in the second journal entry above. Eventually, the balance in the deferred tax liability account will be zero when the asset is fully depreciated and the same amount of depreciation has been recorded for both reporting and tax.

Reporting Deferred Tax Assets and Liabilities
The accounting rules for reporting deferred tax assets and liabilities on the balance sheet require that companies first compute the net deferred tax asset or liability for each taxing jurisdiction (i.e., country or state taxing authority). The company then adds together the net deferred tax assets across jurisdictions and reports that on the balance sheet. Similarly, they add together the net deferred tax liabilities across jurisdictions and report that on the balance sheet.

In the notes to their financial statements, Starbucks discloses that they have $560.9 million in deferred tax assets, and $696.4 million in deferred tax liabilities, for a net liability of $135.5. This amount is reported on the balance sheet as net deferred assets (across jurisdictions) of $134.7 million, which is a line item in current assets, and net deferred tax liabilities (across jurisdictions) of $270.2 million, which is included in other long-term liabilities.

Accounting for income taxes is included in this chapter not only because all companies pay taxes, but because the topic illustrates the length to which accrual accounting is applied. In the case of income taxes, expense is based on reported income, not on the cash paid for taxes. This results in accruing expense and a liability before cash is paid in some cases (i.e., when reported income is greater than taxable income), and deferring expense and recording an asset until after the cash is paid in other cases (i.e., when reported income is less than taxable income). Thus, while accounting for income taxes may seem complicated, it is just another result of the focus of accrual accounting on recording expenses when they occur, not when the cash is paid.

Product Warranties

A warranty is a promise to ensure that over a certain period a product is what it purported to be at the time of sale. A "product warranty" is a warranty that is included with the price of the product at the time of sale. Product warranties begin at the time of sale and can last for any amount of time from (for example) thirty days to a lifetime.

Recall that a main objective of financial accounting is to provide an accurate measure of the profit earned in a particular period. To accomplish this, revenue is recorded when control of the good or service has been transferred to the customer. Expense is recorded (a) at the same time as the revenue for expenses that can be identified with a particular sale, (b) in the period in which the expense is incurred for expense not closely identified with revenue from a particular sale, or (c) allocated across periods for consuming assets that benefit more than one period.

In the case of a product warranty we want to recognize the warranty expense at the time of sale (delivery) because the total product revenue is recognized at that time and the expense related to the product warranty is part of the expense incurred to produce that revenue.

Thus, the company must estimate the amount of warranty services that will eventually be provided for products sold in the current period and record that amount as an expense in the current period.

As an example, assume that a company sold a refrigerator for $1,200 that came with a one-year warranty. The refrigerator cost the company $800 to purchase, and the company expects to incur $25 of warranty expense.

To account for the revenue, the effect on the accounting equation is

$$\underset{\text{Assets}}{\overset{\uparrow\text{Cash}}{}} \quad - \quad \text{Liab} \quad = \quad \text{Perm OE} \quad + \underset{\text{Rev}}{\overset{\uparrow\text{Rev}}{}} \quad - \quad \text{Exp}$$

And the journal entry is

Cash (A)	1,200	
Revenue (R)		1,200

The effect of cost of goods sold on the accounting equation is

$$\underset{\downarrow\text{Inventory}}{\text{Assets}} \quad - \quad \text{Liab} \quad = \quad \text{Perm OE} \quad + \quad \text{Rev} \quad - \quad \underset{\text{Exp}}{\overset{\uparrow\text{COGS}}{}}$$

And the journal entry is

Cost of goods sold (E)	800	
Inventory (A)		800

The effect of the expected warranty expense on the accounting equation is

$$\text{Assets} \quad - \underset{\substack{\text{Liab} \\ \text{Liability}}}{\overset{\uparrow\text{Warranty}}{}} \quad = \quad \text{Perm OE} \quad + \quad \text{Rev} \quad - \underset{\substack{\text{Exp} \\ \text{Expense}}}{\overset{\uparrow\text{Warranty}}{}}$$

And the journal entry is

Warranty Expense (E)	25	
Warranty Liability (L)		25

All three of the previous journal entries are recorded in the period in which the sale (delivery) is made. The first two are likely recorded at the time of sale and the third is more likely made as an adjusting entry at the end of the period for all warranties for products sold during the period.

During the warranty period, part of which may be in a different accounting period, the company records warranty services as they are provided. The effect on the accounting equation is

Assets	–	Liab	=	Perm OE	+ Rev	–	Exp
↓Cash		↓**Warranty Liability**					

And the journal entry is

Warranty Liability (L)	500	
Cash (A)		500

In this case we are assuming that the company paid someone, perhaps another company, $500 to repair a refrigerator that was under warranty. The credit here need not be to cash, it could be to a variety of accounts depending on how the warranty services were provided. The selling company might hire another company to provide the services for them, or have their own employees provide the services. The services might include parts from a parts inventory, or might involve providing a new refrigerator.

As we saw with accounts receivable and bad debts, there is no settling up here. As long as the company has products under warranty, they will have a warranty liability. At the end of each period they should assess whether the liability is sufficient for their obligation or over- or underestimates their warranty obligation. In that case, they would dial down or up their warranty expense estimation algorithm to decrease or increase the warranty liability going forward.

Similar to bad debts, the accounting for product warranties illustrates a method of recognizing expense in the same period as the revenue the expense helped to produce. This is important in order to have an accurate measure of income per period. In this case, the company estimates the warranty expense before it actually happens (when the warranty services are provided) in order to record the expense in the same period as the revenue.

Extended Warranties
An "extended warranty" is a warranty that is sold separately from the product, that has its own sales price, and that, as the name implies, extends the product warranty. Extended warranties normally begin at the

expiration of the product warranty and continue for one or more years beyond.

In the case of an extended warranty, recording the revenue and the associated expense in the same period is more straightforward than for a product warranty. To accomplish this, the accounting rules require that the revenue from the extended warranty is deferred at the time of sale and recognized evenly over the warranty period. The warranty expense is also recognized during the warranty period, so that both the revenue and expense are recognized in the same period.

As a simple example, assume that a company sold a three-year extended warranty for a refrigerator for $120. The sale was made on July 1 and the product warranty is for six months. Therefore, the extended warranty begins on January 1 of the next year and lasts for three years.

On July 1 of the first year, when the company records the sale, the effect of the sale of the extended warranty on the accounting equation is

$$
\begin{array}{ccccccccc}
 & \uparrow\text{Cash} & & \uparrow\text{Deferred} \\
 & & & \text{Rev} \\
\text{Assets} & - & \text{Liab} & = & \text{Perm OE} & + & \text{Rev} & - & \text{Exp}
\end{array}
$$

And the journal entry is

Cash (A)	120	
Deferred Revenue (L)		120

At the end of the first year the company does not record anything related to the extended warranty—they have not yet provided any services.

At the end of the second year, the company records one-third of the revenue as an adjusting entry and the effect on the accounting equation is

$$
\begin{array}{ccccccccc}
 & & & & & & \uparrow\text{Rev} \\
\text{Assets} & - & \text{Liab} & = & \text{Perm OE} & + & \text{Rev} & - & \text{Exp} \\
 & & \downarrow\text{Deferred} \\
 & & \text{Rev}
\end{array}
$$

And the journal entry is

Deferred Revenue (L)	40	
Revenue (R)		40

Also in that second year, if the company provided any services under the extended warranty, they record those expenses. Assume they incurred $100 of expense and paid another company cash to provide the service.

The effect of recording this on the accounting equation is

							↑Warranty Expense
Assets	–	Liab	=	Perm OE	+ Rev	–	Exp
↓Cash							

And the journal entry is

Warranty Expense (E)	100	
Cash (A)		100

As was the case with product warranties, the credit here could be to a variety of accounts depending on how the warranty services were provided.

In contrast to the accounting for product warranties, the accounting for extended warranties is an example of a different method of recognizing expense in the same period as the revenue the expense helped to produce. In this case, the company defers the revenue until the warranty services are provided and the expense is incurred in order to record the revenue in the same period as the expense.

Declaring and Paying Dividends

The final two topics in this chapter are included to illustrate in more detail how a company returns to shareholders some of their investment. The main reason for returning to the shareholders some of their investment is because the company does not need the money to finance their trajectory of profitable growth. If the company were to keep the money rather than return it to the shareholders, they are likely to do one of the following with the money

- grow their current business to the point where it is no longer profitable
- invest in a new business they don't know much about
- invest in U.S. government (low return) securities.

From the point of view of the current shareholders, all of these alternatives are unattractive, they would rather have their money back.

The first method whereby companies return part of their investment to shareholders is by declaring and paying a dividend. There are three dates that are relevant for dividend payments.

The first is the day on which the board of directors of the corporation declares a dividend. This action reduces owners' equity because the dividend now has become a legal liability of the corporation.

If the board of directors declares a $12,000 dividend, the effect on the accounting equation is

		↑**Dividend** **Payable**						
Assets	–	Liab	=	Perm OE ↓**Retained** **Earnings**	+ Rev	–		Exp

And the journal entry is

Retained Earnings (OE)	12,000	
Dividend Payable (L)		12,000

The next date is referred to as the ex-dividend date, and is used to determine which shareholders will receive the dividend. If you purchase a stock before its ex-dividend date, you will receive the dividend payment because the dividend trades with the stock. If you purchase a stock after the ex-dividend date, you will not receive the dividend because it no longer trades with the stock. The dividend will be paid to the previous owner. There is no accounting by the dividend paying company on this date.

The third date is the payment date, when the company issues checks to the shareholders that are entitled to the dividend. Often shareholders have a choice of receiving the dividend in cash or in additional shares.

If the dividend is paid in cash, the effect on the accounting equation is

Assets ↓**Cash**	–	Liab ↓ **Dividend** **Payable**	=	Perm OE	+ Rev	–		Exp

And the journal entry is

Dividend Payable (L)	12,000	
Cash (A)		12,000

Repurchasing the Company's Own Shares

The second method for a company to return to shareholders part of their investment is for the company to repurchase some of the company's outstanding shares. In contrast to paying dividends where all shareholders are effectively withdrawing a portion of their investment equally, a share repurchase only affects investors who voluntarily sell their shares to the company. The investor selling the stock is unlikely to know (or care) who the purchaser is, whether it is the company itself or some other investor.

There are two alternative methods to account for when a company repurchases its own stock. The company can either

- Hold onto the stock as "Treasury Stock"
- "Retire" the stock so that it is as if it had never been issued.

Let's consider both alternatives with the following example. Assume that a company repurchased 100 shares of stock for $20 per share that was originally sold for $12 per share and has a par value of $1 per share. Assume the company recorded all of the cash received when the stock was initially sold in their "common stock" account. The effect on the accounting equation is

$$\uparrow \text{Cash} \qquad\qquad \begin{array}{c}\uparrow\text{Common}\\ \text{Stock}\end{array}$$

$$\text{Assets} \quad - \quad \text{Liab} \quad = \quad \text{Perm OE} \quad + \text{ Rev } \quad - \qquad \text{Exp}$$

And the journal entry is

Cash (A)	1,200	
Common Stock (OE)		1,200

To see the first alternative for later repurchasing these shares for $20 per share, assume that the company holds onto the shares as Treasury Stock. In this case, the effect on the accounting equation is

$$\text{Assets} \quad - \quad \text{Liab} \quad = \quad \text{Perm OE} \quad + \text{ Rev } \quad - \qquad \text{Exp}$$

$$\downarrow\text{Cash} \qquad\qquad\qquad \begin{array}{c}\downarrow\text{Treasury}\\ \text{Stock}\end{array}$$

And the journal entry is

Treasury Stock (COE)	1,200	
Cash (A)		1,200

Treasury Stock is a contra owners' equity (COE) account that is reported on the balance sheet as negative owners' equity. The repurchased stock will remain there until the shares are either retired or resold.

If the treasury stock is resold for $25 per share, the effect on the accounting equation is

			↑Treasury Stock and ↑Common Stock					
↑Cash								
Assets	–	Liab	=	Perm OE	+	Rev	–	Exp

And the journal entry is

Cash (A)	2,500	
Treasury Stock (COE)		2,000
Common Stock (OE)		500

Notice, the company does **NOT** record a gain (or loss) for buying and reselling its own shares.

The alternative accounting treatment for repurchased shares is to retire the shares immediately. Using the same example, if the repurchased shares are retired immediately, the effect on the accounting equation is

Assets	–	Liab	=	Perm OE	+	Rev	–	Exp
↓Cash				↓Common Stock and ↓Retained Earnings				

And the journal entry is

Common Stock (OE)	1,200	
Retained Earnings	800	
Cash (A)		2,000

The first line reverses the original sale of the stock for $12 per share, and the second line reduces retained earnings for the difference between the purchase price ($20) and the original sale price ($12).

We see both alternatives in practice—Treasury Stock on the balance sheet and repurchased shares that are immediately retired—however, the practical difference is very minor.

Part IV – Using Accounting Information

Chapter 15 – Is Accounting Useful for Investors?

The Questions

We have seen throughout this book that accrual accounting not only measures cash and changes in cash, but measures the broader concept of wealth and changes in wealth, regardless of when cash flows. For companies the concept of wealth is referred to as owners' equity and is the wealth that investors have invested in the company as measured by the accountants. These relations are captured by the simple equation

$$\text{Assets} - \text{Liabilities} = \text{Owners' Equity}$$

As is clear from this equation, owners' equity increases when net assets (assets minus liabilities) increase, and owners' equity decreases when net assets decrease.

The argument in favor of an accrual accounting system is that measuring wealth provides more complete information than only measuring cash, and that this more complete information is more useful for investors, creditors and others as they make the decisions they face. However, accrual accounting also requires financial managers to exercise much more subjectivity and judgment than cash accounting. Measuring cash is fairly objective. In contrast, measuring wealth requires making many estimates such as how much

- The company consumed in plant and equipment this year
- The company expects to collect from this year's credit sales
- The company expects warranty promises to cost in the future
- The company will pay retirees in pensions and health benefits
- The company has granted in employee stock options
- The value of inventory or machinery fell during the year

The list goes on and on.

Of course, estimates such as these will always have some degree of error. There are two potential sources of error that are of particular concern. First, estimates such as those listed above may be so difficult to make that even when managers make their best efforts to be accurate, the resulting estimates may not be accurate enough to provide useful information. Second, managers may not make their best efforts to make accurate estimates. Rather their judgments may be influenced (biased) by their personal economic interests, including increasing their salary, earning bonuses, or maintaining job security, such that they provide misleading information.

These two potential problems raise two important questions

- **Is information provided by accrual accounting more useful than information provided by cash accounting?**

- **Do managers attempt to mislead investors by manipulating accrual accounting financial statements?**

In this chapter we focus on the first question, whether accrual accounting provides investors with more useful information than cash accounting. The next chapter focuses on the second question, the extent to which managers may mislead investors by distorting accounting information in response to their economic interests.

These two chapters give you a flavor for what has been learned from the substantial amount of academic research that attempts to answer these questions. But keep in mind, there is only space to summarize results from relatively few of the hundreds of research papers that have been published in the last few decades that address these questions.

The Research Setting
As was discussed earlier, publicly-traded companies are required to provide the Securities Exchange Commission with financial statements quarterly. These statements are available to the public at the SEC website and commonly at the company's website, usually within about six weeks of the quarter end. After the quarter end, but before the company provides its financial statements to the SEC, it is common for the company to issue a press release that announces its earnings for the quarter and provides some context for the level of earnings disclosed. These earnings announcements are a frequent subject of academic research that examines whether and how investors use accounting information.

Much of this research assumes that the stock market is informationally efficient. This means that as new information about a company becomes available, the price of the company's stock quickly and accurately adjusts up or down to reflect, or impound, that new information. If accounting information is useful for investors, it will be part of the information set that stock prices react to, and we should observe a positive correlation between accounting information and stock price movements. Let's look more closely at how this happens.

We begin with the basis for valuing a share of stock. There are various models for valuing common stock, but they all come to the same thing, the value of the stock is based on (a) investors' expectations of the company's future cash flows, (b) discounted at the company's cost of equity capital.

The discounting process is beyond the scope of this book. It is enough to say that the higher the company's risk, the higher the return expected by investors, and the less valuable a dollar of future cash flows will be. In the discussion below we assume that the discounting process is constant for each company across time and focus on investors' expectations of the company's future cash flows.

The return on a share of stock over a period of time is the change in the stock price plus the dividends earned during that period, divided by the stock price at the beginning of the period. This can be represented by the following equation:

$$[(Price_{end} - Price_{beg}) + Dividend]/Price_{beg}$$

There are two general explanations for the return on a share of common stock for a particular company for a particular time interval: compensation for risk (assuming the company's level of risk is constant) and new information about the company that results in a change in investors' expectations about the company's future cash flows.

First, as time goes by, even if there is no new information about the company, the stock price will increase to compensate the investors for allowing the company to use their money. The amount of this compensation varies with the riskiness of the company. If the company is riskier, investors will require more return to induce them to invest in the company. If the company is less risky, investors will require less return to induce them to invest in the company.

Second, when new information about the company becomes available that changes investors' expectations about the company's future cash flows, investors will change their estimate of the value of the company's stock, and as a result demand for the company's stock will change. If the news results in an increase in expected future cash flows, i.e. if the news is "good," demand for the stock will increase, the stock price will increase, and returns during that period will be higher than the expected compensation for risk. If the news results in a decrease in expected future cash flows, i.e., if the news is "bad," demand will decrease, the stock price will decrease, and returns during that period will be lower than the expected compensation for risk.

In some of the studies discussed below, researchers attempt to isolate the return due to information by removing the return due to compensation for risk. The return due to compensation for risk is referred to as the "normal" return, and the return due to new information is referred to as the "abnormal" return. To estimate the "abnormal" return, researchers estimate the "normal" return, and subtract it from the company's total return. This is represented by the following equation:

Abnormal Return = Total Return – Normal Return

If accounting information is useful for making investment decisions, and if the market is "efficient" in incorporating this new information into the price of the company's stock, the company's stock price will quickly adjust up or down to the new information. If the information is net income, the stock's abnormal return will be positive when net income is higher than expected, that is when the income news is "good." On the other hand, the stock's abnormal return will be negative if net income is lower than expected, that is if the income news is "bad."

What can be inferred by such positive correlation between income news and abnormal stock returns depends on <u>when</u> the returns are measured.

Below, we review research on the correlation between income news and abnormal stock returns for three separate intervals surrounding earnings announcements. The results for each return interval can reveal something different about the role of accounting information in the stock market.

Is Net Income Potentially Useful for Investors?
The first return interval examined was the period <u>leading up</u> to the earnings announcement. If accounting information is correlated with stock returns during this period, the researcher concludes that the accounting information in the earnings announcement is <u>potentially</u> useful. By examining this interval alone, the researcher cannot conclude that the earnings announcement was the source of this information for investors, they may have learned the information from other sources.

This question was addressed in one of the earliest studies of "modern" research in accounting by Ray Ball and Philip Brown. The paper was published in 1968 and according to Google Scholar has been cited by more than 7,000 subsequent studies. [1]

When Ball and Brown conducted their study, many thought that accounting numbers in the financial statements provided little information. These skeptics argued that not only were the numbers based on managers' subjective estimates, but they also combined a mishmash of measures made at various points in time, revenue from yesterday, inventory from two months ago, depreciation from several years ago.

Ball and Brown used a very simple research design to provide empirical evidence on whether it was true that financial statements provide little or no information. To understand their study intuitively, imagine that Company A has just reported their net income for the most recent year, and that you (and no one else) have a crystal ball that tells you that Company A will report higher net income in one year when they report income for the current year. What would you do with that information?

If you believe that accrual-basis net income provides meaningful information you would probably use this information and invest in Company A. You would expect that as other investors become aware that income is increasing, they will buy the stock pushing up its value and earning you a positive return. If, instead, you believe that accrual-basis net income does not provide meaningful information you would ignore what your crystal ball is telling you.

This is just what Ball and Brown did, looking backward, with a large sample of thousands of observations. For this sample, they constructed several alternative measures of "unexpected" earnings, i.e., the new information that investors might gain from disclosure of net income at the end of a fiscal year. They then divided the sample into companies that announced "good news" (positive unexpected earnings) and those that announced "bad news" (negative unexpected earnings).

Using these groups, they asked the question: Would it have been useful for an investor to know this information a year in advance? They in effect were asking if it would be useful for investors to have a crystal ball

[1] Ball, Ray, and Philip Brown. 1968. "An empirical evaluation of accounting income numbers." *Journal of Accounting Research*. 159-178.

that told them a year in advance whether net income next year was going to be higher or lower than the previous year. If accrual-basis net income reflects meaningful information, then the "good news" companies in their sample should have higher (more positive) stock returns than the "bad news" companies.

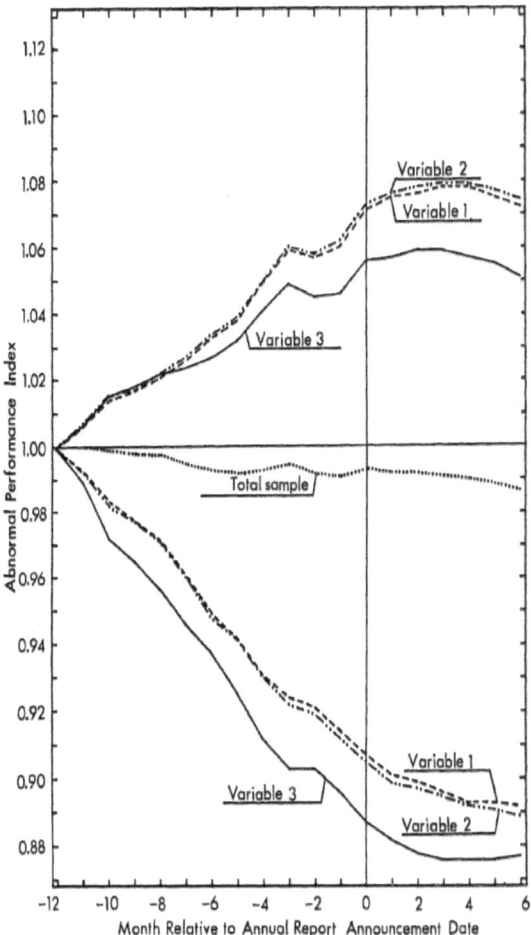

FIG. 1 Abnormal Performance Indexes for Various Portfolios

The results they found are best captured by the very famous figure above. Time is on the horizontal axis, where -12 is 12 months before the earnings announcement, zero is the month of the earnings announcement, and 6 is 6 months after the earnings announcement. The vertical axis is one plus the "abnormal" stock return, and varies from 0.88 (return of negative 12 percent) to 1.12 (return of positive 12 percent). As was discussed above, the "abnormal" stock return is the return earned by the companies after subtracting their "normal" compensation for risk.

The seven lines on the graph report the cumulative abnormal stock returns for three alternative definitions of good news companies (the top three lines), three alternative definitions of bad news companies (the bottom three lines), and for the sample as a whole (the middle line).

The pattern is clear. An investor without a crystal ball would have no information about good news and bad news firms, and so could do no better than invest in the middle line. Such an investor would earn an abnormal return very close to zero (slightly negative in the graph), which means they would only be compensated for risk (i.e., the company's normal return).

In contrast, an investor with a crystal ball would be able to successfully separate the sample into good news and bad news firms. Such an investor could purchase the stock of good news companies and earn an "abnormal" return of about five to seven percent over the next 12 months. Similarly, stocks of the bad news companies will have declined by about 9 to 11 percent over those 12 months.

These results provide clear evidence that it would be useful to know accounting information in advance, and therefore that accrual-basis net income has the potential to provide useful information for investors. However, notice that the vast majority of these returns occur prior to the earnings announcement. This finding indicates that wherever the investors are getting their information, they are getting it slowly over the course of the year. One source could be quarterly earnings announcements, but the company could also release other information during the year that is correlated with accrual-basis income. Thus, these results do not tell us whether accounting information is only correlated with the information used by investors, or whether accounting information is a source of that information, which leads to our next question.

Does Disclosure of Net Income Communicate New Information to Investors?

Next, we move to examining the correlation between stock returns and accounting information at the time the accounting information is disclosed. If accounting information is correlated with stock returns <u>at the time of</u> the earnings announcement, then the researcher can conclude that accounting was a source of the <u>communication</u> of that information. This is because the researcher is looking at returns over a very narrow

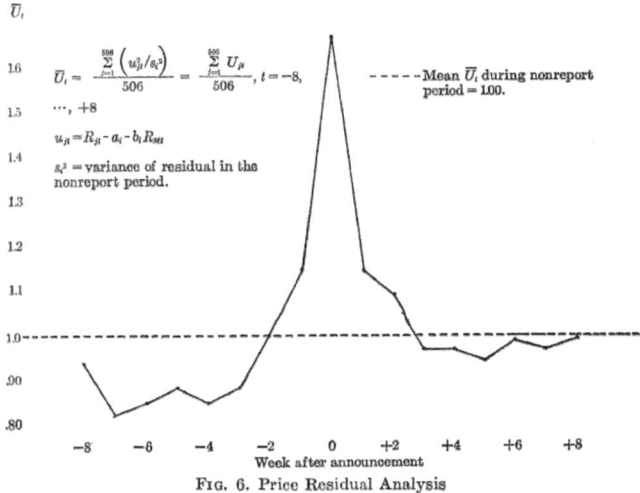

FIG. 6. Price Residual Analysis

period of time in which earnings was announced and little or no other information about the company was disclosed.

One of the first researchers to examine this question was Bill Beaver in a study that was also published in 1968.[2] He compared the stock returns of companies in the week of their earnings announcement with their returns in other, non-announcement weeks. If earnings announcements communicate new information to investors, then we should observe larger than normal price movements and trading volume when earnings is announced.

Beaver conducted this analysis for a large sample of companies, and the graph above gives a good overview of his results. The vertical axis is a measure of stock returns, and the horizontal axis represents time relative to the earnings announcement. Week zero, in the middle of the horizontal axis is the week in which earnings was announced. It is clear from the

---

[2] Beaver, William H. 1968. "The information content of annual earnings announcements." *Journal of Accounting Research.* 67-92.

graph of stock returns that market activity was much higher during the earnings announcement week than in the surrounding weeks. Beaver conducted a similar analysis using stock trading volume and found similar results. Taken together, these results indicate that investors make trading decisions when income is announced, which means that the disclosure of income communicates useful information to investors.

Wayne Morse examined the same question in 1980 using daily (rather than weekly) data.[3] The graph below provides his results. Again, the vertical axis is a measure of stock returns and the horizonal axis represents time relative to the day earnings was disclosed. Day zero in the middle of the horizontal axis is the day earnings were announced.

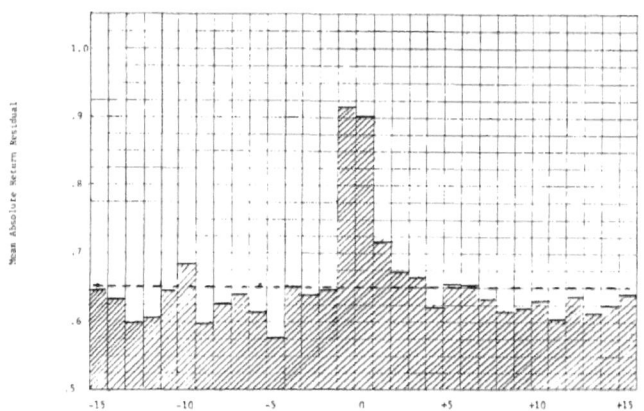

Fig. 1.—Graph of mean absolute return residuals surrounding earnings announcements.
- - - - = sample average.

The results indicate that companies announcing earnings have unusually large returns on the day before the announcement and the day of the announcement. These results corroborate those of Beaver (1968) and provide clear evidence that the announcement of earnings communicates information to investors.

Do Investors "Fully" Use Accounting Information?

Finally, we consider whether accounting information is correlated with stock returns <u>after</u> the earnings announcement. Correlation after the earnings announcement would indicate that investors are slow to react to

[3] Morse, Dale. 1981. "Price and trading volume reaction surrounding earnings announcements: A closer examination." *Journal of Accounting Research.* 374-383.

this information and that the market is not informationally efficient. In this case it would be possible for investors to earn "abnormal" returns using information already available to the public. Below, we summarize several studies that examine this issue, whether investors "fully" use the information in accounting income when it is disclosed to the public.

To help develop some intuition for this issue, assume that Company A just announced its net income for the year. In an informationally efficient market, investors will accurately determine the implications of this information for the company's future performance. Investors will quickly revise their expectations of the company's future cash flows, and the resulting change in demand for the company's stock will quickly impound the new information in the stock's price. Under these circumstances, you would not be able to use this new information to make an abnormal return because by the time you were able to react to the information it will be too late, the information will already be impounded in the stock price.

Now, suppose that for some reason other investors are slow to fully understand the implications of the earnings announcement for the company's future performance, but you are not. Your analysis indicates that Company A will generate higher cash flows in the future than you previously expected, and you decide to buy Company A's stock before the stock price changes. You then wait while other investors slowly to come to the same conclusion as you, bidding up the price of the stock, providing you with a good (abnormal) profit on your investment.

Thus, there are two possibilities when new information is disclosed to investors. In the first scenario, the stock market is informationally efficient and there is no opportunity to earn abnormal returns. In the second scenario, the stock market is not informationally efficient, so that it is possible to invest based on publicly-available information and earn an abnormal return beyond the normal compensation for risk. Below, we summarize three of the many studies that examine which of these two scenarios best describes the way the stock market works.

In the figure from the Ball and Brown (1968) study presented above, we see some evidence that stock returns for "good" news and "bad" news companies continue to "drift" up and down, respectively, for at least the first two or three months after the earnings announcement. This phenomenon, referred to as post earnings announcement drift, was examined more carefully by George Foster, Chris Ohlson, and Terry Shevlin in a study published in 1984.[4] They found that after the earnings announcement, a trading strategy that invested long in the ten percent of stocks with the highest unexpected income and short in the ten percent of stocks with the lowest (most negative) unexpected income, would earn

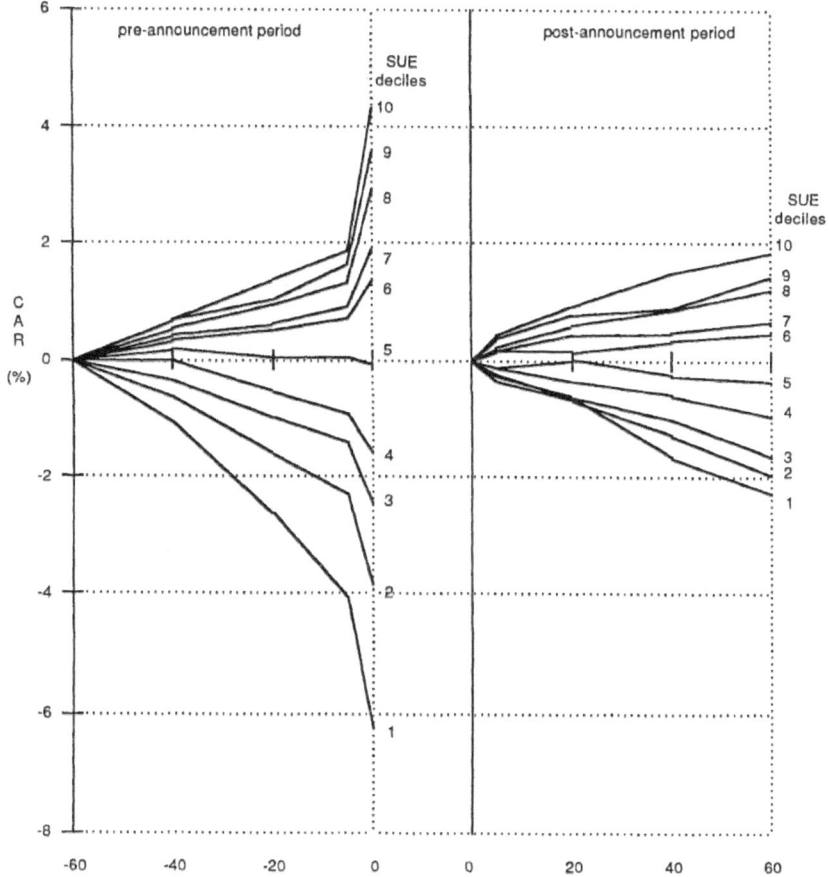

an annualized abnormal return of about 25 percent before transaction costs.

A subsequent study by Victor Bernard and Jacob Thomas published in 1989 examined whether these post earnings announcement abnormal returns were due to variation in risk between good news and bad news

[4] Foster, George, Chris Olsen, and Terry Shevlin. 1984. "Earnings releases, anomalies, and the behavior of security returns." *The Accounting Review.* 574-603.

companies, or to market inefficiency, i.e. that investor response to the new information was delayed for some reason.[5] Above is a figure from their study that demonstrates post earnings announcement drift for their sample.

The figure to the left is similar to that from Ball and Brown (1968). The vertical axis measures of abnormal returns and the horizontal axis reflects the sixty trading days prior to the earnings announcement, which is day zero. The plots on the graph are for ten groups based on the magnitude of unexpected earnings. Group 1 is the ten percent of observations with the lowest (most negative) unexpected earnings, and group 10 is the ten percent of observations with the highest unexpected earnings.

We can see that companies with more positive unexpected earnings (groups 6 though 10) have higher returns during the sixty trading days leading up to the earnings announcement and a further jump in returns at the time of the earnings announcement. Similarly, the companies with the most negative unexpected earnings (groups 1 through 4) have lower returns during the sixty days leading up to the earnings announcement and a further drop in returns at the time of the earnings announcement

The more important graph is to the right. In this graph, Bernard and Thomas have reset the returns for each unexpected earnings group to zero on the day of the earnings announcement (day zero) and plotted the returns for each group over the subsequent 60 days. At the far right we can see there is a monotonic relationship between the magnitude of unexpected earnings and the post earnings announcement abnormal returns.

Focusing on the extreme groups, we can see that group 10, the ten percent of observations with the highest unexpected earnings, has the highest post announcement returns, and group 1, the ten percent with the lowest unexpected earnings, has the lowest post announcement returns. A trading strategy that invested long in group 10 and short in group 1 would earn an abnormal return of about 6.3 percent over 60 days for an

---

[5] Bernard, Victor, L. and Jacob K. Thomas. 1989. "Post-earnings-announcement drift: Delayed price response or risk premium?" *Journal of Accounting Research* 27: 1-36.

annualized return of about 25 percent, similar to the results reported by Foster, Ohlson, and Shevlin (1984).

There are two possible explanations for these abnormal returns. One possibility is that when Bernard and Thomas measured abnormal returns they did not adequately adjust for the riskiness of the stocks, so that the abnormal returns they document are due to risk and not to market inefficiency. The other possibility is that investors are slow to react to the news communicated through the earnings announcement, and that even though there is a reaction at the time of the announcement, that reaction does not fully impound the information in the earnings news. This leaves open the possibility investors can earn abnormal returns by trading on the earnings news that is already available to the public.

Bernard and Thomas conducted careful tests to determine which of these explanations is more consistent with the data, and concluded there was no evidence for the risk explanation, and consistent evidence for the mispricing/market inefficiency explanation.

Many other studies have been published subsequent to Bernard and Thomas (1989) that have found additional evidence of market inefficiency in a variety of settings. The frequency and magnitude of the abnormal returns in many of these studies are difficult to explain by variation in risk alone. Thus, there is substantial evidence that investors do not fully use accounting information at the time it is disclosed.

Is the Accrual Component of Net Income Useful for Investors?
So far, we have seen that accrual-basis net income is correlated with the information that investors use to price common stock, and that some of that information is communicated when companies issue their quarterly earnings announcements. But this does not tell us whether all of the effort put into accrual accounting, keeping track of all those assets and liabilities and making all of the required estimates, provides <u>better</u> information than just keeping track of cash flows.

Judy Rayburn addressed this question in a study published 1986.[6] Using stock returns as a benchmark for changes in expected future economic performance, she compared the correlation between accrual basis income

---

[6] Rayburn, Judy. 1986. "The association of operating cash flow and accruals with security returns." *Journal of Accounting Research.* 112-133.

and stock returns with the correlation between cash-basis income and stock returns. A positive correlation means that when income goes up, stock prices go up, and when income goes down, stock prices go down. A correlation with changes in stock prices that is stronger for accrual-basis net income than for cash-basis income would indicate that accrual-basis net income provides information that is more useful for investors than cash basis net income.

Rayburn estimated linear regressions of annual stock returns on net income, disaggregated (separated) into the cash flow and accrual components. She found significant coefficients on both cash flows and accruals. In statistical terms this means that controlling for cash flows, the accruals in net income are correlated with stock returns. In simple language, this means that if an investor already knows the company's cash flows, they will learn additional useful information if they also learn the company's accrual components of income.

Patricia Dechow addressed the same question in more detail in a study published in 1996.[7] Dechow argued that accrual-basis earnings may be superior to cash flows in measuring company performance for two reasons. First, cash inflows and cash outflows may be mismatched in time if, for example, cash is paid (outflow) for inventory in one period and the inventory is sold and the revenue collected (inflow) in a different period.

Second, even if there is no mismatch, both the inflow and the outflow may occur in the "wrong" period if, for example, cash is paid (outflow) for inventory and cash collected (inflow) for sale of the inventory are both in the period after the sale (transfer of control). In this case, if investors respond to the sale (transfer of control) accrual accounting will better capture the timing of this event than cash accounting.

Accrual accounting attempts to address both of these problems. Revenue is recognized when control of the good or service is transferred, not when the cash is collected, and expense is recognized in the same period as the revenue the expense helped to produce, not when the cash is paid. In this way, accrual accounting attempts to avoid both the "mismatch"

---

[7] Dechow, Patricia M. 1994. "Accounting earnings and cash flows as measures of firm performance: The role of accounting accruals." *Journal of Accounting and Economics* 18 (1): 3-42.

problem and the "wrong period" problem. Dechow conducted three sets of tests to examine whether accrual accounting information is relatively more useful where the improvement would be most expected, i.e., where these two problems are most pronounced.

First, she examined whether accrual accounting is relatively more useful the shorter the reporting period, (e.g., for quarters compared to years). The idea is that the shorter the reporting period the more likely the cash flows will be mismatched or in the wrong period, and the more likely that accrual accounting could result in an improvement. Consistent with this insight, she found that accrual-basis earnings are more highly correlated with returns relative to cash flows for quarters than for years.

Second, Dechow examined whether accrual accounting is relatively more useful the larger the absolute amount of accruals recorded. The idea is that the larger the accruals the greater the difference between net income and cash flows so the greater the potential advantage of accrual-basis net income. In this case she again found that accrual-basis net income is more highly correlated with returns relative to cash flows, which is also consistent with accruals providing investors with useful information.

Finally, Dechow examined whether accrual accounting is relatively more useful the longer the firm's operating cycle, i.e., the longer between purchase of inventory and collection of revenue. The idea is that the longer the operating cycle the greater the likely mismatch between the timing of cash outflows to buy inventory and plant and equipment and the cash inflows from sales. Consistent with the results from the previous two tests, she found that the longer the operating cycle the more informative accrual-based net income is relative to cash flows.

These results, and those of many subsequent studies, confirm the basic assumptions of accrual accounting, that in spite of likely errors in the estimates involved, accrual accounting provides more useful information, and is therefore a better predictor or future cash flows, than just measuring the current cash inflows and outflows.

The studies summarized above provide evidence that (a) accrual accounting has the potential to provide investors with useful information, (b) the disclosure of accrual-basis net income can communicate useful information to investors, and (c) that the accrual component of net income adds to its usefulness. But there is no free lunch here. Not only is accrual-basis accounting expensive, but it also provides managers with a great deal of discretion as they make the estimates required to implement an accrual accounting system. In the next chapter we discuss what the managers may do with this discretion.

Chapter 16 –
Can Accruals Be Used to Mislead Investors?

The previous chapter reviewed evidence that accrual accounting provides information to investors beyond that provided by cash flows. However, accrual accounting also allows managers to use their discretion to make many subjective estimates.

Managers may be influenced by two different motivations as they make these estimates. One possibility is that they use their intimate knowledge of the company to provide the most accurate and useful information possible. Alternatively, they may use the discretion they have within the rules of accounting to respond to their personal economic incentives—to increase their salary, to earn bonuses, or to maintain or enhance their overall reputation. Responding to their economic incentives may lead them to "manage" earnings, and report information that is less accurate, but creates an impression with investors that the company's position and performance is better than the underlying economic reality.

In chapters four and five, we emphasized the importance of the timing of revenue and expense recognition in order to have an accurate measure of income per period that investors can project into the future. Recall that we used the example of how you might report to a bank thirteen months of salary or eleven months of rent instead of twelve when seeking a loan. This misreporting might lead the bank to project into the future that you will have the resources to repay a larger loan than you can support, thereby misleading the bank into making a poor lending decision.

There are two ways in which company managers might similarly mislead investors into projecting too much income into the future. The first is by biasing estimates of expenses downward in order to report higher income. For example, there is not one "correct" estimate for bad debt expense that will be acceptable to the company's auditor. Rather there is a range of acceptable estimates that can likely be defended by the manager if challenged by the auditor. By choosing one of the lowest acceptable estimates in any particular period, the manager can increase income that period to, for example, avoid a loss or meet analysts' forecasts. This applies to all of the many estimates that managers are required to make.

The second way in which managers might mislead investors into projecting too much income into the future is to misclassify a recurring expense as nonrecurring, encouraging investors to ignore that expense when projecting income into the future. This relates to the concept of persistence of net income. When forecasting the future, investors attempt to identify and remove from net income components that are believed to be transitory, i.e., that will not repeat in the future. Recognizing this, the company may combine a recurring expense with an obviously transitory (nonrecurring) component of income. As a result, investors may remove that recurring expense along with the nonrecurring expense when forecasting the future, thereby underestimating future expenses and producing forecasts that are too optimistic.

This chapter reviews research that examines whether managers sometimes behave in this way, opportunistically using the discretion allowed within the rules of accrual accounting to mislead investors. We first review a study that examines this issue in general, and then we review studies that examine more specific methods by which managers might use their discretion to mislead investors.

Do Companies "Manage" Their Net Income?

David Burgstahler and Ilia Dichev addressed this question in an important study published in 1997.[8] The authors reasoned that if managers were exercising their judgment to manipulate accruals, one of the objectives they would attempt to accomplish would be to make sure that net income achieved one or another common benchmark. For example, one common benchmark is zero earnings. Managers normally want to record a profit rather than a loss. As a result, the manager of a company that is in danger of recording a small loss might use his discretion to convert that small loss into a small profit by, for example, underestimating bad debt expense or warranty expense.

Burgstahler and Dichev expected that if such behavior occurs systematically across companies, the distribution of net income across those companies should exhibit a "discontinuity" around zero. That is, we should see fewer companies with small negative income and more

---

[8] Burgstahler, David, and Ilia Dichev. 1997. "Earnings management to avoid earnings decreases and losses." *Journal of Accounting and Economics* 24 (1): 99-126.

companies with small positive income than would be expected by chance.

Another common benchmark is last year's earnings. Managers normally want to record net income that is increasing over time. As a result, if the company is in danger of recording income this year that is slightly less than last year's, the manager might use his discretion to convert that small decrease into a small increase. Again, if many managers behaved in this way, we would expect a discontinuity in the distribution of net income around last year's net income, with fewer companies below and more companies above last year's net income than expected by chance.

Similarly, managers normally want to record net income that is higher than the amount that analysts are currently forecasting. Thus, if the company is in danger of recording income that is slightly less than analysts are forecasting, the manager might use his discretion to increase income to meet or beat the analysts' forecasts. If repeated by many managers, this behavior would create a discontinuity in the distribution of net income around analysts' recent forecasts, with fewer companies below and more companies above the recent average forecast than expected by chance.

In all of these cases, if many managers exercise their discretion to avoid falling short of these benchmarks, a graph of the frequency of companies with certain levels of net income will reveal fewer observations just below the benchmark and more observations just above the benchmark than would be expected by chance.

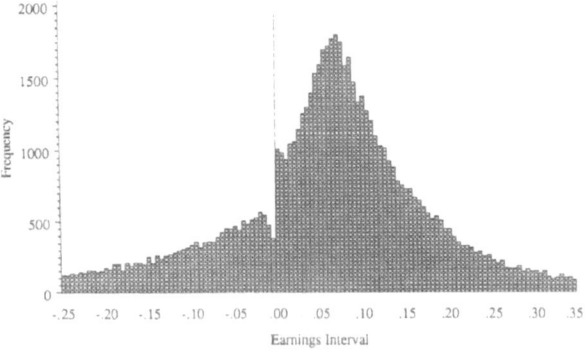

The graph above does a good job of summarizing the overall conclusion of the study by Burgstahler and Dichev. This graph plots the frequency of observations (vertical axis) for various levels of net income (horizontal axis). Normally we would expect this graph to be similar to a standard normal curve that peaks in the middle at the mean and gradually and symmetrically slopes to the sides, as on the right-hand side of this graph. In contrast, the left-hand side of this graph shows a clear discontinuity at zero, more observations than normal occur just above zero profit, and fewer observations than expected are just below zero profit. This discontinuity is consistent with managers using their discretion to lower expense (or increase revenue) to increase net income to be just greater than zero. Burgstahler and Dichev found similar results for the other two benchmarks, last year's earnings and analysts' forecasts.

Occasionally there are controversies in accounting research in which researchers cannot agree on the correct interpretation of a particular empirical result. That was the case with the results from the study by Burgstahler and Dichev. Several later studies argued that Burgstahler and Dichev had provided only indirect evidence that might be consistent with earnings management, but that there were other possible explanations for the pattern they observed.

At the same time, other studies concluded that the original interpretation by Burgstahler and Dichev was correct all along. One of these studies was published in 2013 by two of my colleagues, Dain Donelson and John McInnis, and their co-author Rick Mergenthaler.[9] They examined a unique set of companies that had been sued by shareholders over their financial reporting and had subsequently restated their financial statements.

The idea of their study was to focus on a narrow sample of companies, unlike the broad sample used by Burgstahler and Dichev, where it was known that the companies had managed earnings. Their sample consisted of companies that had been forced to restate their earnings. For these companies, it was clear that they had manipulated net income before the restatement and that the manipulation should have been reversed by the restatement. The graphs below summarize what they found.

---

[9] Donelson, Dain C., John M. McInnis, and Richard D. Mergenthaler. 2013. "Discontinuities and earnings management: Evidence from restatements related to securities litigation." *Contemporary Accounting Research* 30 (1): 242-268.

On the horizontal axis is the difference between reported earnings and analysts' forecasts, and the vertical axis reports the percent of the sample. The vertical line in both graphs is zero, where reported income and the analysts' forecasts are equal.

The graph on the right reports earnings as originally reported. We see that the graph looks very much like the one from Burgstahler and Dichev, with a disproportionate number of companies just above zero, where reported earnings and analysts' forecasts are equal, and a disproportionately low number just below zero, where reported earnings is less than analysts' forecasts. Thus, for a sample of companies that were known to have manipulated their net income, they found results consistent with those reported by Burgstahler and Dichev for a more general sample. This corroborates the interpretation of Burgstahler and Dichev that their results are evidence of earnings manipulation.

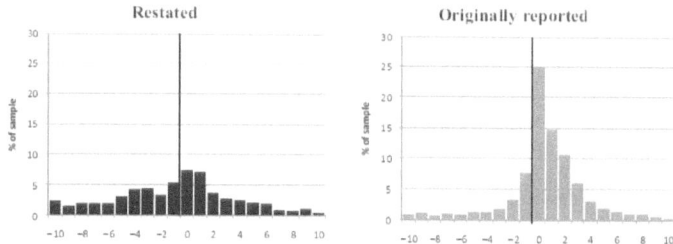

The graph on the left reports the same information after the restatement, that is, after the manipulation has been reversed. In this case, the discontinuity at zero has virtually disappeared and the graph looks more like a normal distribution. Thus, when net income is no longer subject to manipulation there is no discontinuity at the analysts' forecasts.

This evidence does not suggest that all companies manipulate their income all of the time. However, it does suggest that income manipulation does occur, particularly when there is the most pressure to manipulate, when net income for the period absent manipulation is likely to fall just below an important benchmark. In the next section we look more specifically at research on just how managers may go about "managing" or manipulating their income.

How Do Companies Use Accruals to Manage Their Net Income?

Bad Debts

In a study published in 1988, Maureen McNichols and Peter Wilson examined the possibility that managers exercise their judgment over the estimation of bad debt expense to manage earnings.[10] They first developed an estimate of the discretionary component of bad debt, expense, i.e., the incremental bad debt expense due to the manager's discretion rather than the underlying economics of the uncollectibles faced by the company. Using this estimate, they found that managers chose higher estimates of bad debt expense, when income is extreme.

This finding is consistent with managers shifting bad debt expense between periods to increase the likelihood of meeting earnings targets in the company's bonus plan. If unmanaged income is very low, the manager cannot manipulate earnings enough to meet his earnings target and earn his bonus in the current period. If unmanaged income is very high, the manager can manipulate earnings downward and still meet his earnings target and earn his bonus in the current period. In both cases, the manager has an incentive to choose higher estimates of bad debt expense in the current period so that he can underreport bad debt expense in a later period, increasing the chance of meeting the earnings target in the later period.

In a follow-up study published in 2010, Scott Jackson and Xiaotao Liu provided additional evidence on the use of bad debt expense to manage earnings[11] Consistent with McNichols and Wilson (1988), they provide evidence that managers often overestimate bad debts expense, thereby building up a "cookie jar" of recorded expense in the form of a higher balance in the allowance for uncollectibles. They also found that managers use this balance in the allowance for uncollectibles to write off receivables without recording expense, thereby managing earnings upward, when doing so will help them to meet or beat analysts' earnings forecasts.

---

[10] McNichols, Maureen and G. Peter Wilson. 1988. "Evidence of earnings management from the provision for bad debts." *Journal of Accounting Research*, 26: 1-31.

[11] Jackson, Scott B. and Xiaotao (Kelvin) Liu. 2010. "The allowance for uncollectible accounts, conservatism, and Earnings management." *Journal of Accounting Research*, 48 (3): 585-601.

Warranty Expense

In a study published in 2011, Daniel Cohen, Masako Darrough, Rong Huang, and Tzachi Zach investigated the potential for using warranty expense to manage earnings.[12] They first computed an estimate for "unexpected" warranty expense, the portion of warranty expense that is not expected given the past performance and expected future growth of the company. They referred to earnings excluding this estimate of unexpected warranty expense as "unmanaged" and they referred to reported earnings that included this estimate of unexpected warranty expense as "managed."

Following the results reported by Burgstahler and Dichev, they focused on companies whose unmanaged earnings fell below one of three common benchmarks, zero, last year's earnings, or analysts' forecast, but whose managed earnings exceeded the benchmark. They expected these companies to have incentives to manage earnings to achieve one of these benchmarks. They then compared these companies to others without such an incentive to manage earnings. They found that unexpected warranty expense was much more negative (i.e., lower warranty expense and higher earnings) for the companies suspected of managing earnings, consistent with manipulating warranty expense to achieve an earnings benchmark.

Taxes

Computing tax expense for large publicly-traded companies involves many subjective judgments. Because of this, and because of its magnitude, tax provides managers with a good opportunity to manage net income. My colleague, Lillian Mills, investigated whether companies use tax expense to manage earnings in a paper she published in 2004 along with co-authors Dan Dhaliwal and Cristi Gleason.[13]

As companies report their quarterly earnings during the year, they estimate what their tax rate will be for the full year and apply that rate to each respective quarter. At the end of the year, if the manager wants to

---

[12] Cohen, Daniel., Masako N. Darrough, Rong Huang, and Tzachi Zach. 2011. "Warranty reserve: Contingent liability, information signal, or earnings management tool?" *The Accounting Review*, *86* (2): 569-604.

[13] Dhaliwal, Dan S., Cristi A. Gleason, and Lillian F. Mills. 2004. "Last-chance earnings management: Using the tax expense to meet analysts' forecasts." *Contemporary Accounting Research*, 21 (2): 431-459.

increase earnings to meet analysts' forecasts, she may use her discretion to reduce tax expense in the fourth quarter. However, doing so will result in a lower annual effective tax rate in the fourth quarter relative to the annual rate the company had disclosed in the third quarter, providing evidence consistent with earnings manipulation.

Mills and her co-authors referred to annual earnings based on the reported third quarter effective tax rate as "unmanaged" and annual earnings as reported, based on the fourth quarter effective tax rate, as "managed." They found that companies with unmanaged earnings just below analysts' forecasts disproportionately lowered (managed) their effective tax rate in the fourth quarter to generate enough additional income to meet or beat the analysts' forecasts. This result is consistent with Burgstahler and Dichev that some managers manipulate earnings to meet an important benchmark.

Employee Stock Options
Many companies grant stock options to their employees as part of their compensation. These companies are required to estimate the value of the options at the time they grant them to the employees. That value is then expensed over the period during which the employees earn the rights to the options (become vested in the options).

The most common method to estimate the value of these options is the Black-Scholes formula, named after two economists, Fischer Black and Myron Scholes. The Black-Scholes formula is a complex algebraic expression that requires a number of inputs, including the volatility of the underlying stock, the risk-free interest rate in the economy, and the expected future dividends the company will pay. Several studies provide convincing evidence that companies choose biased inputs to the Black-Scholes model to lower the value of their employee stock options and the resulting expense, thereby increasing their income.

I conducted a follow up study with two former doctoral students, Brian Bratten and Casey Schwab.[14] We examined the behavior of companies that changed their option valuation model from the Black-Scholes model to the more flexible lattice model. The increased flexibility of the lattice

---

[14] Bratten, Brian, Ross Jennings, and Casey M. Schwab. 2015. "The effect of using a lattice model to estimate reported option values." *Contemporary Accounting Research*, 32 (1): 193-222.

model could be used either to increase the accuracy of the option values or, alternatively, to further lower those option values to report even less in compensation expense and higher net income. We found that companies used the additional flexibility of the lattice model to lower their stock option expense and increase their net income incremental to the bias already existing in the use of the Black-Scholes model.

Misclassifying Components of Net Income

The studies reviewed above all examine various ways in which managers can use the discretion allowed to them within the rules of accounting to bias expense estimates and manage earnings. A different type of earnings management was investigated by Sarah McVay in a study she published in 2006.[15] She examined whether companies shift expenses from "core" expenses like cost of goods sold and selling, general and administrative expenses, to the non-core expense, special items.

Special items is a generic term that refers to gains and losses recorded by the company for activities not related to their core operations, such as selling used assets or laying off employees. Shifting core expenses to special items is intentionally deceptive (and against the rules of accounting) because investors generally expect special items to be one-time transitory events that have little or no implication for the future, whereas core expenses are likely to be persistent and have significant implications for the future. Thus, by moving core expenses to special items these companies give investors a false sense of the earnings they can expect will repeat in the future.

To see the intuition of this, assume that Company A reports net income of $115 in year 1. Then, in year 2, the company reports net income of $100 that includes a negative special item (loss) of $20. A typical investor is likely to remove the special item from net income by adding it back and conclude that recurring income in year 2 is $120. However, suppose that $5 of the special item is really a core expense. Thus, recurring income in year 2 is actually $115, but investors do not realize this because the company has hidden this recurring expense in the nonrecurring special item. In year 3, when the company reports $120 of

---

[15] McVay, Sarah Elizabeth. 2006. "Earnings management using classification shifting: An examination of core earnings and special items." *The Accounting Review* 81 (3): 501-531.

net income with no nonrecurring items, investors are disappointed because the company did not grow its income from their estimate of $120 of recurring income in the previous year.

McVay found that unexpected core earnings (after controlling for the firm's performance during the period) were higher (more positive) the more negative the company's special items. This is consistent with misclassifying core expenses ($5 in the example above) and including them as part of special items to report core earnings that are artificially inflated (to $120 in the example above).

McVay also reports that companies with large negative special items in one year were likely to have a lower (or negative) unexpected change in core earnings the next year (from the example above, the $5 reduction in core net income in year 3 that disappointed investors). This indicates that the improvement in core earnings in the previous year was both related to the special items recorded that year, and also temporary, thus providing strong evidence that the unexpected core earnings in the first year was due to shifting core expenses to special items.

Disclosure of Non-GAAP Net Income
The studies above examined ways in which managers might bias net income as reported on the income statement following the rules of accounting. The rules of accounting are referred to as Generally Accepted Accounting Principles, or GAAP. Publicly traded companies must report net income on a GAAP basis. However, it has become common recently for managers to disclose alternative measures of income in their quarterly earnings announcement that do not follow the rules of accounting. These disclosures are referred to as non-GAAP (sometimes *pro forma*) income.

Typically, when reporting a non-GAAP earnings measure, managers will remove some items, typically expenses or losses, from net income, suggesting to financial statement users that these items are not persistent and hence do not provide information about the future. These eliminations can provide investors with useful information if managers use their superior information about the company's operations and performance to help investors understand which components of net income are truly transitory. If this is true, the non-GAAP measure will provide investors with better information than GAAP-based net income.

Using our example from the discussion of McVay's study, Company A might make one of two non-GAAP disclosures in year 2. If they were trying to provide investors with useful information, they would exclude the $15 of a truly transitory loss, to report non-GAAP net income of $115.

Alternatively, managers can use these non-GAAP disclosures to mislead investors into thinking the company is doing better than it actually is by eliminating recurring expenses. Returning to our example, if Company A was trying to mislead investors, they would adjust $100 of reported net income upward by $20 that included not only the $15 transitory loss but also $5 of core expenses, to report non-GAAP net income of $120.

Worried about this possibility, the SEC issued Regulation G in 2005, requiring companies to reconcile the difference between GAAP-based earnings and non-GAAP earnings so that investors can clearly see what items managers have removed. The idea is that if investors could see that the $5 expense eliminated from their non-GAAP income by Company A in the example above was a core expense they would not be misled.

Huai Zhang and Liu Zheng published a study in 2010 that examined the extent to which investors were misled by non-GAAP disclosures both before and after adoption of Regulation G.[16] They found some evidence that investors were misled before Regulation G, but only by companies that were not already providing a clear reconciliation between their GAAP and non-GAAP disclosures. After Regulation G, when all firms were required to have high quality reconciliations, they found that investors were no longer misled.

I published a follow-up study in 2012 with Ana Marques, one of my former doctoral students.[17] We examined the interaction between corporate governance and Regulation G, using two common measures of corporate governance, the number of outside directors on the board of directors, and the percent of common stock held by institutional

---

[16] Zhang, Huai, and Liu Zheng. 2011. "The valuation impact of reconciling pro forma earnings to GAAP earnings." *Journal of Accounting and Economics*, 51 (1-2): 186-202.

[17] Jennings, Ross, and Ana Marques. 2011. "The joint effects of corporate governance and regulation on the disclosure of manager-adjusted non-GAAP earnings in the US." *Journal of Business Finance & Accounting*, 38 (3-4): 364-394.

investors. The idea is that these "outsiders," independent board members and institutional investors, will pressure managers to behave better, making them less likely to use non-GAAP measures to mislead investors. Previous research had found that these two governance mechanisms were associated with less earnings management. We investigated whether these governance mechanisms were also associated with less abuse of non-GAAP disclosures before and after Regulation G.

We found evidence that investors were misled before Regulation G, but only by companies with weaker governance (fewer outside directors and institutional investors). Similar to Zhang and Zheng (2010), we found no evidence that investors were misled by non-GAAP disclosures after Regulation G. We concluded that Regulation G was necessary and useful for protecting investors, but only for companies that had weak corporate governance in place.

Do Companies Use "Real" Activities to Manage Their Net Income?
The research summarized above provides substantial evidence that managers use the discretion they have within the rules of accounting to manage investors' perceptions of the company's performance. In this section we examine several studies that provide evidence on whether managers also manage earnings by making "real" decisions, such as producing extra inventory or reducing discretionary expenses such as research and development or advertising. In a survey of chief financial officers published in 2005, John Graham, Campbell Harvey, and Shiva Rajgopal report that 80 percent of survey respondents said they would reduce discretionary expenses for advertising, research and development and maintenance in order to meet the company's earnings targets.[18]

Sugata Roychowdhury was the first to provide empirical evidence in support of these survey results in a study published in 2006.[19] Roychowdhury first replicated Burgstahler and Dichev, showing the discontinuity in the distribution of earnings at zero (the break between profit and loss). He then focused on companies that recorded a profit for

---

[18] Graham, John R., Campbell R. Harvey, & Shiva Rajgopal. 2005. "The economic implications of corporate financial reporting." *Journal of Accounting and Economics, 40* (1-3): 3-73.

[19] Roychowdhury, Sugata. 2006. "Earnings management through real activities manipulation." *Journal of Accounting and Economics* 42 (3): 335-370.

the year that was slightly greater than zero, the companies most likely to take some action to avoid reporting a loss. He tested whether these companies exhibited unusual behavior in three accounting variables.

First, he found that these companies reported lower than expected cash from operations. This is consistent with temporarily offering sales discounts to boost revenue and profits, while at the same time having the effect of lowering cash inflows relative to what would have been expected otherwise by the growth of the company.

Second, he found that these companies had higher than expected total production costs for inventories. This is consistent with temporarily producing more inventory in order to spread the fixed costs of production that period over more units and thereby lowering cost of goods sold and increasing income.

Finally, he also found that these companies had temporarily lowered discretionary expenses on advertising, research and development and selling, general and administrative expenses, again increasing income.

Taken together, the results in Roychowdhury's study provides evidence that income can also be managed by exercising discretion over real activities, i.e., by operating choices.

Daniel Cohen, Aiyesha Dey, and Tom Lys published a follow up to Roychowdhury's study in 2008 that examined the effect of the Sarbanes Oxley Act on earnings management.[20] The Sarbanes Oxley Act was passed by Congress in 2002 following major accounting scandals in the U.S. (e.g., Enron and Worldcom). Among other objectives, the Sarbanes Oxley Act was intended to increase the oversight of companies so that they had less opportunity to manage earnings using discretionary accruals.

The authors found that companies' use of discretionary accruals to manage earnings was increasing prior to Sarbanes Oxley. In contrast, they found that after Sarbanes Oxley the use of discretionary accruals declined significantly, while the use of the type of real earnings management documented by Roychowdhury increased. This indicated that Sarbanes Oxley was successful in reducing accrual-based earnings

---

[20] Cohen, Daniel A., Aiyesha Dey, and Thomas Z. Lys. 2008. 'Real and accrual-based earnings management in the pre-and post-Sarbanes-Oxley periods." *The Accounting Review* 83 (3): 757-787.

management, but that managers were successful in finding other ways to manage earnings.

Finally, Amy Zang published a paper in 2012 that provided additional evidence on how managers make trade-offs in their use of accruals and real activities to manage earnings.[21]

First, she found that companies are more likely to rely on real earnings management when managing accruals is constrained, such as when the company faces more scrutiny of their accounting practices or when the company has made substantial use of accruals management in the recent past.

She also found that companies are more likely to rely on managing accruals when real earnings management is constrained, such as when the company faces strong competition, is in a less healthy condition, is being closely monitored by institutional investors, or is incurring greater tax expense in the current period.

Finally, she provides evidence that managers fine tune their accruals management after the end of the fiscal year taking into consideration the extent to which they were able to use real earnings management during the year.

Thus, it appears that managers have several tools available to manage earnings to the level they wish, and that they use these tools in a comprehensive and sophisticated manner.

Summary
The review of some important published papers in accounting research in this chapter and the previous chapter began on an optimistic note. The evidence indicated that accrual-basis net income, as well as both the cash flow and accrual components of net income, provides useful information for investors. However, the published evidence also indicates that corporate managers can use the discretion that comes with accruals, as well as other supplementary communications, in a variety of ways to mislead investors. Further, the evidence indicates that managers also use

---

[21] Zang, Amy Y. 2012. "Evidence on the trade-off between real activities manipulation and accrual-based earnings management." *The Accounting Review* 87 (2): 675-703.

real activities as a complement to the discretion they exercise over accruals to manage earnings. So, where does this leave us?

We shouldn't lose sight of two facts. On one hand, accounting information is the only highly disciplined quantitative information about companies that investors and creditors have to help them make decisions, and there is substantial evidence that it is useful for that purpose, at least on average.

On the other hand, financial reporting is a complicated communication game. On one side are corporate managers who have more information than outsiders about what is going on inside the company, but who also have economic incentives to be less than completely forthcoming. On the other side are financial statement users trying to make important economic decisions with imperfect information provided by managers who may well be responding to their personal economic interests.

Thus, while accounting information is useful on average, it is up to each financial statement user faced with a decision about a particular company to decide how much reliance to place on that company's financial statements and the corporate managers who produced them.

www.ingramcontent.com/pod-product-compliance
Lightning Source LLC
Chambersburg PA
CBHW021354210526
45463CB00001B/99